Nkomo
The Story of My Life

Nkomo

The Story of My Life

Methuen · London

First published in 1984

© 1984 Joshua Nkomo

Printed in Great Britain
for Methuen London Ltd
11 New Fetter Lane, London EC4P 4EE
by Richard Clay (The Chaucer Press) Ltd
Bungay, Suffolk

British Library Cataloguing in Publication Data

Nkomo, Joshua
  Nkomo.
  1. Nkomo, Joshua   2. Politicians—Zimbabwe—
  Biography
  I. Title
  968.91'04'0924   DT962.82.N5

ISBN 0–413–54500–8

Printed and bound in Great Britain by
Robert Hartnoll Ltd. Bodmin, Cornwall

For my wife, maFuyana,
who has stood by me through it all

Contents

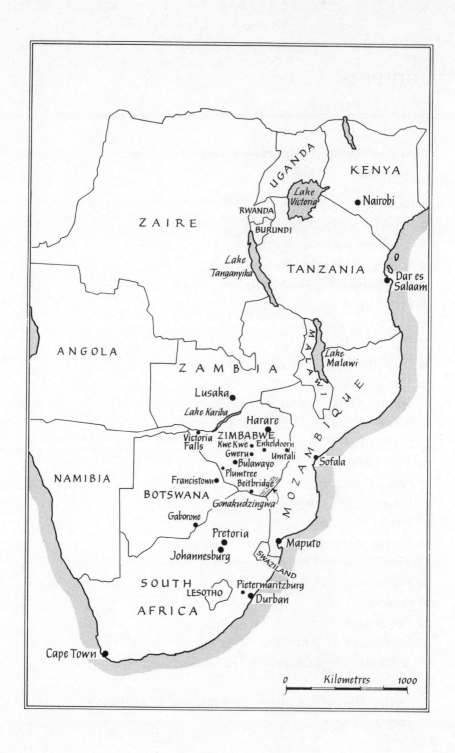

KENYA

ZAIRE

UGANDA

RWANDA
BURUNDI

Lake
Victoria

• Nairobi

Lake
Tanganyika

TANZANIA

• Dar es
Salaam

ANGOLA

ZAMBIA

MALAWI

Lake
Malawi

Lusaka •

Lake Kariba

Harare •

ZIMBABWE
Kwe Kwe • Enkeldoorn •
Gweru •
Bulawayo • Umtali •

Sofala •

Victoria
Falls

MOZAMBIQUE

NAMIBIA

BOTSWANA

Francistown •

Plumtree •
Beitbridge

Gonakudzingwa

Gaborone

Pretoria •

Maputo •

Johannesburg •

SWAZILAND

SOUTH

AFRICA

LESOTHO

Pietermaritzburg •

• Durban

Cape Town •

0   Kilometres   1000

Illustrations

Note on African Placenames

Many of the placenames in this book have changed, or reverted to older forms, with the end of the colonial period. Where the change is simply the correction of a European misspelling of an African name, I have used the modern form – Gweru, for example, not Gwelo. Where the name has completely changed I have used that which was in use at the time I am writing about: to do otherwise, I think, would be to try to rewrite our history.

The main examples are:

Southern Rhodesia (briefly Rhodesia) is Zimbabwe
Northern Rhodesia is Zambia
Tanganyika is Tanzania
Bechuanaland is Botswana
Nyasaland is Malawi
Salisbury is Harare (which was formerly the name of an African township of Salisbury)
Lourenço Marques is Maputo

Nkomo
The Story of My Life

Introduction

From my earliest youth I thirsted for freedom. When I became a man, I understood that I could not be free while my country and its people were subject to a government in which they had no say. In middle life I fought for national independence, and I was sixty-three years old when, in 1980, Zimbabwe emerged as the last of Britain's African colonies to win nationhood. Yet even then the cause of freedom for the people had not prevailed. We had won our national right to independence, but our human rights were still suppressed.

This book is not a history – one day, if I am spared, I may contribute to the writing of one with a happy ending, but this story has no end. Instead it is the personal record of a life that has played a part in history, and it is also the work of an active politician who wishes to see things change for the better in the lives of the ordinary people of his country. I have been called 'Father Zimbabwe'. Whether I deserve that title is not for me to say. But by a dozen years in prison and half as many in exile I believe I have earned the right to speak up for freedom while it is still endangered – this time not by far-off colonial rulers, nor by a settler population who will, I hope, now play their full part as citizens of a new nation, but by my former colleagues in the liberation struggle.

Our war of independence was longer and more cruel than any yet fought in Africa, because it was unnecessary. The white people of Southern Rhodesia, outnumbered at least twenty to one by the blacks whom they refused to acknowledge as their fellow-citizens, must have known in their hearts that they could not in the long run perpetuate their rule. The British government had the constitutional duty to make the settlers obey the law, but declined to do so. We had no alternative to taking up arms. By their prolonged resistance, the settlers themselves fostered bitterness not only between themselves and the black majority, but also between the various African factions struggling for justice in prison or in exile.

Hardly a family in our country was unaffected by the bloody war that was forced upon us. Tens of thousands of young people grew up knowing nothing but chaos and disruption – living in danger, in the bush, in exile, in makeshift camps, outside the steadying framework of established communities, the focus of their lives the false glamour of the gun. The war was necessary, and I do not regret my part in it. The price of freedom can never be too high. But the end of the fighting, and the start of the task of building a nation, was the time to draw the divided people back together again, to emphasise the work that can only be done in unity. Instead Zimbabwe's first government, born out of the rivalries of those years in exile and in prison, set out to impose a narrow sectarianism. It did not really attempt the task of binding up the nation's wounds.

The leaders of the party that won (by questionable means, but let that pass for now) our first elections believed that I symbolised the national unity that they rejected. So I became the focus of their anger, perhaps of their envy. The party I lead was repressed, the people who look to me for guidance were brutally treated. After a direct attempt on my life, which seemed likely to be repeated and to be successful, I was persuaded that I could best serve my country by surviving – and that meant leaving it for a while. The greatest irony of my life is that I have written this record of it in Britain, the country that for so many decades refused our people the freedom they fought for. But the right to publish my memoirs is one that I gratefully claim even from my former oppressors.

Chapter 1
Leaving Zimbabwe

Just before dawn on 8 March 1983, I crossed the dry river-bed into Botswana, driven into exile from Zimbabwe by the armed killers of Prime Minister Robert Mugabe. Over the decades of our struggle for freedom I had grown used to the hostility, even the hatred, of governments representing the tiny white minority of my fellow-citizens. But nothing in my life had prepared me for persecution at the hands of a government led by black Africans. This book will, I trust, make clear what had gone wrong and why. But first I must explain how I got away and lived to tell the tale.

Over a year had passed since I was dismissed, on trumped-up charges, from the government of Zimbabwe. All that time Robert Mugabe and his party colleagues had sought, without success, to link me and my party, Zapu, to the armed bandits operating in the western province of Matabeleland. Instead of trying to prevent the unrest that was inevitable after fifteen years of armed struggle, the government seemed intent on creating rebellion and suggesting that I was at the head of it. In the rural areas thousands of people – many of them my supporters, many innocent even of that offence against the ruling party – had been massacred by the Fifth Brigade, the force specially trained by North Korean advisers to operate independently of the official army and police.

Whole villages had been burnt to the ground, cattle slaughtered, women raped. Soldiers who had fought gallantly under my command for our country's freedom were arrested and tortured. Some were tried, acquitted by the courts – and then redetained without trial under the arbitrary laws inherited from the colonial period. My family and my friends were threatened, my passport was impounded, my speeches calling for unity and justice were methodically suppressed as the press and broadcast media were brought under total state control. But still the ruling party could not provoke me to disloyalty towards the nation I had struggled to liberate.

Prime Minister Mugabe had publicly called for violent action against my person. He said, quite falsely, that I was trying to overthrow his government. Speaking of my party, he said: 'Zapu and its leader, Dr Joshua Nkomo, are like a cobra in a house. The only way to deal effectively with a snake is to strike and destroy its head.' On Saturday 5 March 1983, his men at last moved against me in person. Despite instructions from the police that I should report to them every time I left my house in Bulawayo, I was taking various precautions: that Friday night I had spent with relatives in the eastern suburbs (the former European area of the town, my own home being in the more crowded western district that was formerly reserved for Africans).

On Saturday morning came the news that the old African townships were cordoned off by the army and the police, while the men of the notorious Fifth Brigade were conducting searches within the cordon. Early in the afternoon we heard that my own house had been searched, that the Fifth Brigade commander had checked that it was indeed my home, and had left.

I was furious at this invasion of my home, and I resolved to go there and check it out. My hosts urged me not to go but, seeing that I was determined, my wife insisted on coming with me. I told my security man to drive off across the deserted town. As we approached the cordon of soldiers and police he flatly refused to go on, saying that if by any chance he survived what was bound to happen, he would get the blame for exposing me to danger. My wife agreed with him, and for almost two hours we drove aimlessly around the deserted city, discussing what to do. In the end caution prevailed, and we drove back to the former European suburb where we had spent the night.

About 8 p.m. there was a telephone call. There had been shooting at my home, and sporadic fire was continuing in the neighbourhood. My driver and two other members of my household were known to be dead: there might be more casualties, but nobody was certain. The Fifth Brigaders were still asking the neighbours where I was, but those who knew were not saying. Never before had I wished that I were dead, but I wished it then. I wished I had died when Ian Smith's raiders had attacked my house in Lusaka and missed me by an hour. Then I would have died at the hands of the enemies of my people. But now the attempt on my life was being made on the orders of the African government of Zimbabwe, by people claiming to act on behalf of the nation that I had worked for decades to create. It was the bitterest moment of my life.

Later it became clear what had happened. The Fifth Brigade men had entered my house, searched it and found me absent. They had then questioned my people about where I was, and on getting no reply had shot three of them out of hand. They had then rampaged through the house, smashing up the kitchen and aimlessly breaking the furniture. Apparently for their amusement they had also damaged three of my cars, putting rifle-butts through the windscreens and ripping the upholstery.

This was sheer, unprovoked murder and hooliganism, directed at me but striking at people whose only offence was to have served me loyally. Robert Mugabe had decided to have me out of the way, and he evidently did not care what method was used. But I hold the legitimate government of Zimbabwe innocent of this atrocity. Mugabe was acting not as prime minister, but as leader of his party, Zanu. I had once asked him directly: 'What is the supreme organ in Zimbabwe?' He had answered: 'The supreme body in Zimbabwe is the central committee of Zanu (PF), my party.' I told him that could not be so: that the supreme organ of the country could only be its elected parliament, speaking for all the people. As the prime minister chosen by parliament, Robert was the top man of the country. But as leader of his party he was just a politician like me, with the same rights but no more. As leader of Zanu he acted outside the law: but the law and the constitution of Zimbabwe remain in force, and I hold the ruling party, not the lawful government, responsible for the attempt on my life.

It was my wife maFuyana who determined what I was to do. 'It appears to me,' she said, 'that your friends have gone out of their minds. Now that they have come straight out to kill you, you have got to leave. If you survive abroad you can return, and help the country out of its present problems. If you stay you will die, and there will be no repairing the damage that will do Zimbabwe.' I pleaded with her that we should stay together, since if I left her alone they might well kill her and the children too. But she insisted that nobody should leave their country in time of trouble unless it was absolutely necessary. It was her duty, and the children's, to stay and see things through. But equally it was my duty to go, since only if I survived would there be a hope of peace and reconciliation. She was weeping: when I argued that I too should stay she accused me of being selfish. And so I gave in to her argument. Once more I was heading into exile.

To leave Zimbabwe was the toughest decision I ever had to take. I knew my enemies would say I had run away, and I expected they would invent stupid stories about my flight. That clown Herbert Oshewokunze, the minister of home affairs, told the newspapers I had 'escaped' disguised as an old woman. People will believe anything if they believe that. Who ever saw an old woman of my height and my weight, with a clipped moustache and one of the best-known faces in all Africa? And if the police had information about this large old lady, why did they not arrest her? Anyway I did not escape, I decided to leave and I left. For a year I had lived the life of a hunted animal. I could hide no longer. On the Monday I had been summoned to report to the police: if I reported, the killers would follow me from there, and if I did not report I would be declared a fugitive suspect, with every soldier and policeman in the country licensed to shoot me out of hand. Those were the arguments for leaving. I resisted them until my wife's words sank in. Then I said, 'Right, I'll do it.' I did it, and surprised even myself.

Once the decision was taken, we sent our people out to reconnoitre the roads, first to the south-west and then southwards, towards the Botswana border fence which is, at its nearest, about a hundred kilometres from Bulawayo. All that Sunday the men kept coming back to report that it was impossible to pass. Every few kilometres there were road-blocks and men with guns, soldiers or police or men from the security service and the Fifth Brigade.

As commander-in-chief of the Zipra army during the war against the previous regime, I had acquired some knowledge of military tactics and – more important – of the military mind. I knew that every minor road would be blocked. But something told me that they would never expect me to do the simple thing and drive right down the main highway towards the border. That is just what we did. At half-past midnight we set off down the road to Plumtree, beyond which the main road and railway pass on to the Botswana frontier-post. The timing was chosen to pass through Plumtree at about 2.30 or 3 a.m., when soldiers in any army are inclined to take a nap. That was the chance we took, and it worked. I must add that the only people to know of the plan were my wife and the young men who accompanied me. I deliberately left my son and daughter, and her husband, out of it. It was best they did not know, in case of repercussions later.

The leader of our group was Makhathini Guduza, a member of the central committee of Zapu. He drove off first in the truck, a half-ton pick-up with a canopy, together with one man. They were unarmed. I rode behind in the station wagon with Jackson Moyo and three other young men: we had two AK rifles and three pistols ready for use. Guduza's vehicle kept about two hundred metres ahead of ours, so that we could clearly see each other's lights. We had arranged a simple set of signals. If he saw something suspicious on the road, he was to stop and keep on all his lights including the brake light. If he then switched everything off, it meant that all was clear, and we were to pull up to him for a discussion. But if he left all his lights on the four passengers in my car were to get out and move clear of the road with our weapons, and our driver was to move cautiously ahead.

If it came to fighting, the plan was that one of the boys would stick by me, and the others were to fan out right and left before opening fire, to give the other side the impression that there were a lot of us. Then I as commander was to shout, 'Close up!', and on that word of command we would retreat, join up, and try to work our way forward around the obstacle in the direction of the border. We were perfectly ready to shoot if it came to that: I did not like it, but there it was.

So we drove out through the former white suburbs to join up with the main road. In Bellevue, just before we picked up the highway, we passed a single car. Between there and Plumtree, a distance of just under ninety kilometres, we met no others. Ten kilometres short of Plumtree we stopped: Guduza went ahead to scout, and I and my three boys took up defensive positions on the roadside. In Plumtree, we knew, there was a government force of about two thousand men. Guduza came back and reported that they seemed to be there all right, but asleep: there were no police on the road, and the townships were dead quiet. I said, 'Let's go,' we sandbagged the pick-up, and I got in the back with three guards and the guns. That was how we drove right into Plumtree, turning left at the township as we entered it, and so on southwards on the Mpandeni road. Now it was only ten kilometres to the border. We knew this was the riskiest part, but our headlights showed nothing but the rabbits jumping around.

Next we had to find the place where we knew the border fence was unguarded, and this was where we made our first mistake. We turned down the wrong track, and found ourselves at a dead end by a little country school. I took the risk of waking up the teachers, who directed us back towards the highway – and there once again we took a wrong turning, which we realised when the lights of Plumtree once again came up in front of us. As we turned back the sky was starting to brighten in the east, and we knew there was very little time. But at last we identified the corner, drove down the dusty track and came to the village we were looking for. A countrywoman, up early fetching water, pointed to the line of trees and the river-bed just beyond them that marked the border. We drove down and turned left at another track, stopped at the bank of the dry Ramakwabane river, and walked across to the two border fences on the Botswana side. I am no lightweight, but the boys pushed and I climbed the fence, and at last we were over in no-man's-land, and up again to the Botswana fence. It was exactly twenty past six in the bright morning when I climbed down the wire onto the safety of Botswana soil.

From then on it was all welcomes. The chief of the nearest village had been my pupil for a while back in 1939, when he lived on the Zimbabwe side of the border. He greeted me and sent for the local headmaster, who organised transport to take me to Francistown, where the police took over. By 9 p.m. that night we were safe in Gaborone, the capital, and lodged on the orders of the president of Botswana in a small house. For the past two days I had barely rested. Now the tension was over, and I fell into the unconsciousness of deep sleep.

Chapter 2

An African Heritage

My parents were born when my country was still free. The government was in the hands of the people, directed by custom and tradition. My father, Nyongolo, was born about 1880, my mother five years later. They were children when Cecil Rhodes and his column of raiders raised their flag on the hill of Harare: around that hill spread the city of Salisbury, now called Harare once again.

They were teenagers when the occupation was completed in 1897, after the superior weapons of the settlers, assisted by British troops, had subdued the combined resistance of the Shona- and the Ndebele-speaking peoples. At the end of that war the commander of the invading soldiers sent out his men to shoot and kill at least two thousand natives, at random, 'to instil fear of the white man by the native'. The settlers then established a 'loot committee' to share out the cattle and other livestock, and to parcel out our land into estates.

I was myself seven years old when the British government handed over effective power to the settlers of what was then Southern Rhodesia, who chose self-government in preference to becoming a fifth province of South Africa. From that time on the nation was dominated by a tiny section of its population: the struggle against minority rule was to be the problem of my life. But the benefit of this new form of government was that it defined, once for all, our national borders. In the old, pre-colonial days the territories of each of the peoples in the land were defined only by custom: their vagueness led to raids and counter-raids in search of cattle, food or women. Now there was no reason why all of us should not unite and develop an unquestioned sense of national identity.

I was born on 7 June 1917, the third of eight children. Alice was born in 1910, then Paul (who sadly died in 1939), then myself, Joshua. After me came Mackenzie, who left us and may now be living somewhere in South Africa; then twin girls (but only Othilia survived infancy); then Stephen; then Edward, the last-born, in 1927.

My parents were Christians, workers for the London Missionary Society at the settlement of Tshimale, in Matabeleland. They were among the first of our people to be married in church, and my father's elder brother, Mapokwana, questioned the wisdom of such marriages, saying that the limit of a single wife restricts the growth of the clan. Just after Alice was born, the missionaries sent my father to be trained as a teacher at their Tiger Kloof School in South Africa.

My mother told me again and again how she and my father worried about me as a baby. For almost the whole of my second and third months of life I caused them sleepless nights with my screaming. My parents consulted a traditional doctor, who gave me some of his medicine. The result gave my parents a new cause for concern. I became unnaturally quiet, unable even to cry like a normal baby. They thought I might even have lost the power to speak, but the doctor assured them that there was nothing to worry about, I would talk when the time came.

This made me a late talker and a shy child. I could not keep up with the other children, and kept running back to my mother. I adored her; I was a mother's boy. My weakness made me backward in our games, and at the sport of stick-fighting. I was slow to follow the other boys in herding, first the calves and then the full-grown cattle. Even when I went to school and found myself coming first in all my classes, from Standard 1 to Standard 6, I felt the other boys were better than me.

In later life that lack of confidence has been both my strength and my weakness. Because I felt the others were ahead of me, I always struggled to keep ahead of their standards. But because I had so much trust in my mother I have believed I could rely on other people as I did on her. In all my dealings with people I have acted trustingly, and have found out too late when I have been betrayed. My comfort has been to trust in and be trusted by the masses.

After three years of study in South Africa, my father Nyongolo returned to find that the mission station at Tshimale was being run down. The white people had chosen it for their own area, and the missionaries had decided to move their school to a nearby community, named after its chief, Bango. It was a lovely place, in the high rainfall area of the Matopos foothills, south of the city of Bulawayo. The rivers Semukwe and

Tshatshane flowed nearby from the Matopos, bringing year-round water for the people and the livestock. In this delightful place I was born, and so were Paul, Mackenzie and my sister Othilia. As children we swam in the pools and raced in little canoes. We snared small game, birds and rabbits and squirrels, and even the little beavers. There were steep slopes of water-polished granite, where we would slide on makeshift sledges made of *iSikhukhukhu*, a shrub with slippery branches. In due course the white people claimed it too for their own, and once more we had to move on.

Bango's village was like many others in Africa, a cluster of homes, spaced out 500 metres or more apart. Each home was made up of several round huts. My father, having only one wife, had five huts for the whole family. Chief Bango himself, with five wives and many more dependants, had twenty-five or thirty huts, simple structures of upright poles plastered with the clay that we call *udaka*, and conical roofs of grass thatch. The focus of the home was the kitchen hut, with its central hearth and three stones to support the cooking pots. There were no windows and no chimney, so the smoke had to find its way out through the gap between wall and roof, where ears of grain were stuck so that the smoke could cure them against weevils.

The community at Bango lived by subsistence farming. Each man tilled as much land as he could handle, and kept as many animals as he could get. Father, although a teacher, was entitled to farm like any other member of the community, and his travels to South Africa had brought him into contact with better methods of farming. Luposwa, one of Chief Bango's brothers, had similar experience of better ways of farming, and together they produced much more than most local subsistence farmers. Together they began trading in their surplus grain.

Soon my father and Luposwa Bango became the proud owners of one of the little two-wheeled donkey carts that we called Scotch carts: later they bought a much larger trolley-wagon, with four wheels. Gradually their improved farming methods spread to the other farmers of the community, and the partners began to buy grain in bulk and sell it to the white miners and traders nearby. With their extra earnings they bought more cattle, sheep, goats and donkeys.

Father's income came from his farm and his trade. But he continued to teach as well, and he and his partner Luposwa Bango became preachers together in the mission church. The missionaries did more than spread the gospel. They actively promoted the building and maintenance of local primary schools, teaching arithmetic, English and Sindebele as well as religion. The mission provided books, slates and chalk, and paid the teachers – although the pay was as low as ten shillings a month.

The school building was erected by the whole community, and served also as a church. The benches were simply logs with their tops flattened, set up on sticks for legs – or sometimes they were low walls, fifteen inches high and six inches wide, that the children sat on. The blackboard was black clay plastered directly onto the wall and polished with a smooth stone.

By no means all parents wanted their children to go to school, especially if they were girls. Sometimes the missionaries made gifts to the family to entice the children to school. In most local communities only about a quarter of the people went to church, most of them being women; only a small proportion even of them formally became Christians. Most people stuck to their traditional religion, which the white people mistakenly described as ancestor worship; in fact the African people of what is now Zimbabwe worship almighty God who is a spirit, and with whom they communicate through their ancestors.

With my brothers and sisters I started my education before I was old enough to go to school. Father gave lessons to us and a few neighbours' children, teaching us reading and writing. I did not like it at the time, since it interfered with my games, but I felt the advantage when the school years began and I had a start on the other children. Before my school-days I had learned a lot, too, from my mother's readings from the Bible, and they had a great impact on me, coming from someone I loved so much. It was not until later in life that I saw how the Israelites' occupation of Palestine resembled that of our country by the white settlers, and began to become disenchanted with the story that told how that occupation was sanctioned by God.

Our upbringing was strictly Christian. There were

Bible-readings, hymns and prayers every night before bed. We were taught not to eat any food prepared for our neighbours' traditional worship, and strictly instructed never to touch liquor or tobacco – injunctions that I have respected all my life. My wife has brought up our children in the same standards – I would wish to have done so myself, but I have been so many years absent from my family, in exile or in prison. As I have grown older I have remained a religious man, but not so much specifically a Christian. That there is a God I devoutly believe – but a God of all mankind, not just of a selected people.

Going to school with the other children of the community was a relief, sitting in the classroom with a number of others. It was freedom not to be right under my father's eye and subject to his rages, when he would throw chalk and even the slates at us if we could not remember the previous day's lesson. There was safety in numbers, with a teacher who did not know me so well.

When I went to school my mother wanted me to look smart, and bought me some short trousers. This was an embarrassment, since all the other boys wore the *amabhetshu*, a little loin–cloth of skins suspended round the waist by a thong. (Girls wore a small cotton skirt, and in those early days neither boys nor girls wore a top, until later vests and blouses began to be the rule.) So each day I left home in my shorts, but with my little *amabhetshu* in my satchel, and on the way to school I would hide behind a bush, pull off my shorts and slip on my leather garment. Then on the way home I would do the same the other way round, making sure that none of my school-mates knew what I was up to.

Once the effort to please my school-friends earned me a big beating. In our house there was always a big 14lb bag of sugar for the tea and coffee my parents drank as teetotalers, and I was used to taking spoonfuls of it to make delicious cups of sweet water. It seemed to me a good idea to share this delicacy with my friends, and have a supply of sweet water for everyone. So I stole a half bag of sugar, took it to a pool of clear water, tipped it in and stirred. My friends and I were very disappointed to find that the pond tasted no sweeter and was full of mud as well: and when Mother found what I had done I got a thorough thrashing.

As I grew older my circle of friends widened, including children who did not go to school as well as those who did. In the long evenings and under the moonlight we played games, and gradually my early backwardness fell away and I gained confidence. For the boys there were special gatherings in an area set aside outside the fence of a home, where the older boys told us boys' stories, and sometimes men would tell us of bygone wars, how to hunt, how to use our sticks for defence or attack, how to share the special parts of the animal set aside for men after it has been slaughtered. We would pass the roast pieces around the group of boys, each one taking a bite in turn, in a ritual of brotherhood.

The girls, for their part, would gather inside the yard of a home to hear from a grandmother what girls needed to know – how to prepare different foods, how women of old used to manage family matters even better than women of the day. Sometimes too there were gatherings of boys and girls together, always in the girls' meeting place, where we would hear old stories – *insimu* – with moral lessons for the young. These tales influenced me as much as the Bible: they are the oral history of our people, passing our knowledge down from generation to generation.

It was the duty of the boys to herd the cattle, sheep and goats, and we were proud of our special rights at milking time. It was the boys who decided whether the milk from a cow that had newly calved should be drunk by us in our male enclosure or sent to mother for the use of the whole family. As the greatest of treats, we would milk a cow directly into our mouths – I loved the foam of it, and the gentle warmth of the fresh milk.

Our animals were individual beings to us, not just possessions. I could recognise the footmarks of our own cattle, and distinguish the lowing of our own oxen and the bleating of our own sheep – though how that was possible I do not know any more. We loved our beasts so much that it was hard to part with them for slaughter or for sale. Father got our agreement to the sale of our favourites only by a trick: he would point to a group of cows or of oxen and ask if we agreed to the sale of one from that group. When we returned from school we would find that the missing one was our favourite after all, and the house was almost in mourning.

Between the ages of eight and fourteen I became much attracted to the traditional religion of our people. With my friends I would steal away from home in secret to the ceremonies of our non-Christian neighbours, joining in the dancing and the singing, and even partaking, despite my parents' strict orders, of the food that had been specially prepared for the ceremony. To me their worship was more lively and attractive, and seemed more serious, than that I had seen in the Christian church. It went on without a break, sometimes for two or three days and nights, maybe even more.

In Bango's community both the Ndebele and the Kalanga languages were spoken interchangeably within the community. The Christian word for God was translated as *uMlimu* in the Ndebele and *Mwali* in the Kalanga language. This God, it seemed to me, was the same whatever language was being used, and the same too in the Christian and the traditional faiths: I could not understand why there had to be such a clear line of demarcation between them – but I was too young at the time to question what my elders told me.

It was later that I made the connection between religion and nationalism. I learned that the missionary Robert Moffat had been the interpreter when the so-called agreements were made by which Cecil Rhodes claimed to have been granted rights by the last king of our country, Lobengula. I learned too that Moffat had previously said of Lobengula and his regime: 'This savage kingdom must be destroyed if Christianity is to take root in this area.' Lobengula and his councillors asserted that they had never agreed to the concessions that Rhodes, through Moffat as interpreter, claimed to have been granted. But the only man who could say what had really transpired was Robert Moffat, and his Christian conscience.

As the spirit of Zimbabwean nationalism came to the fore again in the early 1950s, I examined for myself the power of the traditional faith of my people, and visited the shrine where Mwali resides in the Matopos hills. Well before dawn, at about 3 a.m., William Sivako and Grey Mabhalani Bango, the nephew of the chief of my father's village, accompanied me to the place called Dula. We were led by a frail old man along an ancient track: some twenty others were with us, each bringing his own problem.

The place was an overhanging slab of granite. The old man, our guide and leader, told us to squat down a few metres from the rock-face: he squatted in front of us, between us and the rock. He commanded us into a soft rhythm of clapping. Suddenly a voice like that of an ancient man began to call us by our names: 'You, son of Nyongolo, and you, son of Sivako, and you, son of Luposwa Bango – what do you want me to do for you? How do you expect me to accomplish it? When I told King Lobengula what not to do, he did it. I told King Lobengula not to fight against his cousins who were coming into the land, his cousins without knees.* But Lobengula ignored my instructions, and he fought against his cousins, I know,' the voice went on, 'he was compelled by some of his chiefs who wanted to destroy him, he listened to them and not to me.'

I replied, as leader of the group: '*Babamkhulu*, grandfather, we have come to ask you to give back this land to your children, the people of this land, including the cousins against whom Lobengula fought.'

'Yes, my children,' said the voice, 'I will give you back your land. It will be after thirty years, and it will be after a big war in which many will die.'

Mabhalani broke in: 'But grandfather, give it back to us now, we pray, you have the power to do it.'

But the voice was firm: 'It cannot be given to you now, I say it will be given after thirty years, and after war. That is because Lobengula failed to heed my word. My children of Bechuanaland will get back their land before you, because Sikhume Khama listened to my word and did not fight his cousins.'

About sunrise we heard the wind blowing strongly but we did not feel it. The voice said: 'Goodbye, my children.'

I cannot explain this event, but it happened and the prophecy came true. The other people accompanying us witnessed it: their own problems were not attended to, and they left amazed. We, for our part, left disappointed because the answer to our prayer was gloomy. For thirty years I kept the secret that the voice had foretold a long and costly struggle.

---

* 'The people without knees' was a term applied to early white visitors whose legs were mysteriously concealed by their trousers.

At this place in the Matopos hills all our rulers, from the Monomotapas four centuries ago to Lobengula, the last of our kings, have paid homage, and so have the ordinary people. During the years of colonialism the people continued to go there, respectful of their old religion. In 1974, when I was released after more than ten years in prison, I was told that the voice of the shrine had issued a message. It had said farewell, and ceased speaking to the people, but their complaints and pleas would still be heard. Perhaps as people become more 'civilised', God takes a step back.

Towards the end of our dry season, in August, September and October every year, the people attend upon the shrine to pray for rain, health and peace. I once spent a week in attendance at this festival, and I was left in no doubt of the faith and sincerity of the African religion. Men and women dedicate themselves for a period to the shrine, sleeping in the open, rolling in the ashes, singing and dancing all the time. The Christian religion seeks life after death for the individual, while our African religion seeks rain, health and peace in the world for all mankind.

Chapter 3
A Little Learning

Before I even began to study I had learned one big lesson. There was something upside down in my country. To me, Father was the greatest man in the world. But there were people who treated him disrespectfully. When he met one of these people on the road, he would take off his hat and stand aside, but they would not take off their hats in return; at best they would nod their heads and pass on, barely noticing him. These were the pale people, the Europeans, *Amakhiwa*. I understood almost without being told that they had taken something from us. Later I discovered that what they had taken was our country.

Setting that right has been the ruling passion of my life. It was my father who set me the example. Until I was six, as I have told, we lived in Chief Bango's village, in the Matopos foothills. But all that area of good farmland, with its regular rainfall and beautiful grass for cattle, had been claimed by the white people for their own use.

The end of the First World War brought big changes to Southern Rhodesia. My father's brother, Mapokwana, had fought with the British army in France, so my family was well informed about it. The returning soldiers brought with them the terrible Spanish flu — I believe that epidemic, which spread all around the world, killed more people than the war itself, and it caused many deaths in our country. Immediately after the flu came the great drought, when the rains failed for two years running, and the land dried up. The cattle were weak from lack of food, and they could not resist disease. (These droughts are the curse of our country.)

Being only a small child I did not understand all this. Indeed what I remember is eating meat often. Our cattle were so lean that nobody would buy them, and it was better to slaughter them for food than let them die of thirst and lack of grass.

But the big change that came to our lives was a result of the end of the fighting in Europe. There was a big inflow of immigrants to Africa, and some prisoners of war remained in our country and did not go home to Europe. The land designated as 'white areas' began to fill up, and there was great pressure on the black people living there, on their ancestral lands. In the area round Bango new white farmers settled, and the established farmers began to work their land more intensively. Heavy hut taxes were levied on our homes. The white farmers began to demand that the residents work free of payment on their land, in lieu of rent. The areas available for arable farming by Africans were cut down. We were forced to reduce our livestock. Life became unbearable.

Father decided, in 1923, to move away to what was called a 'native reserve'. He had been told that the reserves were places where Africans would be free – 'where the white people would have nothing to do with us'. But he was wrong, and later he proved it. In the reserves the natives were just occupiers, not free owners. The white administrators, the native commissioners, controlled everything that mattered. The numbers of cattle Africans could own were regulated, as were the types of crops they could grow.

The place we moved to was called Mbembeswana, about eighty kilometres south of Bango but still in the district of Matopo (which is now called Kezi). We left Bango in early winter. It was very cold. We loaded our goods onto the Scotch cart, and the journey to our new home took two days. The place was dry, flat land, very bushy, cut by ravines but with no hills or other landmarks. A boy who strayed far from home after the cattle could easily be lost in the bush: there were wild animals, hyenas, leopards, wild dogs, even lions. The place was dry. Instead of getting our water from free-flowing rivers, we drew it from bore-holes, and it tasted chemical, like Epsom salts.

The thing that hurt most was losing all the friends I had made at Bango. There was one shock in particular that still makes me sad. Apart from my elder brother Paul, there was another big boy in our household, and I had always thought of him as my brother too. His name was Kwebe, and he used to sing and tell stories and show us how to do things. But when my father announced that our family was going to move, Kwebe said firmly that he was not coming, he was going to stay. At that moment I realised that he was not my brother at all, but an orphan whom my parents had taken in and brought up as one of their own. We all tried to persuade him to go with us, but he was determined. So my father gave him two head of cattle for his own, and we went off without him. It was the saddest day of my childhood when we said goodbye. I never saw or heard of him again. It has happened to me several times in my life that I have had to separate from people I especially loved. That was the first time, and the worst.

But even my father could not make a success of farming at Mbembeswana, especially in those dry years. He looked for a better place to live. There was a neighbouring chief, about thirty kilometres away from Mbembeswana, called Ntelela Malaba. He was an old friend of Father's, and a qualified teacher: they had been together at the mission at Tiger Kloof in South Africa. Malaba invited Father to join him in his area as he felt it was better than Mbembeswana. This was early in 1925, and the rains came in torrents that year, even in the dry lands of the Matopo district. The wagon got stuck in an overflowing water-course, and it took us two days to travel the thirty-two kilometres to our new home. After struggling for almost five hours to pull out the wagon and the Scotch cart from the water-course, we left behind a crate of fowls which had been taken off the wagon during the crossing, and I had to be sent back for it on a donkey. I was terribly frightened, but I tried not to show it. The landscape of Malaba was not as flat and bushy as Mbembeswana. The village of six homes surrounded a little hillock, which protected us from the usual easterly prevailing winds. Directly south of Malaba village, of which we were part, stood a prominent lone hill, Nyashongwe, with a huge rubber tree which made it a spectacular landmark, and useful to us as herd-boys.

Within a year of our arrival, the people had built a community school, just like the one at Bango. I was a big boy now, but I continued to change into my leather *amabhetshu* when I went to school, which was barely two kilometres from our home.

In the reserve we very rarely saw a white man in those days. There was Mr Kennedy, the trader who kept the store and lived there all the time. Every six months the native commissioner came to collect the taxes – £1 a year for each adult male, and some other small taxes for veterinary services. It was the commissioner who first arrived in a wagon that moved without any animal to pull it, giving off an exhilarating smell that I later learned was petrol. When the first aircraft was seen over our village I was out with the cattle: my friend and I dived under a bush in the stream-bank, terrified lest the white people in the air should see and harm us. I could not have known then that one day I would travel millions of kilometres in aircraft to countries that I had not dreamed of.

Once again our family made progress. Father's improved farming methods soon produced a surplus of grain. With Chief Malaba as his partner he started trading again, with big customers close at hand in the Legion and Antelope gold mines. I led the donkeys that pulled the trolley full of maize bags, and admired European houses and machines around the mines. It was there that I first encountered electricity.

Father was doing business, the donkeys were tethered, and I had nothing special to do. On the outskirts of the mine compound I wandered up to a white overseer's house, deserted and in a bad state of repair, the windows broken and the doors wide open. I could not resist looking inside, and there I saw something very attractive. From the ceiling of each room hung a bowl or dish, white inside and green outside, with a strange translucent shine. I thought them very beautiful – I supposed they had been left behind, and there could be no harm at all if I took one home to Mother, who would surely find it useful as well as pretty. So I climbed on a drum which was lying about to take down the beautiful bowl, and was astonished to find that it was tied to the roof with a very strong twisted wire. I gave the wire a tug – and there was a terrible flash and bang that made me fall off my drum onto the floor. I never told Father about this awful adventure, and it was not until several years later that I understood I had been trying to rip out the shade of an electric light with the current still switched on.

After two years, in 1927, we moved again. The government had built a new dip tank at Chief Bidi's area. This was the first dip tank in the neighbourhood. My father was appointed supervisor of this dip, which served both the Bidi and Malaba communities. We had to move to Bidi's so that Father would be close to his place of work. The area dip supervisor became an extra white visitor to our area, and cattle buyers began to visit regularly. Father used to give them things – eggs, milk, sometimes even a goat or a sheep.

For us children the white people usually left a few tins of food, such as canned meat, or jam, tinned fish or something like that for a treat. But they never gave the tins to us directly. They would leave them on the ground near where their fire had been, and they would always leave them open. Maybe it was kindly meant: perhaps they did not want to give presents to individual children, but hoped that we would share them out fairly among ourselves. Maybe they thought we did not have can-openers, or know how to open things. But leaving tins open, so that the ants could get in, or dirt could fall in from the fires and dust, seemed an insult. It is the kind of thing that leaves a mark on a child's mind.

The girls were spared this type of experience, because they were always with Mother doing those jobs which are regarded as reserved for women. They helped Mother to pound maize, millet or other small grain, cooked and fetched firewood and water. Father incurred the neighbours' disapproval by doing jobs reserved for women, fetching firewood and water for the family in his Scotch cart. If it was an emergency, he would bring water on his bicycle, which he had just acquired.

I was the weakling of the family, suffering regularly from pains in my stomach or in my head. Father heard of a traditional doctor travelling in the neighbourhood, and asked him to inspect me. After the doctor's visit and treatment I recovered almost at once, and Father gladly paid his dues. I became truly interested in the doctor, fascinated by the songs and the dancing which were part of this treatment. He asked Father to let me accompany him, and I went along on his local journeys, digging and cutting roots and herbs at his instructions.

Seeing my real interest, the doctor said he would teach me his art. I began to learn the dances, and to grind the bark and the herbs for his medicines. In my young mind I thought that one day I would become a wonderful doctor like my teacher, Mathimulana Nyathi, who came all the way from far-off Rusape, in Mashonaland. He did not speak Sindebele well, but I was told and believed that the Shona people were skilful in traditional medicine. At home when he was there, we had fresh goat meat every day, since traditional doctors could not do without it; that too I enjoyed.

Father was not happy about my new plan. He had long discussions with the doctor, which I did not like although I could not understand them. Father's face told the tale – he did not approve of traditional doctors, and finally he took me home and that was the end of it. It was a great sadness to me.

The chief of our community, Ntelela Malaba, was an important man, especially on Wednesdays, the day of his weekly court. Men, and sometimes women, would come to his *enkundleni*, his place of judgment. Father and a number of other men attended to help the chief hear the cases. Every man was entitled to cross-question both the accused and the complainant, acting both as prosecutors and as the jury.

We children sat and listened, and sometimes were told to move away. We did not understand why this was so, but later I realised that there were certain cases that the elders did not want us to overhear. But we never moved far off when the court was in session. At the end of the hearing there would be a goat or two slaughtered, or even an ox. We would not miss that meat.

Bidi remained my parents' home from 1927 to the end of their lives. Mother died there in 1942, her heart broken by Paul's sudden death three years earlier. Father died there in 1954. Their graves stand alone in the bush, far from any home. As I write, in the great drought of 1983, I have news that the cattle of the district are dying of hunger and disease, and the people are on the point of starvation. The dip is unused because the government will not supply the necessary chemicals to people whom it regards as 'dissidents'. I cannot send food to my own cousins, Sihle and his wife, although their children are suffering from malnutrition, because the authorities say that food supplies might be diverted to sustain the rebels.

As official dip supervisor, my father had eventually qualified for a shotgun permit and the right to shoot game. After his death I had to hand the gun in to the district officer. I did not apply for a licence to keep it, since I knew I would be refused. I never claimed compensation for handing it in to the government office. I thought they could have it free, if they denied me the right to inherit it.

The family decision that shaped my whole life was to send first my elder sister Alice and my brother and then me to boarding school. My father was now disillusioned with life as a teacher: teaching was badly paid, and he did not see it as productive work. He wanted us to learn a useful trade, and the government had just opened the first two schools in the country for teaching Africans manual skills.

Tjolotjo Government Industrial School in Matabeleland (like its counterpart Domboshawa in Mashonaland) taught handicrafts, agricultural science, building skills and so on – all based on a grounding in literacy. Tjolotjo seemed an immense distance away from our home, being sited some 110 kilometres on the far north-west side of Bulawayo. My elder brother Paul went off there first, and I was impatient to follow him in 1932. He started a course as a builder, but I was still needed at home: Father by now had built up his herd to about a thousand head of cattle, maybe a couple of thousand goats, and a big herd of sheep. I was the elder herd-boy in charge of the cattle, watching them, seeing they did not stray too far, inspecting them for ticks and infections. My sisters too helped with the livestock, although it was not the custom for girls to do that sort of work. Father employed a few young people to work for us. But they were not just employees, they became practically members of the family. If I got a new pair of shorts, the other boys would get the same, and they got a little pay as well.

Most of these children who worked for us had parents who did not want them to go to the formal schools – perhaps because they were not Christians, maybe for other reasons, or because they did not see the point of learning to read and write. As I and my brother and sister were taught by my father before we went to formal schools, so Father taught these young people in his morning classes together with Stephen and Othilia. Some of them got a better education that way than they would have done at the mission school.

I was fifteen when I went away to boarding school at Tjolotjo. I took the new bus service to Bulawayo: I had in my pocket the £6 annual fee for Tjolotjo school, and a little money for the journey. It was the greatest adventure of my life. There were a few hours to wait at Bulawayo, which seemed an enormous place, shining with its electric street-lights. I did not even know where to buy the ticket for the rest of my journey, and wasted some time asking for one in the row of little Indian shops near the station. I think the shopkeepers thought I was being silly, and it was some time before one told me to go back to the station and buy my ticket at the ticket office there.

The next stage of the journey was by train, fifty kilometres to Nyamandlovu, the nearest station to the school. From the station we started walking, at about 3.30 in the afternoon. I was much the youngest of the young people in our group. What I did not know was that it is seventy kilometres from the station to the school. So on we walked. I was carrying my little bundle with my blankets and some provisions, but I had no shoes. At first the soil was sandy, but at dusk we got onto rocky ground – and all the time I was expecting to see the electric lights of a town in front of us, for I was sure that such an important place as a boarding school would have electric lights.

It seemed like the middle of the night when some of the bigger fellows decided we had done enough, and we would stop for a rest. We just lay down on the ground for three or four hours, then up and on again. My feet had blisters, and the others must have been pretty impatient with me. But some of them even helped by carrying my blankets and provisions. The sun rose and became blistering hot, we crossed the river Gwaai by the ford, and came to a little store where we bought some biscuits and things. But still we were not there. Then in through a gate, and neat fields spread out beside the track: and suddenly a chicken ran across the road in front of us, there were huts and houses on each side of the road, and we had arrived. It seemed like the longest journey in the world, and it had lasted from 3.30 one afternoon until about 1 p.m. the next day.

The best thing was to find my brother Paul. He showed me how to register: then I collected my school uniform, and I felt really important when I had put on the shorts and shirt. I imagined I was in the police or something, and I felt like a big man. But in fact I was the youngest student in the place, since most of them were grown men in their twenties. The first letter I wrote home to my mother was to ask her for two shillings and sixpence to buy tennis shoes. It seemed like an awful lot of money, but I could not go around barefoot. In fact my mother sent me a big sum of money, ten shillings, and I bought the tennis shoes and put them on with the khaki shirt and khaki shorts, and sent a photo of myself wearing all that back home. My mother was very proud of me.

But the first classes were terrible. I had learned to write on a slate, but I had never written on paper. Now we were issued with pen and ink, and exercise books to write in. It felt very uncomfortable. The teacher, a very interesting old man called Titus Hlazo, sat us down and started us off with a test. He wrote up on the blackboard: 'Write five sentences about a cat.' I read it, I got my pen and dipped it, and wrote in the exercise book: '1. Write five sentences about a cat. 2. Write five sentences about a cat. 3. Write five sentences about a cat. 4. Write five sentences about a cat. 5. Write five sentences about a cat.'

When I had finished I stopped. The others were still writing. I could not understand how they were taking so long about it. Mr Hlazo came and looked over my shoulder. 'Have you finished?' he asked. When I said yes he got furious. 'Savage! Savage!' he said. He waited until the others had finished their little compositions, then he explained that he wanted me to think of five different things to say about a cat, all on my own. I had never done that kind of thing before, and my English was very limited.

It took me quite a while to realise what I was meant to do, but then I picked it up and got to a good standard quite fast. The one thing I did badly was spelling. In my final Standard 6 examination the dictation piece had the word horse four times: I spelt it differently each time, and all my spellings were wrong. But my composition was good, and my arithmetic was ace. I came top in the whole country in the arithmetic exam one year, although I was much younger than all the other students. After a while I began to be top in my class all the time. I would perhaps have got overconfident. But ever since I was sickly as a little boy, before the traditional doctor gave me the herb medicine, I had never been quite sure of myself. Because I was unsure of myself I always worked very hard, so as not to fall behind the others. I think if I had had more confidence I would never have done as well at school.

The toughest time at Tjolotjo was from Monday morning to Friday midday, when we had to speak English the whole time.

Friday afternoon and all weekend, we were free to speak Sindebele: but of course we talked among ourselves in our own language even when we were not meant to. It was terrible not being able to say what we really meant except when there were no teachers around.

The classroom subjects were more than the old three Rs – reading, writing and arithmetic. We also did English, Sindebele, history and geography. But the purpose of the school was to teach crafts. Since my brother was doing the general builders' course, I decided to specialise in carpentry and joinery. In fact I got pretty good. If I move into a house now and find that the doors do not fit, or the joints are springing on a piece of furniture, I still know how to put it right, and that pleases me. I take pleasure in a well-made piece of woodwork: it is something you can never forget.

I suppose Paul and I were star pupils. By the end of my five years at school we were teaching the younger boys ourselves, and I enjoyed watching their progress. All the time the school was growing, and we hardly went home in the holidays. We paid our fees by working on the school extensions. I became the school bugler, proudly sounding reveille in the mornings, and hoisting and lowering the Union Jack each morning and evening.

The school used modern methods, but the teachers tried to be realistic, and not to encourage the use of expensive farm implements that we would never be able to afford on the farms we were going back to. For example, we developed with the teachers a method of drilling seed-furrows with oxen. The animals pulled a wooden cross-bar, with logs attached to it at right-angles, so that they made lines in the direction that the ox was walking. Then, using a measuring-stick, the seeds just had to be sown the right distance apart along the lines and the field was perfectly planted. The great advantage was that any farmer could make one of these things without spending money on anything but a few nails and some rope. Even the poorest people could improve their crops by methods like these: more people should be thinking now about such methods, instead of concentrating on expensive tractors and imported machinery. It was 1936 when I left Tjolotjo. But I did not go into the building trade as had been planned. I dare say there were several European building contractors who would have been glad to employ a qualified craftsman, especially since the wages they paid to Africans were so much below what they paid to the coloured people who usually did that sort of job in those days. But we took after our father: we wanted to work on our own account. With the money saved up from working on the school buildings and as a building sub-contractor in Bulawayo, my brother bought a second-hand bus and started operating. I learned to drive as quickly as I could, and on 19 October 1937, when I was twenty years old, I qualified as a driver of public service vehicles. I was tremendously proud of my licence, and I still have it. But I must admit it was an uncertain life.

Just once, in the hope of earning some extra money, I accepted a job as a lorry driver. My employer was a white man from Francistown in Bechuanaland – or rather he said it was in Francistown, until I got there and found it was a little place about 24 kilometres out of town. I was put in a tiny hut in the yard, and the man said he had no money until he could get hold of a load of maize that was stored about 320 kilometres northwards at Maitengwe. He showed me his old Chevrolet truck and told me to go off and pick up the load. So in I jumped and drove off, all by myself, across wild country with nobody about, and in the most terrible heat. The road got worse and worse, and I began to get anxious. Then sure enough the engine began to boil. It was only then that I thought about tools, and the spare wheel, and water. I stopped, and of course there were none of those things. So I waited until the engine went off the boil, and drove on very slowly. As it boiled up again I saw a little village beside the road, and stopped to ask the women for water.

They had no water: they said they had to walk thirty kilometres just to get enough to drink themselves, and they certainly could not spare me any. At last, after a lot of talking, I gave them sixpence – a lot of money for me – for a gallon drum of rusty water. Then, quite by chance, I thought I recognised the accent of one of them, and thanked her in Kalanga, the language most people spoke at Bango. She was astonished: where was I from, who was I, what was I doing in a truck? I explained, and the good lady gave me my sixpence back and said I could have the water with her blessing.

In the end I got the load of grain, which was far too heavy for the truck, and on the way home of course there was a big hissing sound and the back tyre went flat. I stayed by the road for two days, with no food and practically nothing to drink, until at last a couple of other trucks came along. The drivers were wonderful. They understood perfectly that my boss had cheated me, and they gave me food and fixed my flat tyre so that I got back to Francistown. The first thing I did was to hand in the keys and tell the white man I was off home. I did not even ask for my pay; I just walked into town and took the train back to Bulawayo, and that was the end of that.

So I was back in Bulawayo without a penny. Again I got a driving job, this time delivering bread in a half-ton van belonging to Osborne's Bakery on Grey Street and 6th Avenue. The owner was a Mr Macintyre, who afterwards became Minister of Finance of the Federation of Rhodesia and Nyasaland. I was the only African driver: the other four vans were driven by coloured people. My pay was £4 a month, and I thought that pretty good – until I found out that the coloured drivers were doing exactly the same work and getting £12 a month.

It was not that I resented the coloured people getting that money; in fact I thought they deserved anything they could get. They were very badly treated. Most of them were the children of white men and local African women, and their fathers used sometimes to pay them to use another name. The Africans did not accept them either, and the municipality used to pretend they did not exist, and never built houses for the coloured community. They more or less survived, living alongside the Indians, whom the whites also found it hard to classify. The coloureds' only privilege was that they could buy white people's liquor, while Africans could only get home-brewed beer, so the coloured men would buy bottled beer and whisky and sell it to the Africans.

When I discovered about the difference in pay, I went to Mr Macintyre and asked why it was. He was quite patient, I suppose. He explained first that I was a native and the others were coloured; second, that natives did not need beds and wheat bread and knives and forks, because they were happy with just a couple of blankets and some mealie porridge and a plate to eat off. I told him that if he would pay me £12 a month I should be very happy to sleep on a bed and eat meat with a knife and fork. So of course he sacked me, and I went back to my brother, whose bus was getting worn out by this time.

I kept alive by tackling all sorts of odd jobs – a bit of dealing in livestock, a spell of teaching in a rural school, anything to keep me going. But I knew by now that I had to improve my education if I was to have a satisfying life, and that was how I came to go off to South Africa to see the world.

Chapter 4
Seeing the World – South Africa

Those years of knocking about at odd jobs were invaluable to me. They taught me to find my way around as naturally in an African city as in the countryside, and they taught me how to make my own living. But I was not satisfied with being a driver and carpenter: I wanted to qualify as a carpentry instructor. Yet it was 1942, I was twenty-five years old, and there was no imaginable way for a Southern Rhodesian African to get such a qualification in his own country. The first secondary school for Africans was not found until 1947.

To advance my qualifications I set my heart on going to Adams College in South Africa, which is where I began my studies again after three years' break. This college sounded a wonderful place, perhaps because it was so far away. It was founded and run by an American Methodist society, the American Board Mission, in the countryside forty-one kilometres outside Durban in Natal. One special attraction was that it was near the sea – nobody I knew, not even my father, had seen the sea. Getting there became my great ambition.

The first problem was to get enough money together. The fees were £22 a year, but of course one needed much more than that for travelling, clothes and living. I had saved £25 from various jobs, my father gave me £10, and Mother quietly handed me £7 15 shillings for the train fare. Off I went, not knowing what to expect but hoping for great things. At Plumtree, on the Bechuanaland border, I joined the train for the long journey south, travelling just behind the engine in the coach marked 'Reserved' that was set aside for Africans.

It was an immense journey, across the dry country of Bechuanaland and into the hill country of the Transvaal, with its rich white-owned farms, to the mining country of the Reef at Johannesburg. In the carriage I met four other young people who had joined the train earlier, and these were the beginnings of friendships that changed my life. Two were from Bulawayo: Moses Siqalaba, already qualified as a teacher, who stayed on in South Africa and never returned home; and Alex Ndebele, a young man of great promise who died young. From Salisbury, the capital of Southern Rhodesia, were Enoch Dumbutshena, my long-time friend and now Chief Justice of the High Court of Zimbabwe, and Herbert Chitepo, who also became a brilliant lawyer – having been my friend, he later became my great adversary, until he was murdered by his own associates in Zambia in 1975.

The meeting began on a false note. All of us had friends or relatives living in one or another of the native townships of Johannesburg, and I am afraid that at first I put on airs like a much older and more experienced man, with nods and winks indicating that I knew my way around the city and had often been there before. After a while I realised that they too were all on their way to Adams College, so I confessed that I was going there as well, and we laughed and became friends. We were so few, the first students from Southern Rhodesia to have the luck to get to college.

At Johannesburg we had a whole day to wait for the connecting train for Durban. We hardly dared leave the station, into the huge, bewildering city. We watched the miraculous electric trains, coming and going to the suburbs all day long. But the formal racial segregation of South Africa made no special impression on me. It was exactly the same as at home, except that in Southern Rhodesia there were fewer signs written up to tell people where to go. You just followed the rules automatically in those days.

It was Siqalaba, the oldest of us, who showed that the rules could be challenged, if not broken. On the train to Johannesburg he insisted on walking into the dining car and sitting down to be served. The black waiters were embarrassed: they kept whispering to us that it was no use, we should move out before there was trouble – but we sat there until the white supervisor came along and ordered us to get out. Yet the result of our little demonstration was that, when we ordered our meals in our own compartment, the dining-car staff made sure that we were well served, exactly on time. The protest had earned us respect, even if it did not get us our meals in the white people's dining car.

It was in Durban that things really began to seem different.

We were met at the station by someone from home – Stanlake Samkange, who later became a historian and a professor. He took us to McCord's Hospital, which had been built by American missionaries for African patients, and to our amazement one of the white American doctors invited us to lunch. We sat down at table with the doctor and his wife and some other guests, and it was very pleasant. That night we slept at the doctor's house, comfortably, as his guests. That was certainly something that could not have happened at home, and I began to believe things were going to be good. I remember I had a new tin mug that I had brought with me for drinking out of on the journey. I began to think that Adams College was too grand a place to turn up at with a tin mug. But I had packed it away in one of my suitcases, and I could not get at it in order to throw it away.

But as we arrived at college next day, by taxi with our cases on the roof, it all seemed terribly untidy, covered with long grass and weeds that were growing up in the January rains. The buildings were scattered around a big campus – the chapel, the library, the teachers' college, the high school, and finally the girls' dormitories and the vast block where three hundred boys slept. The first meal was just maize porridge with a little sugar, not European food at all, and there was a great rush to reserve a plate and a mug for each pupil. I was certainly glad I had not been able to find my own mug to throw it away: without it I should not have had anything to drink out of. And I had imagined I would be ashamed of it in that fine college I was now attending.

I began in the carpentry class. The instructor showed us how to make a dovetail joint: the other students chiselled away at their wood, but I at once did the job so that the corners slotted smoothly together. The teacher was amazed, until I told him that I had myself been instructing a class in my last school. He decided soon that there was nothing he could teach me, and recommended that I be transferred into the academic side of the college, which was quite separate. So, a week late, I began on the academic curriculum of Latin, maths, physical science, English and Zulu. I was completely behind in Latin, and could never catch up, so I dropped it. In the other classes I did fairly well, but I was no longer the star I had been at Tjolotjo.

The embarrassing thing was that none of the other students in my class was over seventeen, while I was twenty-five and in the beginners' class. Beginners had to do odd jobs around the place, tidying and keeping things clean. I was given the job of sweeping the pathway between the girls' quarters and the dining room: the girls all giggled when they saw this grown-up man doing the juniors' work with his broom. My class teacher, Mr Ngobese, made jokes about me: 'Nkomo's only here to get away from his wives,' he said, and everyone else thought it very funny. Worse, our class teacher, Miss Jukuda, a nice Xhosa girl, was only twenty-three and a graduate already. I am not a small man, but it made me feel very small.

I wanted to give up. During my first term I got news that Mother was very sick at home, and I got there only just in time to be with her on her deathbed. It was a week's travelling time, and I very nearly did not go back at all.

In my second school vacation I discovered that my carpenter's skill could make me a lot of money in Durban. I began turning out nice little four-legged stools with soft leather seats. In wartime, luxuries like that fetched a good price, and I had £40 in my pocket at the end of a month, when, unfortunately, the government prohibited the use of hardwoods except for war purposes, so that was the end of my enterprise. But I had made enough for another year's fees, and I was pretty pleased with myself.

Suddenly everything changed. One day, with all 1,000 young people gathered in school assembly, the head blew his whistle for silence and called out: 'Is there any student who has a driver's licence?' The only one to stand up was Nkomo, in the junior class. It turned out that the school secretary had bought a car but did not know how to drive. So at last I could make myself really useful.

The school secretary was Julia Hoskin, the widow of a major in the army. She was Norwegian, a beautiful woman with a beautiful heart. I fetched her from home in the morning, took her back for lunch, returned her to her house in the evening, and the rest of the time I was free to use the car myself. Mrs Hoskin invited me to share her meals, and we discussed everything together. I worked in her garden, especially on the roses that she loved – not as an employee, but like a son.

I drove Mrs Hoskin to visit her husband's grave: on two occasions the car refused to start as we were leaving that sad place. Each time she went back to the grave and arranged the flowers and returned to the car, it would not start. One day, the principal of the college called me to his house, and looked very solemn when I arrived. He was called Senator Edgar Brooks, a very religious man and an important figure in Natal politics. He asked me to kneel and pray with him, which I did. After we had prayed together he asked whether I would promise to tell him the truth about a painful subject, however difficult it was. I said yes, of course. Then the senator started asking me about the nature of my relationship with Mrs Hoskin – I honestly did not understand what he meant by that, and told him frankly that I honoured her and respected her as a mother.

Perhaps it was naive of me, but I was terribly shocked by what Senator Brooks then told me. He said a member of the staff, an Afrikaner called Mr de Koch who was Dean of Men and in charge of all male students, had reported an improper relationship between myself and Mrs Hoskin. If true, that would have been a crime under South African law. But to me it was just disgusting. I insisted that I must go at once and tell Mrs Hoskin what had been said. The Senator completely believed my denial, I am glad to say, and he instructed Mr de Koch to apologise in person to both Mrs Hoskin and me. But after that our friendship could no longer feel free, although I continued working for Mrs Hoskin. I felt very unhappy and hated to see Mr de Koch around the college.

I spent three years at Adams College, and despite its obvious inadequacies I very much improved my academic standard there. Since it drew students from all over central and east Africa, I got to know people from other countries, as well as facts about those countries. Yet I do not think any lesson was so important as the one Mrs Hoskin taught me: that white people too were human beings, if you could somehow get through the barriers that society erected to stop us being friends.

The question was, where to go next? I could not train to be a teacher, since my father had rejected that profession. I considered becoming a minister of religion, but found the missionary societies had no nominations for Southern

Rhodesia. After a long search I found out about the Jan
Hofmeyr School of Social Work. It was a foundation set up by
liberal South Africans – Hofmeyr himself was a millionaire
friend of Field-Marshal Smuts who left part of his vast fortune
for the education of Africans. The school was associated with
but not part of the main University of the Witwatersrand in
Johannesburg, and it had the great advantage, for someone
with my piecemeal academic background, of giving a diploma
to successful students who could subsequently go on to take a
full degree by correspondence, which is what I eventually did.

Once again the fees were the big problem. The school
charged £60 a year, which put it out of reach of practically all
Africans who could not get some sort of grant either from their
government or from a mission. I had my £40 saved up from the
period making stools, and I applied for a grant to the African
Welfare Society in Bulawayo, which came up with £20 for the
first year. I reckoned that with a bit of luck I could earn what I
needed to live on in Johannesburg, so I applied, and was
accepted. In January 1945 I set off from Durban to start this
new big-city life.

Mrs Hoskin took me to the station in her car. As the train
began to move she pushed a plain brown envelope in through
the window of my Africans-only compartment. The train pulls
out of Durban station on a curve, so you cannot wave for long
to anyone who is seeing you off. I was round the curve out of
sight by the time I could open the envelope. It contained a
cheque for £180 – a full three years' fees at the Hofmeyr. It was
not just an extraordinarily generous financial gift. It was also a
statement of faith that I could complete the full diploma
course. It was the finest thing anyone had ever done for me,
and there was no possible way I could repay it. When I told my
father of it he was deeply moved. As a token of his gratitude he
sent Mrs Hoskin a present of two gold sovereigns. I was very
much distressed to hear of her death four years later.

In Johannesburg I plunged into the hard work of my new
course, so very much more difficult than anything I had done
before. But however hard I studied I could not help getting
caught up in the life of that great city, in those years after the
European war ended and before the Afrikaner government
(elected in 1948) began its work of repression, which continues

today. The Hofmeyr School had no student hostel, so I rented a room at the Bantu Social Centre, which was meant mainly for visiting students like myself. The centre served no meals, so I ate at a restaurant called the Blue Lagoon, kept by a light-coloured Xhosa woman, very respectable, called Miss Taise. It was at the restaurant that I met a student from the Witwatersrand University called Nelson Mandela, that great man whom the South African government has kept in prison for so long. Later I was allowed to take a room in one of the Wits university hostels, and another student whom I made friends with there was Seretse Khama, the late president of Botswana.

Life in the big city was too fast for us boys from the country. The South African government made it very difficult for people from different backgrounds to mix freely. All their policies were designed to emphasise the so-called differences between the many peoples of the country: Zulus were not meant to mix with Xhosas, even though their languages are practically identical – and very like our own Sindebele too. Social life was fragmented along these tribal lines, and official policies encouraged that. It was hard for an outsider like me to fit into that strange system. Anyway I badly needed money to live on. The YMCA employed social science students to do welfare work in the army camps, looking after the young black recruits (who, since this was South Africa, were never allowed firearms). It was well paid, £20 a month, and you got a free uniform and free travel.

Only at the weekends did I really have any time off. There were very few pastimes open to someone like me. The only pleasant open space Africans could use was the Zoo Lake, a beautiful park where you could relax (provided you sat on the grass, not on the white people's benches). When they closed the gardens to black people it was one of the first signs of hardening apartheid, and it was very much resented. The other relaxation was to go to the great rallies organised by the African National Congress in one or other of the townships almost every weekend. I was very much impressed by the speeches, and by the sheer mass of people. But I was not yet really political: I was still trying to work out the social theories I was learning at the Hofmeyr.

At that time Johannesburg was already a dangerous place, although I think it is much more dangerous now. There were black gangsters called *tsotsis* in the townships, and everyone was terrified of them. I only had one bad experience with gangs myself. I was walking home after YMCA duty, after midnight, wearing my new hat that I was very pleased with. A gang of youths came up and began to jostle me, pushing and threatening with broomsticks, until my hat fell off. At that moment a late tram (for white people only) came down the track, and I managed to scramble across the tramlines just as it passed, leaving the young hooligans on the other side. When the tram was clear they were gone, and my new hat with them. I went into a grocer's shop that was still open nearby and told the white grocer what had happened. He was sympathetic and telephoned for the police. I waited an hour but no policeman came. I had described the boys in the gang. They were white.

My last year in South Africa was 1947. Most of it I spent in Durban, doing the fieldwork for my diploma in social work. There I came up against all sorts of problems that shocked me, with my rural background. There were poor people with no jobs and no chance of getting land to farm. There were women with babies, abandoned by their men and without grandparents or relations to rely upon for help. There was drunkenness and vice of every kind. I could study the problems, offer my sympathy (although the theory was that social workers should not get emotionally involved in their clients' problems). Sometimes I could get a little help for hard cases from one charity or another, and I had some success in arranging the adoption by African families of abandoned children – something that no social work agency had tried to do before. But I began to understand that social workers can only patch the holes in society. They cannot prevent the fabric being weak. Only the government could do that, and the government of South Africa was not governing for the people, but against them.

Durban, and the whole of Natal province, is mainly English-speaking, while most white people in Johannesburg speak Afrikaans. On the personal level I, like most Africans, found the Afrikaners much easier to get on with. They expected black people to know their place, which was inferior. But once that was established they could be friendly enough, and talk away freely. The English-speakers were theoretically more liberal, but when it came to social contacts they were much less free. If you tried to talk to them they would get embarrassed and quickly find something else to do. In Johannesburg practically all the Africans I knew could speak Afrikaans perfectly, because they were used to talking with the whites who spoke that language. But very few Durban Africans spoke English easily: they never got the chance to talk at length with native English-speakers.

The English word was 'segregation', the Afrikaans one 'apartheid'. In 1948 the Afrikaners won a big parliamentary majority, after many years of rule by the English-speakers, and they set to work at once to make apartheid a reality. There was a big controversy while I was in Johannesburg about what they called the 'locations in the sky': that was what the newspaper headlines always said, and at first I could not make out what it was supposed to mean. Soon I found out.

The new policy of the Afrikaner National Party was to push all Africans right out of the white areas, to force them to live apart (that is what apartheid means) in their own locations, and only come into the white districts as daytime visitors. But the rich white people who lived in the high-rise apartment blocks in the middle of town did not want to have to do without their black servants late at night or early in the morning. If the servants had to travel home at night and travel in at dawn, how could these well-off whites (most of them English-speakers) have their dinners served and their breakfasts prepared?

The English-speakers tolerated the African servants living illegally on the top floors of their apartment blocks. The Afrikaners said the 'locations in the sky' should be closed down and the servants sent off to live in the African townships. It was ridiculous, complete hypocrisy, for the English-speakers to claim that their policy was more liberal than the government's. All they wanted was cheap labour all the time.

A much more serious issue was constantly raised at the African National Congress rallies that I attended at the weekends. In the Cape province black and coloured people had the right to vote on the common roll, along with everyone else.

The Nationalist government, under Dr Malan, the prime minister, wanted to take the vote away from these people. The blacks and coloureds appealed to the courts against this government policy, and won their case. Then the government changed the constitution, increasing the number of senators so as to get the necessary majority in both houses to exclude the non-whites. I never forgot this. Later on, when the British tried to persuade us in Southern Rhodesia that we should accept a token minority of seats for black voters in the assembly, I remembered how the white South Africans had used their majority to get rid of the token black representation in their own parliament.

All these were at the time just personal impressions. I was thirty years old, and I had still not started to make myself a political philosophy. I was finishing my education and trying to sort out my own private life. In Pietermaritzburg, while doing my fieldwork, I met a lovely young Zulu girl, Violet Xaba, and we decided to get married. We even started to make the wedding arrangements, and I was just about to write to my father to tell him the good news and ask his advice. Then, to my surprise, he wrote to tell me he was getting married himself; he was lonely, he had met a very good and suitable young woman, and he hoped I agreed with his plan. I wrote back at once to say how pleased I was – Mother had been dead for over five years now, and I knew how lonely Father had become.

I went home for my father's wedding, and something very remarkable happened. I met a young woman and we fell in love. I knew we had to marry – although in fact we waited until 1949, when I had some security to offer her. I was very unhappy to let Violet down in this way, and it was some time before I got my courage together and wrote to tell her we could not get married after all. I was so relieved when she wrote back, telling me that she too had met someone else whom she really wanted to marry more than me. We are still good friends. When my daughter Thandi was married in 1983, Violet travelled up from South Africa for the ceremony, and I was pleased to see that she is still an attractive woman.

My marriage was the best thing I ever did in my whole life. In the thirty-four years of our marriage we have spent less than half the time together, but we have had a perfect understanding all the time. My wife has always borne the main responsibility for such property as we have owned: more, she has kept our family together, because all of us have always been confident that she would be there whatever happened.

Names of married women are very private things among our people: I suppose I was almost thirty before I learned that my own mother's name was Mlingo Hadebe. My wife was given the Christian name of Johanna, but that is not what I call her. The name I use is an honorific form of her maiden name – maFuyana. She is the younger sister of my father's second wife. She is also a devout Roman Catholic, and that was the only problem about our wedding. I was at the time a devout Methodist (I have explained that my religion is wider now). After much discussion we ended up having three weddings – a civil marriage to make it legal, then one blessing by a Methodist clergyman and another by a Catholic priest, our dear friend Father Schmitt (whose tragic death I shall have to tell of later). We have four children of our own – Thandi, born in 1954 just after my father's death; Ernest Thuthani, born in 1956, Michael Sibangilizwe, in 1958; and Louise Sehlule, in 1964. But we have three more children in the family, and I will explain why. My father and his second wife, maFuyana's elder sister, had three girls and two boys by the time of his death in 1954, when he was almost seventy. We adopted the three oldest, Patrick, Regina and Clara. We have always treated them as though they were our own children, and we have been amazingly lucky through all these turbulent years that all have survived.

My father's youngest son, Siponono, was wounded in action against the forces of Ian Smith's illegal regime in the mid-1970s, when he was just over twenty. He was recovering from his injuries in hospital outside Lusaka, in Zambia, when it was attacked by bombers of the Rhodesian Air Force. Siponono was killed outright.

Chapter 5

The Return of the Native Son

I had done well at Hofmeyr College, the missionaries had passed on good reports of me, and the people who ruled our country wanted suitable Africans to sort out some of their post-war problems. A job was waiting for me as soon as I got home at the beginning of 1948. I did not come up to my employers' expectations; indeed I hope I may have confirmed some of their worst fears.

My employers were the Rhodesia Railways, whose lines ran all over Northern and Southern Rhodesia, and half-way down through the protectorate of Bechuanaland to connect with the South African network. The vast majority of their employees were from Northern Rhodesia, Nyasaland or Mozambique. Very few were recruited in Southern Rhodesia itself, where the main marshalling yards and administrative headquarters were situated in Bulawayo, capital of the western province of Matabeleland. The migrant worker system enabled the employers to use the employees as though they were just implements. As far as Rhodesia Railways were concerned, there was no difference between a spanner and a black man. They were both useful on the railways, and they could both be easily replaced.

The key to the system was the compound. When Cecil Rhodes first started employing migrant workers in the South African mines, they were housed in compounds, great barracks ringed round with a high wall, the entrances guarded. That way the workers could be controlled, and the smuggling of gold or diamonds out of the mines could be kept in check. The railways took over the system. It was cheap and convenient for them, and it enabled the employers completely to rule the workers' lives. They supplied the food, laid down the hours of work and the hours of leisure, and could even turn the water supply on and off as they wanted.

Yet, despite being far from their homes and physically under the thumb of the railways, the employees had begun the rudiments of a trade union organisation to improve their working conditions, and in 1946 they had organised a successful strike. I had not been home while it was on, but I read the baffled accounts of it printed in the white-owned newspapers, and I was fascinated. Like the employers, I did not understand how it could have happened, and I was employed partly in order to make sure that nothing like it happened again.

The new department that I joined with my new social work diploma was called the Department of African Affairs: it was what a normal company would have called the personnel department. I was described as the chief social worker, and I was meant to train some welfare assistants. My superiors had not decided how I should work, exactly what I should do or what my status in the company was. In fact I was probably the first university-trained person, black or white, whom the railways had ever employed. This was confusing for the managers, and that was my advantage. I had to create my own job, and I did so in ways that the employers had not at all expected.

Most of the people under the African department were the compound policemen. That led to a wonderful comedy. Every morning the policemen would line up in their uniforms for inspection. But I did not wear a uniform; I wore an ordinary suit. There was nothing for the inspector to inspect. I gave up going to the little parade: there was nothing they could do about it. Instead of going to the office where I could conveniently be inspected, I started the day with some home visits to families, on welfare business. The inspector called me in and asked me: 'Why were you not present on line-up?' I answered that I had a job to do, I had to make my calls when people would be at home. He decided I was some new sort of animal, and left me alone.

Then there was the office problem. They had given me the job without thinking that I needed an office to do it in. I occupied some space on the police bench for a while, which was inconvenient for the policemen, then I put my case to the chief of the department, not just for an office but a typewriter too, to prepare my reports. It was difficult for him, since there had never been an African with an office before. After a while he found me a room that had previously been occupied by a compound manager, and that was all right. Then one day some technicians turned up to pull out the telephone: 'You are not supposed to use the telephone,' they insisted. But I stuck it out, saying that without a telephone I could not contact the other departments and so on, and they went away. Soon I had to go to Northern Rhodesia, to Lusaka, to look after welfare problems there, and while I was away they came in and took the phone out. That was the kind of interference I got.

The people running the new department were selected because they had, by their own standards, rather liberal opinions. Dr West, the head of the African department, was a leading member of the African Welfare Society, a charity that had given me a grant for my education at the Hofmeyr: Mr Cordell and Mr Longhurst, his deputies, certainly wished Africans well on the personal level. But I do not think that any of them at any time even dreamed that better relations had to mean, in the long run, creating a single community in a nation of which they and I would be equal members, no more and no less.

There was a young white man called David Fyfe in the department who worked closely with me, especially on encouraging the young people. He was a scoutmaster, and used to organise sports and social activities, which was very useful. After a while he was appointed a welfare officer, above me. He had no training at all, and education only up to school leaving certificate level. He was paid £100 a month. I, with my degree, was paid £12, the same rate as the coloured delivery drivers I had worked with before I went south for my education. But African graduate teachers were getting only £8 or £10 a month, so I was very well off by African standards. The point is that European pay rates were ridiculously higher than ours.

Despite their privileges in pay and living standards, the white people who worked directly with me were well-meaning enough, and they were not unusual in that. This was a time of liberalisation in racial attitudes, coinciding with a huge wave of immigration from Britain into Southern Rhodesia after the war. The white population of the country doubled in the seven years after 1947, to about 170,000 – and Europeans tended to keep their liberal views for a few years after arriving in Africa, only to abandon them once they became absorbed in the settler community.

But there were plenty of whites who could not stand the idea of an African getting promoted. When the railway headquarters moved into a new office I was given a proper place to work, with a telephone and a typewriter. I could see the white people looking at me and wondering how I was going to organise all that. This did not bother me, nor was I upset when they formed their tea club – I suppose they put a little money in to buy tea and biscuits, and when the time for break came they sat in their rooms and had their cup.

One day a tremendous wind blew up. I was out on my visiting rounds, and when I came back I found an African man in my office pumping up a Primus stove, with a kettle and teapot and cups and all. I asked him whatever he was doing, and he answered: 'The boss told me it is too windy for the stove outside, so I was to come in here and make the tea.' I told him to get out at once. But outside the stove still would not go, and the white fellows did not get their tea. They told the man off. He said there was nothing he could do, Nkomo had said he could not use his office.

The white clerk, a Mr Spearpoint, had the nerve to come to me and say: 'Mr Nkomo, I want the man to make my tea in here.'

So I said: 'Make the tea in my office? Why can't he do it in your office? I am not even a member of your tea club. If I was a member I might let the tea be made in my office. But you haven't asked me to join your club, so you can make your tea somewhere else.'

There was an official complaint about me to head office: but the head people backed me up and said the other office staff would have to put up with me.

In a while they began employing Africans for clerical jobs, so the white clerks got used to seeing black people handling papers around the office. I was a sort of spearhead for the employment of black people, and I did not mind facing up to the insults that went along with that.

It was the way they treated the ordinary workers and their families that I found most damaging. It was part of my job to visit people in their homes, and quite often I would find some tiny child alone in the house with its baby brothers or sisters. I would ask the oldest child where its mother was, and the answer would be: 'She has gone to collect her rations.' African workers were not trusted with the full amount due to them in pay: they would have something deducted from their wages, and in return they would be entitled to a ration of maize meal, salt, sugar and so on. Of course the families had really bought these things and paid for them. But the way it was presented was that the workers' wives were given hand-outs of food. Even the children were led to believe that they were wholly dependent on the railways. The idea that food is something that you have to budget for, that people are free to spend their own wages as they like, was not respected when it came to Africans. It was an irresponsible part of a bad system.

This was one of the first issues that I tackled in my second job, which was as president of the African Railway Employees' Association. This was in fact the black railway workers' union, but there was no way in which African trade unions could be recognised or registered. It had been founded just before the strike of 1946, and had not really managed to do much since then. Its members and committee were all fairly simple working people, and they did not know how to organise a membership register and run a union organisation. Almost as soon as I arrived at the welfare office, the general secretary, Sigeca Ndlovu, came to me and said: 'We have this organisation, can you help?' So I did my best, and when there were elections for a new committee in 1948 they elected me president. The railway administration was not at all happy about that. But although unrecognised, the union was not actually illegal, and there was nothing they could do about it.

I was determined that, although I had a job in the administration offices, I was not going to be part of the railway management. I did my welfare work conscientiously, and reported on the right forms and so on. But when there were management meetings I did not go. I said: 'I am an employee, not a manager: I do not help make policy in this organisation.' I had plenty of relations and personal contacts in the Bulawayo African townships, but I chose not to live there. I had a room in the railway compound, like any other worker, and I ate the same food as all the other workers. It was pretty dirty and ill-organised until I helped the people to get rotas going for washing clothes and dishes, and cleaning up. I had lived better in the Bantu Centre in Johannesburg.

The management people were not surprised that I chose to live with the workers. They had come to believe that living in the compound, eating coarse food and not enjoying luxuries were part of the African way of life. It did not occur to them that we would prefer to live better if we got the chance. It was convenient to them to take that view of us. It became part of their way of life. I understood that, and it did not make me angry. But I resolved to confront them. It was impossible to persuade them to change. They had to be made to change.

That was why I took on a third responsibility, on top of my job as welfare officer and my position as president of the railway union. In South Africa I had become very interested in the African National Congress, which was just starting to move on from being a body which merely complained about the way things were to one which developed a concrete programme for change in society. The Southern Rhodesian ANC was at this time, in 1948, a weak organisation. It had perhaps 5,000 or 7,000 members, and there had recently been a row in the committee. But there were some excellent people who were trying to make it more active – Clement Muchachi, Jerry Vera, Aaron Mabeza, 'Old Man' Dliwayo and Edward Ndlovu. It was pretty much like it had been with the railway union: they just came to me and asked for help in getting things organised. I was promptly elected president of the ANC as well, my predecessors having been Enoch Dumbutshena and Stanlake Samkange.

It was our mission to make people believe that things could be changed. That was not easy: there was a tremendous amount of apathy. We held our general meetings in the Stanley Hall, the only public hall in Makokoba township. If we did well, a hundred people would turn up. On a bad day there were so few people that we used to meet in the little library – it was as bad as that. Even the committee, whose members were ordinary working people and a few farmers, did not really believe that anything could be changed; the white people were so strong and well organised, we were so weak. I travelled round the country meeting as many people as I could – I had the advantage of a railway pass, but often I had to go by bus to remote places. Muchachi used to walk miles through the bush to get to tiny places and spread the word that there was, after all, an alternative to just accepting the condition of life that the white government imposed upon us.

All we could do about people's grievances at that time was to find out what they were and formulate them, writing things down for the first time, organising petitions and complaining about what was wrong. I typed out resolutions and memoranda on my railway typewriter, on every imaginable subject. But whether it was labour relations or voting rights or land questions, or simply personal grievances, all communications to the authorities had to be addressed to the secretary for native affairs in the government. He very rarely bothered to reply. Half the time we did not even get an acknowledgment. African protests did not matter. It was discouraging. But we continued.

It was that experience of ordinary people's difficulties, in all walks of life and in every corner of the colony, that convinced me that no partial political reform could set matters right. Through my railway work I came to know not only Southern Rhodesia but Northern Rhodesia with its different form of colonial government, and Nyasaland with its apparently more well-intentioned protectorate system. I saw that the people were denied not only their rights but also their responsibilities: they were treated as children and expected to behave like children. It was an attitude of mind as demeaning to the rulers as to those who were ruled. It had to be changed, and nobody was going to change it except ourselves.

In 1952 I unexpectedly discovered that the government of Southern Rhodesia needed me after all, even if they did not want me. The British government was trying to organise a new federation of the three separate territories in what it called Central Africa – the two protectorates of Northern Rhodesia and Nyasaland, and the 'self-governing colony' (whatever that might mean) of Southern Rhodesia, my homeland. They organised a conference in London to prepare for this new arrangement, and somebody in the British government – I have been told that it was the prime minister himself, Winston Churchill, but I do not know if that is true – insisted that the Southern Rhodesian delegation should include at least a token black representation. So suddenly I found myself the possessor of a brand-new passport, on an aircraft heading for Europe. This is a story that needs explaining.

After the Second World War, and the independence of India that immediately followed it, the British saw that they could not go on running their colonial empire in the same old way. Independence for the colonial peoples would have to come one day. Meanwhile they wanted to reorganise the colonies so that they would be easier to run and presumably more profitable. One way to do that, they thought, was to amalgamate several colonies into one federation. In our part of the world the British Labour government, which was voted out of office in 1951, had studied the plan for a Central African Federation of the three territories, but had not decided to go ahead with it.

Mr Churchill's new Conservative government were sure they wanted federation. For the white minorities in each of the territories it was a logical move. Northern Rhodesia had its rich copper mines, and needed cheap migrant labour to work them. Nyasaland had a surplus population and a long tradition of sending migrant workers abroad. Southern Rhodesia had a big food surplus and a much bigger white population than the other two territories – and the whites controlled their own internal affairs. By putting the three together, the British hoped to get rid of a load of responsibility, and the local whites hoped to be able to hold onto control of the whole area. The big companies, based in London and Johannesburg, that controlled the Northern Rhodesian mines and the Southern Rhodesian farms, thought such an arrangement would guarantee their profits for a long time ahead.

We in the ANC suspected the idea was a bad one, but we were desperately short of reliable information on what federation really meant. The only news we got was in papers owned by companies committed to the preservation of white interests. (There was at the time no radio service for Africans in Southern Rhodesia, although we could listen to the service from Lusaka in Northern Rhodesia; but that too was really just European news edited for African consumption.)

The one contact we had with other affected people was at the house of the Indian representative in Salisbury, a Mr Singh – he was not called High Commissioner, since the colony was theoretically not independent, but he had diplomatic status. He invited the leaders of the African National Congress in Northern Rhodesia down to Salisbury for a reception. Their leader was Harry Nkumbula; also present was a quiet, serious young man who impressed me very much. His name was Kenneth David Kaunda, and he struck me as a deep thinker and kindly man.

The British government, before imposing federation on the three territories, had to go through the motions of discussing it with the people who lived there. The constitutional and racial position was very different in each of the three. Nyasaland had only about 4,000 whites in a population of 2.4 million. Northern Rhodesia had 37,000 whites in a population of 2.9 million. Southern Rhodesia had 135,500 whites among 2.2 million. In the two protectorates, the constitution made it plain that the interests of the African inhabitants were 'paramount': the British government was meant to be a sort of trustee for the Africans.

But since 1923 the whites of Southern Rhodesia had run the country exactly as they wanted. They had their own army and air force, and in practically every way the place was as much an independent nation as the Dominions of Canada, Australia, New Zealand and South Africa. The Southern Rhodesian prime minister regularly attended the conferences of the Dominion prime ministers. The only reason why it was not formally acknowledged to be an independent nation, ruled by whites, was to keep it out of the hands of the South Africans. So it remained in name but not in practice a colony, flying the Union Jack and theoretically subject to British rule.

At the time, in 1952, I was aware of these things but I did not really regard them as important. There were plenty of more immediate problems to deal with in my three full-time jobs. But one day, sitting with my wife in my little house at Number 3 Railway Compound, I saw a car pull up outside the door. I recognised it as belonging to the Reverend Percy Ibbotson, a minister whom I knew very well indeed. He was the secretary-general of the African Welfare Society, of which I had by now become (in addition to my other offices), a committee member.

Mr Ibbotson was a very decent man, so I at once went out and invited him in. He seemed a bit tense, and after a while he asked if I would mind taking a walk. Once outside, he revealed that he had a message for me from no less a person than Sir

Godfrey Huggins, Prime Minister of Southern Rhodesia. I had in fact once seen Sir Godfrey. That was when he came on an official visit to the Tjolotjo Government Industrial School, in about 1934. I remembered that his shoes were beautifully polished, and that he was disappointingly small for the man who was head of the whole country. I was the boy who hoisted up the Union Jack and broke it smartly out of its bindings as it reached the top of the flagpole. Apart from that we had not been in touch.

The message now was that the prime minister was inviting me to join the Southern Rhodesian delegation to the forthcoming London conference to prepare the federation of the Rhodesias and Nyasaland. But what, I asked, was he inviting me as? As a prominent person, said Mr Ibbotson. I replied that I was not a prominent person, just a young man, and I could certainly not give an immediate answer. Then began a few days of frantic activity. I told my wife, then called an emergency meeting of the ANC executive and asked their opinion.

The discussion was heated. We knew the African leaders in Northern Rhodesia and Nyasaland were deeply hostile to federation. Both those territories had begun to make progress towards self-government, with a few Africans elected by one way or another to their legislative assemblies; they did not want federation with 'self-governing' Southern Rhodesia, which had no constitutional provision that African interests were paramount. But our own ANC had, as I have said, mainly concentrated on trying to give voice to specific grievances among our people. We had not progressed to the point of considering political or constitutional changes.

The big question in my colleagues' minds was what the prime minister wanted me to do if I did accept. That I did not know. So I went back to Mr Ibbotson and asked him: he did not know either. He in turn went back to Sir Godfrey Huggins, who replied that he had nothing specific in mind for me to do: he did not even want to know my opinions in advance. All he wanted was for me to be a member of the Southern Rhodesian delegation. This I passed on to my executive, and after some more discussion they decided that I should go to London and oppose the federation.

We were all highly suspicious, believing that Huggins must have some subtle plan – we did not know that it was just my black face, not me, that Sir Godfrey Huggins was inviting. One other African name was on the list, that of Jasper Savanhu, from Salisbury. He was an executive with the Argus newspaper group in the capital; beyond that I knew nothing at all about him.

Thus, more or less at random, I was pushed onto the international stage. I went home to tell my father, who approved, and bought myself suitable clothes for London in April. Then I found myself at the little airport of Bulawayo, ready for the first of the many flights that I have since undertaken. We flew in a Dakota to Livingstone in Northern Rhodesia, to meet our colleagues from Salisbury and pick up the British Overseas Airways flight from Johannesburg to London. My companion on that first leg was the same Mr Macintyre who had sacked me as a bread delivery driver fifteen years before because I complained that the coloured drivers for his company were getting three times as much pay as me. I did not mind, but it must have been embarrassing for him.

We slept the night at Livingstone, in a rest-house at the airport, and at breakfast very early next morning we met the party from Salisbury. Inevitably I sat down with Jasper Savanhu. He was not a graduate, as I was, but he was very much more sophisticated than me, and had in his work spent a lot of time socially with white people. I remember that he put a hard French roll on his plate and cut it so that the plate jumped off the table and clattered down onto the floor. The white delegates elaborately pretended not to notice these blacks who did not know how to use their knives and forks.

The flight, in an old Hermes aircraft, took thirty-six hours to London in those days, by way of Brazzaville, Kano, Tripoli, Rome and London. We all sat right at the back of the aircraft, with Sir Godfrey Huggins in the last row of all. I noticed that he seemed nervous when we took off. When he went to the lavatory it was the same one that I used. I thought about how that could happen on a BOAC plane, but not in any place that Huggins himself was in charge of.

All the same, I was very careful to do things just as they should be done. The meals came on airline trays, and when

1a. 1949: Joshua Nkomo and maFuyana, after their wedding. (*Parade*)

1b. 1949: the Rhodesia Railways African Recreation Club Committee: front row, second from left, Joshua Nkomo; front row, centre, David Fyfe.

2a. Nkomo in 1983 outside the last remaining house of the Railway Compound where he lived from his marriage until 1953. (*Nicholas Harman*)

2b. Nkomo at Stanley Hall in 1983, the centre of Bulawayo's political life in the 1950s. (*Nicholas Harman*)

2c. The grave of Nkomo's parents and his brother Paul. (*Nicholas Harman*)

3a. 1960: nationalist delegations of the NDP (Southern Rhodesia) and UNIP (Northern Rhodesia) return to Salisbury after constitutional talks in London. *L. to r.*: Robert Mugabe (NDP Publicity Secretary), M. Sipalo (UNIP General Secretary), Joshua Nkomo (NDP President) and Kenneth Kaunda (UNIP President). (*Parade*)

3b. 1962: wearing characteristic NDP hats in Salisbury are, *l. to r.*: Robert Mugabe, Stanislas Marembo, Joshua Nkomo, Maurice Nyagumbo and Dr Terence Ranger.

4a. 1961: Joshua Nkomo, president of the NDP, walks out of talks on a proposed constitution for Southern Rhodesia. He is followed by the NDP treasurer-general, the Rev. Ndabaningi Sithole. (*Parade*)

4b. 1962: Joshua Nkomo, returning to Salisbury from New York, had a triumphal reception at which a spirit-medium presented him on behalf of the freedom fighters of the 1890s with a ceremonial axe, a symbol of resistance. He was also given the name *Chibwechitedza*, 'the slippery rock'. (Lionis Lambiris – *Parade*

mine arrived I would always read the paper a bit before I began to eat. That gave me time to observe how the white man in the next seat took all the little covers off the things, and which knife he used for which course. At that time, on my first visit to the big world outside Southern Rhodesia, it was very important to me to seem in control of what was going on: only much later did I learn that self-confidence comes with doing things your own way, and not imitating other people.

That first flight was an astonishing experience. Those old aircraft did not fly up over the clouds as they do today, and the turbulence of the air amazed me. We took off from Kano just at dusk, as the sun disappeared; as we rose into the sky it came up again above the horizon and shone straight in at the window, pink and gold and beautiful. Then came the first sight of London, the city I had been taught was the centre of the world. It turned out strangely unimpressive, but no less interesting for that.

We drove in along the old Great West Road, where the small houses were lined up side by side like those in Makokoba township – a dreary beginning. Huggins and the senior delegates were lodged in the Hyde Park Hotel, which was very grand. Junior members were tucked modestly away, so that Savanhu and I found ourselves in a little bed-and-breakfast hotel somewhere near Charing Cross station: but it was the first time I had stayed in any kind of hotel, and that was something. There I set out to try to understand these British people who had been so remote a feature of my life at home.

I had always wondered who did the work in England. In Southern Rhodesia even the lower-grade white employees had servants: you would not have thought a white man even knew how to make a cup of tea for himself. But here, in the hotel lobby, were white people carrying my bags and calling me 'Sir'. At home no black man was ever called 'Sir'. Even black teachers were called 'Teacher'; 'Sir' was for whites. Next morning a white lady – *Nkosikazi*, Princess, was how we had been taught to address white ladies – came to my room and began to sweep up and collect the laundry. I thought I had better get out and explore this place where things were upside down.

My great good luck was that one of Huggins's delegates was a born Londoner, and a very decent man. Mr Eastwood was not senior enough to be kept very busy on conference business, so he took on the task of showing off the city he was so proud of. He had worked as a lad in Petticoat Lane, the street market in the East End. We went there almost at once, and I thought it very grubby and not at all what you would expect of an imperial capital – but I was delighted to see that things were like this. We went to Westminster Abbey and to the Chapel Royal at Windsor, and walked on the graves of kings. They showed me where King George VI was newly buried, and the place reserved for his widow beside him. (I still, incidentally, have a great admiration for the Queen Mother, that dignified lady.)

I began to think about Christianity and power. At home, becoming a Christian meant giving up our own old ways to follow white clergymen and a white Christ. Our religion, in which we approached God through our ancestors and the history of our people, was said to be primitive and backward. But here in England the ancestral tombs in the churches signified the continuity of the nation, and I could not see what was so different about that. Of course I did not on this first visit start to form a theory of colonialism, or anything as abstract as that. But I felt inside myself that the Christianity I had been taught was, whatever its other virtues, mainly a way of imposing the white man's authority.

I had always wondered what the difference really was that put white people in authority over black people. At home it was impossible to know whites well enough to find out. But now I began to suspect that the difference was in the texture of our hair and the colour of our skin, nothing more. I admired the Britain I saw. It seemed to me in those days that here was a place where people accepted their position in society – where the man who carried your bag at the airport carried it with a little swing of pride that he was a good bag-carrier. But it seemed to me extraordinary that anyone should try to export this system to other countries. I felt that the monarchy was holding it all together – I still feel that about England – but I could not see what this monarchy had to do with my people.

I learned from that first visit out of my own country to get away from the official hotels and the official ceremonies as much as I possibly could: wherever I went thereafter I tried to visit the people, as well as visiting the country. But there was business to be done, and that took some sorting out.

One of the first events was an official British government reception at Claridge's Hotel. I assumed that if you invited people for a reception you gave them something to eat, but I got nothing but some little sausages and prawns, and went to bed hungry. Then there was a banquet – I inquired in advance whether that meant food, and was relieved to find that it did. After all the courses had been cleared away, the conference chairman, Lord Salisbury, proposed the toast to the Queen. I would have liked to drink to her, but there was nothing in front of me but a glass of champagne. Since I never touch alcohol I raised the glass to my lips and put it down untouched.

The conference itself began with a nasty shock. I turned on the radio news to hear the BBC reporting the arrival of the three delegations from the three territories of the future federation. The man noted that the Africans from the protectorates of Northern Rhodesia and Nyasaland were boycotting the conference. The announcer then went on to report that the Labour party had strongly condemned the attitude of the Southern Rhodesian delegation, which included 'two African stooges'. I did not know exactly what a stooge was, but it sounded bad. I had always been told that the Labour party was sympathetic to black people, and now it was calling us names without even asking our opinion.

Savanhu and I were completely isolated. We did not know our way around London, we had very little money and no idea how to get in touch with the press or the BBC. We had heard that Dr Hastings Banda, the Nyasaland African leader who was based in London, was lobbying against federation and the way the conference was being organised – but we had no way to contact either him or the Northern Rhodesian delegation.

So we were entirely dependent on the BBC and the British papers to inform us and help us to decide what to do. We decided that if we simply boycotted the conference like the other Africans, we would just be ignored. So we thought it best to attend the opening session, then immediately state our reasons for withdrawing and walk out. Savanhu agreed to speak for both of us, and off we went to the conference.

The name of the British minister who took the chair made it easy for me to object to its aim. He was Lord Salisbury. The capital of Southern Rhodesia was named after his grandfather, who was prime minister of Britain when Cecil Rhodes captured it in 1980 – and he was personally a large shareholder in companies that stood to make big profits, at the expense of the Africans, if federation went through. Throughout my career I found myself dealing with Conservative ministers who had family and personal links with the old colonial traditions. Even Lord Carrington, who chaired the Lancaster House conference in 1979 which preceded the independence of Zimbabwe, had previously been a director of a huge company with colonial interests.

Lord Salisbury began by stating the advantages the British government saw in federating the three territories. I noted that, in all that gathering, Savanhu and I were the only two black people. When Salisbury sat down, I jogged Savanhu's elbow: he shifted in his seat, but did not rise. If the moment passed it would be too late – so I got to my feet myself, quite unprepared, and began to speak.

I announced that I and my colleague were withdrawing. We were doing so in support of the stand of our friends from Northern Rhodesia and Nyasaland. But before I withdrew I wished to make my own position clear. I had been invited as an individual – I did not claim to speak for Mr Savanhu – and not as a member of Sir Godfrey Huggins's delegation. Indeed Sir Godfrey had not inquired what my position was. As its president I had consulted the executive of the Southern Rhodesia African National Congress, and I stated categorically that the ANC rejected the idea of federation. Then I walked out, and Savanhu followed.

This stand won me a bit of the sympathy that had been lacking when the Labour party described me as a stooge. Various sympathetic British people got in touch with me to express their support, and I was able to have short meetings with Dr Banda – a stern figure, very reserved, like most Malawians. People like Fenner Brockway, Commander Fox-Pitt and the Reverend Michael Scott all gave their support, and I was able to talk to a few interested journalists. But even those intelligent and liberal people in Britain could not see why I was so strongly against federation. They knew that race relations were easier in the other territories, and that African political advancement had begun there. They argued that, if Southern Rhodesia went into the federation, the more relaxed attitudes of the other places would gradually affect us too.

It was very hard to explain to them what our struggle was really about. I think they saw it through the perspective of South Africa, or perhaps even of the United States – that what was wrong was segregation, or apartheid, whatever you called it – that if race relations were made a bit less rough, progress would gradually and naturally follow. But I knew perfectly well that if there was federation it would mean more power for the largest group of white people within it, and that meant the Southern Rhodesian electorate that had been voting for Sir Godfrey Huggins, and against African progress, solidly ever since 1933. In fact federation would mean a setback for the small progress that had been made in the two other territories, and would not make things the slightest bit better in the south. Even those people in Britain who wanted to sympathise with me thought I was being too gloomy. Subsequent events proved that I was absolutely right.

The united opposition of the African populations of the three territories did have some effect. The Labour party came out squarely in opposition to federation, and so did a large number of church and trade union groups in Britain. Then, when I got home, Sir Godfrey Huggins and his government gave me an importance that was more than I personally felt I deserved – although I was delighted to take advantage of the opportunity they offered me.

Arriving home, at the airport in Bulawayo, I was quite fiercely questioned by the local journalists, and one thing I said made a sensation. I was asked what I would do if federation went ahead, and I answered: 'If the whites persist in handling us the way they are doing, they must not be surprised if one day we pay them back in their own coin.' This was taken as a most brutal threat. Jasper Savanhu put out a special statement, published by the Argus newspapers who employed him, saying he dissociated himself entirely from such sentiments. (Later Savanhu was to accept a job as a 'deputy minister' for housing in Huggins's federal government. But he was not even allowed to build a house for himself in a white area, and after a while the poor chap had to resign and admit that collaboration did not work because the whites would not let it.)

I stated that I had only promised that the whites would be treated exactly as they had treated other people: if they did not want to accept their own coin, they should not pay other people in it – or did they think there was something wrong with the white man's coin? That only made the government angrier. They took away my passport and impounded it. I was becoming a bit of a celebrity.

Chapter 6
First Offence

Since the government and the white-owned newspapers had decided I was a nuisance, a lot of Africans and a few white people sympathetic to the African cause decided I was worth supporting. Early in 1953 the British government organised another review conference for the federation, in London, to examine the arrangements. This time all the delegations were all-white: African opposition was taken for granted and ignored. After what I had done last time, Sir Godfrey Huggins and his colleagues were not going to invite any more token Africans to join their team. Instead, a group of private people in Bulawayo raised a subscription to send me to London to lobby against federation. Taffie Zibuya Moyo made a loan of £350 which, I fear, has still not be repaid.

There was one problem. The government was still holding the passport issued to me for the first trip. I asked for it back, and was told I must make my request in person to the minister for native affairs. To make the visit more formal, I was accompanied by two fellow-members of the African National Congress committee, Amos Mazibisa and Edward Ndlovu.

Mr Fletcher, the minister, quite politely opened our meeting by asking why the ANC wanted to send me to London. We answered that it was essential to express to the British people, whose government was imposing this federation, the opposition of the black people of Southern Rhodesia. At present the British were hearing only the views of the white electorate, which was entirely unrepresentative of the nation. Mr Fletcher then asked my colleagues to withdraw.

'Are you insisting on going?' asked Mr Fletcher.

I said I was, it was essential.

'But why?'

'The people want their views expressed,' I said.

Fletcher looked genuinely puzzled. 'We have elevated you by inviting you to the last conference. I am a minister – we have pulled you up to our level, so that you could speak for your people. Now you are letting the people pull you down to their level. Why are you tolerating this?'

I said to the minister: 'Either we rise as a people or we remain down as a people. You cannot pick out one man and raise him above the crowd.' Mr Fletcher, I knew, spoke Sindebele well: I quoted to him our proverb: '*Akulaqunga olukhula egumeni* – the tall grass cannot grow on the beaten pathway.' Mr Fletcher did not reply. He put his right hand to his jacket pocket and pulled out my passport, which he handed to me. I took it. Mr Fletcher's hand remained extended. Very much surprised – this was not at all a normal thing – I took his hand and shook it. 'Good luck,' said the minister. I turned and left the room to join my African colleagues.

In London, after the long flight, I had contacts prepared and friends to meet, and we moved around Britain together addressing meetings organised by Labour party groups, churches and trade unions. It was for me a new sort of excitement, working together with others in a common cause. The Reverend Michael Scott had founded the African Bureau to support our cause. Fenner Brockway, MP, was on our side. There was a great meeting at Central Hall, Westminster, packed with sympathetic people, and there were long miles of travel to many other places.

Looking back, it seems surprising that British government officials and politicians did not pay more attention to what we were saying. I met a few of them on both my London trips, but the conversation never progressed much beyond polite chit-chat. They would have saved everyone a lot of trouble if they had listened to us, but I suppose they genuinely did not know the extent to which I reflected African opinion in my country. The ANC was, after all, still a small organisation.

Even broadly sympathetic people in Britain had trouble understanding the real depth of my opposition to federation. They were aware of the threat that, if Southern Rhodesia stayed out of the federation, it might be swallowed up by South Africa, which would have wiped out all hope of African progress. Sincere well-wishers argued that, since Northern Rhodesia and Nyasaland, with their huge African majorities, were inevitably going to move forward to independence, we in the south should join with them and use their progress as a base for our own struggle for freedom. They were well-informed and realistic: they knew the whites in Southern Rhodesia had their own army, air force and police, and they did not believe this solid armour could crack if we took it on unaided. But I, and the people I spoke for, believed that what people demand cannot be suppressed.

It was Sir Godfrey Huggins himself who explained what federation was really about. He stated that his aim was to create in Central Africa a new partnership between Europeans and Africans, a partnership like that of the rider and the horse. That was very honest. The white man was to ride, the black man was to carry him. That was what we were up against. I had to fight that idea in my own country, and I had to persuade people abroad that our opposition would be determined and effective.

At home once more, I found that the government of Southern Rhodesia had become seriously alarmed, or perhaps just angry, at my activities. They looked for a way of getting back at me, and thus laid the foundation of my new reputation as the spokesman of African opinion. It was pure chance that led to my new fame.

In England, as usual at the end of public meetings, there had been all sorts of people handing out leaflets. I had accepted them more or less at random, and stuffed them into my briefcase with my other disorganised papers. When I arrived in Bulawayo the customs took away those papers, and among them they found a couple of copies of a pamphlet that I had not even read, emphasising the contrast between black and white people's housing in Southern Rhodesia. This gave the government the chance to put me on trial for importing subversive literature. I was summonsed to answer the charge at Bulawayo magistrates' court.

I was, at first, frankly rather alarmed by having to appear in court. I was a respectable citizen, and I did not like being put on trial. So I inquired about getting a lawyer, and found that although there were law firms perfectly willing to act for me, I would have to put down £400 in cash before they started. That much money I did not have, so I decided to defend myself in person.

What the government did not expect was the amazing show

of public support for my defence. From all over Southern Rhodesia people came to stand in the street and cheer when I went in and out of the court. Bulawayo was blocked solid. The police had no idea what to do – the people were perfectly law-abiding – and they could only try to keep the traffic moving and the crowds orderly. In fact the policemen behaved very well, with no aggression. Inside the magistrates' court it was the same. The presiding magistrate at first put me in the dock, like any criminal. Then I requested more room to arrange my documents. The magistrate politely agreed, and allocated me the place usually occupied by defending counsel, right alongside the prosecutor. The prosecutor himself was polite too. I laughed aloud the first time he answered a point of mine by referring to me, in English barristers' style, as 'My learned friend'. I was tempted to return the compliment, but managed to keep to the rules and not seem impertinent. The upshot was that the magistrate found me guilty, cautioned me and granted me a discharge. It was hardly the victory the government had hoped for. My own triumph was in the streets, with those thousands and thousands of people from all over the country. Factories closed because so many of their workers had taken time off to go to court: white people found their domestic servants missing, gone to Bulawayo for the trial. There had never been anything like it before.

The government, by putting me on trial, had helped to rally African opposition to their plans for federation. More of our African people began to see that they must no longer merely complain about particular grievances; they had to move on to criticise the system itself, to develop a political programme on their own account. For a start, we began to coordinate our action with that of the African parties in the other territories threatened by federation. In particular we managed to organise a meeting with the African National Congress of Northern Rhodesia, in the border town of Fort Jameson. Our side was represented by myself and Chalton Ngcebetsha. (Mysteriously, after Chalton and I had arrived by train, Stanlake Samkange arrived by chartered aircraft: I have never known who paid for that, or who organised it, but Stanlake was there.) From Northern Rhodesia came Harry Nkumbula, Kenneth Kaunda and Simon Kapwepwe, another opportunity to renew contacts with those people whose struggle was so like ours, but also so different. The beginnings of a united African resistance were in sight.

But then a new distress fell upon me. On a Saturday in July 1952 I addressed a meeting in the township to reaffirm our opposition to federation, and returned home afterwards to our little home at 3 Railway Compound. My wife was upset: our son Temba, who was six months old, would not stop crying whatever she did. We took him down to the hospital, where the doctor examined the boy, gave him some medicine and told us to bring him back on Monday. Monday never came. On Sunday night Temba died.

The police had the duty of dealing with any sudden death in the compound. On Monday morning they came in their official van to take the body to the mortuary. They were decent and sympathetic. I rode in front with the white police officer. My wife rode in the back with some women friends and the little body: the women were keening in sorrow.

We drove out of the compound, over the maze of railway lines, and past a group of shunters, white people. Hearing the wailing, one of them, a young lad, asked the policeman what was wrong. 'A child has died in the compound,' said the officer gently.

'So where is this dead animal?' asked the shunter.

The policeman pushed his window up to silence him, and drove on, deeply embarrassed. Partly to spare his feelings, and more to spare my wife's, I said nothing. Until I wrote this down here today I have never allowed anyone, even my wife, to know that this thing happened when our first son died.

Chapter 7
The Long Haul Starts

Temba's death was a shattering blow, more to my wife even than to myself. I had my work developing the rudiments of a welfare organisation for our people. It kept me extremely busy, often away on my travels recruiting candidates for the training courses I was organising, or coping with my trainees' needs. MaFuyana was at home in our tiny house, mourning and with not nearly enough to distract her. She badly needed a change, but there seemed no way I could provide it.

Then an unexpected opportunity arose. I had come across some members of the Moral Rearmament movement just before these events, and at first I had been attracted by their ideas. The movement – usually called MRA, sometimes the Buchmanites, after its American founder Frank Buchman – advocated a woolly and sentimental belief, that if people would only be totally honest with each other on the personal level, political problems would disappear; they were also violently anti-Communist, which was, I suppose, how they managed to collect and spend what seemed to be huge amounts of money from the United States.

I had pretty soon lost interest in the MRA people, because they talked to me as if I were a baby. But all of a sudden, in the middle of our distress, they invited maFuyana and myself to their international conference at their headquarters at Caux, in Switzerland. I mentioned the invitation to maFuyana and she thought it would help if we could get away and start to forget what had happened. So I accepted for both of us, and I suggested that my social worker colleague, Jerry Vera, should come along as well – Jerry was then and long remained a very close friend of mine.

So off we went to Europe. It was a tremendous journey – first to South Africa, where we stayed with an MRA supporter in a white suburb, which I suppose was illegal, since I certainly was not employed by him. Then we flew in a huge old chartered aircraft, which was bitterly cold, by way of Benghazi, Rome,

Amsterdam and London. The plane was so unreliable that one of the engines had to be shut down because of an oil leak just as we were crossing the Alps (I tried to keep this from maFuyana). Then we took the train from London to Geneva, and on to Caux.

The meeting mostly consisted of people getting up and telling everyone else about their private thoughts, and it was often very embarrassing. I was alarmed, after about a week, when it was suddenly announced from the platform that Mrs Nkomo was going to speak. MaFuyana did not have much formal education, and I frankly thought her English was not up to addressing an audience of about a thousand people – we had hardly ever talked English together, since there was no reason why we should. But her speech was, for me, the best thing about the whole conference: she had prepared her notes, and spoke clearly and to the point. It was a revelation. I had no idea she could do it, which only shows how much married couples may have to learn about each other.

But I became increasingly bored, and wanted to get away from the sentimental atmosphere. They had a technique by which the participants were meant to sit and think quietly, then write down what God had told them and read it out. I thought the politest way to make my excuses was to sit and listen to God, then write down that He had said we were to leave Caux and get back to our work in Southern Rhodesia. The organisers did not like that at all, and they tried to ignore me. They wanted to have everyone there for the end of the conference, when Dr Buchman himself would come and speak. I accused them of insincerity, because they would not respect what God had told me. In the end I had to make my complaint at a public meeting, and finally they agreed that we should leave before the end. (Some other Africans there had much the same experience, which made me certain that the MRA people were not sincere.)

So back we went to Southern Rhodesia, by way of London. The journey was yet another pleasure, my wife and I travelling as tourists together by way of Malta, Wadi Halfa, Khartoum, Juba, Nairobi (where we spent the night), and on via Dar es Salaam to Salisbury. We certainly saw a lot of Africa along the way – unlike on aircraft now, where you are whisked from place to place with no idea of what lies between. The whole trip was a tonic, after the tragedy of our child – and whatever I thought of the MRA people, they helped me to see what a strong person my wife is, and to set her up again for life at home. It was about this time that she developed her knitting and sewing into what became practically a one-person industry, and kept her occupied during all those long years while I was away, at work, in exile or in prison. And Thandi was born in 1954. So whatever I have missed in life through my work, I have always been confident that a happy home awaited me, if I could only find time to be there.

Now in 1955, I settled down again seriously to develop the first-ever social welfare services for Africans in Southern Rhodesia. Dr Philips, the director of the Hofmeyr School, had given me a sound theoretical background. My personal task was to apply it in circumstances that no theorist had foreseen, to exploit the very limited resources that the railway company made available in order to develop our people's enormous potential for helping each other.

There was a dire shortage of trained Africans in practically every field, including my own. So I concentrated on setting up successive six-month courses, to train welfare assistants to take responsibility for personal and family problems throughout the massive international rail network. The courses attracted people from other walks of life as well – from the municipal councils that ran our country's vast housing schemes, from the police, from the teaching profession. I was able to provide the basis of theory that they needed to organise their own often very sound ideas. I carefully kept politics as far as possible out of my work, which made it a bit unreal. The biggest social problem of all was the policy that reserved the right to live in urban areas to white people, so that all Africans were there only by permission of the boss.

But I could not keep politics out of my life, even if I had tried harder. The Central African Federation had been created, despite the united efforts of all valid African spokesmen to prevent it. My main contribution to federal politics was intended to show them up as a farce. I stood in the first federal elections for one of the token black seats, reserved for African candidates (provided they qualified on the grounds of education or property ownership) but voted upon by an electorate almost 99 per cent of which was white. Indians and coloured people also had the right to vote on this 'B' roll, along with the few 'qualified' blacks of whom I was one.

Of course I was soundly beaten. Mike Hove, an African colleague of Jasper Savanhu's with the Argus newspaper group, got about 30,000 votes and I got about 15,000. Most of my support came from Africans and Indians (the coloureds were so disillusioned that they barely bothered to vote at all), but the result showed that several thousand whites must have voted for me without telling anyone. The real point was that, as the demonstrations at my trial for importing subversive literature had shown, I had massive African support, but the rigged electorate excluded the vast majority of the people from voting. The electoral system was absurd, and my defeat proved it. That was what I had intended. Afterwards I and the few other members of the African National Congress who were qualified to hold voters' cards sent them back to the returning officer, stating that a qualification for voting that brought only about 400 Africans onto the register with tens of thousands of whites was ridiculous.

My conviction grew that the whites would never give us our rights until they were forced to do so. I could not help feeling that my work for the railways was a sham – I was trying to patch the cloth of social problems, when what we needed was a whole new blanket. By 1953 I could take it no longer, and I decided to resign in order to serve full-time as general secretary of the Railway Employees' Association. This I did for three years. I began to believe that if more Africans could acquire property and qualify that way for the right to vote, it might lead to political progress. In any case, I wanted freedom to spend as much time as I needed on ANC business, and to travel as widely as possible about the country.

I set up in business as a real estate dealer and insurance salesman. I studied the books that told how it should be done, and the benefits that would follow for my clients. But the theory simply did not match the facts. In urban areas Africans were not allowed to own land, merely to rent it on leases of various lengths – I myself moved out of the railway compound, first to the supposedly 'superior' township of Barbourfields, in Bulawayo, then later into a house that I built for myself on a plot at Pelandaba, where Africans were allowed to take 99-year ground-leases. My home is still in Pelandaba, and it still suffers from the occasional flooding and frequent water-shortages that arise because the land was never properly surveyed as a whole when the estate was originally allotted for occupation by Africans.

The rules by which Southern Rhodesia was governed simply did not permit the emergence of the 'African middle class' which some liberal white people said they wanted to create – in any case the whole idea of class is alien to our people, among whom distinctions of that kind simply never arose in the rural villages where we all have our roots. We could not buy real estate. Insurance policies take decades before they bring their holders any significant wealth. I soon lost faith in the business activities I had launched into. I made very little money, which was hard on my family. And all my hard work for the ANC had sadly little result at the time.

In those early days of federation, the government of Southern Rhodesia was in the hands of people who passed for liberals, by local white standards. The prime minister was Garfield Todd, a New Zealander with a missionary background, and at one point I had hoped that he would allow some measure of African progress. But he was a member of a parliament dominated by that everlasting white electorate, whose main concern was to preserve its short-term privileges.

Whenever things got hard, Todd would tell his friends of his would-be liberal principles, then go on to act tough in order to prove to the electorate that they should go on trusting him. When there were justified strikes by African workers in the Wankie colliery, and on the railways, in 1956, it was the Todd government that sent in the police with dogs to put the strikers in their place. When the country's rising prosperity after federation raised African incomes so that it looked as though several hundred more of them would qualify for inclusion on the voters' roll, it was Todd's government that raised the property qualifications, pushing even the comparatively prosperous Africans back to the bottom of the pile.

I only once met Todd during the time he was prime minister. He came not as a politician but as an evangelist to address a Gospel rally in Barbourfields stadium, near my home, and I was asked to interpret for him into Sindebele, for he spoke no African language well. The people were surprised when they heard Nkomo stand up and start to speak Todd's words. He said in particular that the Christian religion was vital both to spread the word of the Gospel, and because it made people more amenable to being ruled! It seemed extraordinary to me that Todd should have chosen to present that as his Christian message.

I do not at all mean that Todd was a bad or an unkind man: indeed all his friends told me of his decency, and quite a lot of those friends were Africans. He brought up his children well: his brave daughter Judy even became a member of my party, Zapu, before being thrown out of the country by the Smith regime. But the white people at that time, with very few exceptions indeed, could not see that Africans would not be content with gradual progress and small advances. Even the most liberal of them thought only in terms of slowly bringing a few elite Africans up so that they could take a small share, as junior partners, in what was bound to remain the white man's government. They lacked the imagination to understand the anger that comes from not being allowed to govern your own lives.

Even on a personal level they seemed blind to how we felt. A particular friend of mine was the Reverend Ibbotson, the missionary who had brought me the invitation from Sir Godfrey Huggins to the first London conference, and who was active in all sorts of charities and good works for Africans. One day I was travelling in his car from Bulawayo to Salisbury, and we stopped at lunchtime in the small town of Norton. Ibbotson went in to the dining room, which was of course for whites only. Once inside, he asked the waiters to bring out food to me in the car, so that I would have something to eat at least. This was thoughtful of him, and it is true that by no means all hotels would have allowed their waiters to bring food out to a black man in the car park.

But what it meant was that, while Ibbotson had his nice lunch off a table with a cloth, I got a coarse plate with all sorts of scraps of cooked meat piled onto it and covered with gravy. Ibbotson did not give the matter a moment's thought: he never mentioned it, and I am sure it never crossed his mind. He had campaigned for a long time to make hotels obliged to serve Africans as well as Europeans – but what he wanted was separate African facilities, not equal facilities for everyone.

It was attitudes like this that built up a tremendous head of resentment against all Europeans among our people. If white people are sometimes unfairly treated in free Zimbabwe – and sometimes they are, and I very much regret it, and have always tried to put that right – it is the fault of those unthinking attitudes. Ibbotson was once employed by the Todd government to prepare some pamphlets telling white immigrants how to behave in the new country where they had just arrived. One memorable piece of advice he gave was that whites should never in any circumstances allow their black servants into the lavatory in their house, not even in order to clean it. If the servants saw the white man's lavatory they might come to think that maybe white people had the same needs as black people. That should never be allowed.

The early years of federation brought prosperity to Southern Rhodesia, and a wave of white immigration. The federal government spent the largest share of its budget where it would benefit the white electors, most of whom lived in our territory. Roads and housing and airstrips – and of course the army, air force and police – were all greatly expanded and modernised.

The African leadership sank into apathy. It was very difficult to get a lively meeting going. As I travelled around meeting the leaders of African social organisations – church groups, sports clubs, welfare societies – I continually encountered the same people running several of them at the same time. The organisations were beginning to develop very dangerously, along local or tribal lines. One important group was the Matabeleland Home Society: it excluded those who were not Ndebele. So in response someone founded the Bakalanga Kwayedza – the Kalanga Dawn society, for members of that language group.

In the African townships the young people went in either for boxing or for football; they were the only recreations. The Matabele Highlanders would be playing the Mashonaland Football Club, with supporters speaking different languages. There were boxing clubs exclusively for the Zezuru, for the

Makaranga, for the Manyika – all tribal groups, in this case from the Shona-speaking people. I constantly fought against this trend, urging the organisers not to associate tribal names and tribal feeling with such an aggressive sport as boxing, since it could only build up bad feeling for the future if you set young lads punching each other in the face for the honour of the tribe. There were, after all, plenty of other sorts of loyalty that could be encouraged instead of tribal loyalties. I had some, but not enough, success.

Much more fruitful was the political work of building opposition to the new restrictions that were gradually being imposed on country people by the government. The Land Husbandry Act of 1951 was presented as a device for 'improving' African farms in the so-called Tribal Trust areas. It gave district commissioners powers to limit the numbers of cattle and other livestock that African farmers might own, and to restrict the acreage that they might plant to maize. Certainly there was overcrowding and land hunger in the African country areas. This was a direct result of European immigration, and of more extensive use by Europeans of farmland they already owned: as a result, more and more Africans were driven into the districts set aside exclusively for them, which were of course those where the land was poorest and the rainfall lowest.

The way the Act was enforced grew stricter following a series of resolutions passed by the European Farmers' Union in 1954 and 1955, which claimed that unless African production of food was restricted, white commercial farmers would be unable to survive. African labour was cheap, especially on family farms. Africans produced 80 per cent of the commercial beef in the country. Small African farmers did not produce much maize each, but only a few surplus bags of grain from each of them would swamp the market and drown the white farmers' profit margins. It had for long been illegal for any African farmer to grow the most important of all commercial crops, Virginia tobacco – Africans were only allowed to produce the cheaper Turkish leaf, mainly for local consumption.

Now practically every sector of African farming was hit by new restrictions. This gave us the real grievance that we needed to get political action going again. The ANC in that period was against everything the government did, whatever it was. We even opposed the compulsory dipping of cattle – something absolutely necessary, as I knew, being the son of a dip supervisor. We opposed it not because it was bad in itself, but because it was at the dip that the officials recorded how much stock each farmer had, and those records were the basis for destroying cattle when the order came for destocking.

At the same time as this rural resistance to growing government repression, a new wave of activists was springing up in the towns. In 1955 there was formed in Salisbury the Youth League, a group of militant young people among whose leaders were James Chikerema, George Nyandoro and Edson Sithole. They were joined later by a group including J. Z. Moyo, Lazarus Nkala and Joseph Msika. In 1956, bus fares in Salisbury and Bulawayo were raised suddenly by twopence a ride: this gave the Youth League the specific grievance they needed to mobilise popular anger against government oppression in the cities. They organised a boycott of the bus services. Since Africans lived in townships far from the factory districts, this was the equivalent of a mass illegal strike. The focus of the protest was Harare African township.

The boycott turned into mass demonstrations: the police tried to break up the gatherings, the people resisted, and soon there were riots in the streets. Buses and cars were burnt, the roads were blocked, the power of the African people was demonstrated – and the more the police acted, the more resentment they caused. First in Salisbury, then in Bulawayo, the government was faced with something like organised rebellion – something that the complacent white politicians had always said could never happen. Parliament replied by bringing in new measures of discipline, like the Unlawful Assemblies Act: this in turn increased popular resentment, and created a new political spirit among our people.

The African National Congress proved quite inadequate as a channel for this mass resentment. With a few other members, I had persuaded the executive to hold an inquiry into how we could change our obviously irrelevant posture on most issues; but I could not continue as president of a failed organisation, and I resigned. But the Youth Leaguers had plans for me.

They organised a meeting of their own executive, in

Salisbury, telling me that they had invited three of us of the older generation, ex-presidents of the ANC, to attend: the others were my friends from Adams College, Enoch Dumbutshena and Stanlake Samkange. I was asked to act as chairman of their meeting. But the choice of a new president was to be undertaken in an entirely neutral fashion, and they had invited a senior man from Northern Rhodesia, Mr Yamba, to take the chair for that part of the proceedings. What they had not told me was that, although Dumbutshena and Samkange had been invited to the meeting, both had declined their invitations.

The agenda proceeded, and after some time the choice of a president came round. I vacated the chair, and Mr Yamba took over. I heard my name mentioned: someone said 'Seconded', someone else said 'Nominations closed', someone else said 'Carried'. I protested mildly: Yamba asked me whether I was a member of the African National Congress, to which I answered that I was, but the future of that organisation was in doubt. 'That's all right, then,' said the acting chairman. I had been hijacked into the presidency – and so, on 12 September 1957, the new African National Congress was formed. To mark the occasion we left the meeting place – it was in Mai Musodzi hall, which still stands – and marched around in the open air. By some freak a sudden hurricane broke over us, lifting roofs into the air, tearing away our small banners, and practically knocking us to the ground. It was a stormy start for a stormy organisation; mysteriously enough, the same thing happened at the next year's congress, in Bulawayo.

The new ANC was very different from its predecessor. Its committee included several people who, since the Harare bus riots, were not in the least averse to violence for political ends. With myself as president, the executive included James Chikerema as vice-president, George Nyandoro as general secretary and Joseph Msika as treasurer. Francis Nehwati and Stanislas Marembo were also members. The new constitution committed the organisation to specific political objectives, including in particular rule of our country by the majority, which meant by black people. For the whites, this meant revolution. But there was – I must emphasise this – absolutely no intention to exclude white people as such from a full share in the national life. Guy Clutton-Brock in particular gave us significant help with drafting the new constitution.

The best tribute to the new party came from the police, who immediately started to watch our movements carefully and to interfere with our meetings whenever they could. But our organisation took root and grew whatever the authorities might do. Support for the nationalist cause within our own country was no longer in doubt. What we needed now, if our national struggle was to succeed, was support from outside.

The world was changing fast. In 1957 Ghana became the first of Britain's African colonies to achieve independence: it was manifest that others would be following soon; sooner than the British expected. With other national movements in our own part of Africa, there was no difficulty making contact: we had our links with the nationalists in Northern Rhodesia and Nyasaland, the other parts of the federation, and we soon established friendly liaison with people in Tanganyika.

To travel further and extend our knowledge would be both hard to organise and expensive. Once again, as in 1952, the Indian representative in Salisbury gave us really significant help. The World Assembly of Youth, an international, mainly student, organisation of which we knew very little, was holding its assembly in New Delhi late in 1957. Mr Singh must have contacted its secretary-general, a Swedish citizen called David Wirmark, and from him the ANC received an invitation to send a delegation to the assembly. I was no longer strictly a youth, being by now forty years old. But I was still the only member of the ANC executive to hold a passport – the same one the government had given me as the 'stooge' of their London fiasco – so it was decided that I should go to represent our country, as leader of a delegation of one. So once again I set off on my travels. It was the start of a long period of exile.

Chapter 8
The First Exile

Visiting India for the first time, I moved at last to a nation that had freed itself from British imperial power. Ten years previously, in 1948, the Indians had finally hauled down the Union Jack and replaced it with the symbol of their own sovereignty. Our organisations for national independence in southern Africa were called congresses in homage to the Indian National Congress, the main instrument of that country's own liberation – and the man who inspired that Indian Congress was Gandhi, himself brought up in South Africa. Gandhi's methods were not appropriate to our own special national situation. But his movement's achievement was an inspiration to us, showing that independence need not remain a dream.

The ideal was noble. The reality, as so often in the business of international travel, was more complicated. I flew first to Nairobi, then across the Indian Ocean to Bombay, where I was to catch another plane for New Delhi. But the plane was late into Bombay, and I was stranded for several hours in that immense, hot city. You could feel the poverty: independence, I could clearly see, does not of itself cure ordinary people's problems. I telegraphed ahead to New Delhi, to warn the organisers of the World Assembly of Youth that I would be late. The cable never arrived, or was lost. I got into Delhi airport late at night. There was nobody to meet me and I had no address to go to, so I told the taxi driver to take me to the cheapest possible hotel. I had practically no money at all, and I felt sorry for myself. From the window I looked into the exotic street and wondered about those teeming millions of people. A small boy threaded his way through the traffic to a traffic island, where he mysteriously lay down. An hour later I looked out again and saw that he was sleeping there. It put my own discomfort in perspective.

Over the coming years of exile I would often arrive penniless and late at night in strange cities, to find a bed where I could. In New Delhi that time the other delegates, I suppose, had allowances from their organisations at home, but we had not thought about that, and I gradually dropped my standards from the initial taxi ride to buses, then cycle-rickshaws, then donkey carts. It was many years before I obtained the financial backing that enabled me to travel in some comfort – and I never got used to the hand-to-mouth way of life that was necessary in those times. That was an inescapable part of the way I have served Zimbabwe.

The World Assembly of Youth itself was largely concerned with student politics, which did not greatly concern me. But for the first time I met delegates from many other countries and cultures of which I knew almost nothing, and I began to make friends at once. I got on especially well with two people from Britain. One was Charles Longbottom, who later became a Conservative member of parliament. The other was Maurice Foley, who also helped me in London: he became a Labour MP, and I was let out of prison for a talk with him when he was one of Harold Wilson's ministers in 1968. The closest friend I made in New Delhi was an American, Frank Ferrari, to whom I have been obliged for kindnesses ever since. He later gave me all sorts of support while I was in New York seeking to draw the world's attention to my country's problems at the United Nations.

As leader of a delegation of one from a country few people knew much about, I had the honour only of a formal introduction to the prime minister, Pandit Nehru. But what was truly impressive was the great parade that the Indians organised for their guests, with Nehru and his colleagues standing up on the high saluting-base amid a throng of young people from all over the world – surrounded by what seemed like millions of Indian people, glad and proud to be showing off their new nation. It was dignified and magnificent, and it made a great mark on me.

I returned home to another sad family event. During my absence, my wife's father had died, after a long illness, and maFuyana was deeply distressed. My father-in-law, Silwalume, was a grandson of Mapisa, who had been chief of the council of Lobengula, last king of our country. His death broke a link with the days before we were ruled by the settlers. By the time I arrived, his formal funeral as a Roman Catholic was over.

There followed, according to African tradition, the long discussions that mark the death of the head of a family. But I could not stay for that. The African National Congress had been invited to send a representative to the All-African People's Conference organised in Ghana by Kwame Nkrumah. MaFuyana was distressed and needed my presence. Moreover, while I was on party business I could earn no money, and she and the children were not well off. But if we were seriously interested in independence we could not turn down Nkrumah's invitation, and I was still the only ANC leader with a passport. I had to go.

It is difficult now, perhaps, to remember just how important Ghana's independence early in 1957 was to all Africa. Nkrumah was a magnetic personality. He had defied the British, served his time in prison, overwhelmingly won elections, been released, and come to power. Ghana's constitution at independence was strictly on British lines, with Nkrumah as prime minister under a governor general.

Now, before a year was up, Nkrumah was discarding that formula and taking office as executive president of the nation, head of state as well as of the government. The ceremony to mark that changeover was timed to coincide with the meeting of the All-African People's Conference, whose organiser was the legendary George Padmore, the West Indian who had worked for decades in London to foster belief in a free Africa, and many of whose friends were biding their time in prison for their inevitable release as heads of sovereign African nations.

There were at this time only four independent nations in all of Africa south of the Sahara – Ethiopia, Ghana, Guinea and Liberia. The rest of the delegations were from nationalist organisations, – what would now be called African liberation movements. There was Patrice Lumumba from what was still the Belgian Congo, an endless talker, passionate about his own country, although he seemed completely uninterested in the rest of Africa. There was Holden Roberto from Angola, impressive but something of a playboy. The Tanganyikan delegation was led by Oscar Kambona, that from South Africa by Tennyson Makiwane. From Kenya came Tom Mboya, one of the greatest of the many potential leaders whom Africa has lost.

The southern African delegations had one special problem. The African National Congress of Northern Rhodesia had split: a dynamic group of younger people had divided off into what was called the Zambesia Front, led by Kenneth Kaunda and sharply critical of the older group under Harry Nkumbula. We had to decide which group to recognise as members of the congress, and we chose Kaunda. There then arose the question of who should sit on the conference steering committee to represent the southern Africa region. After some debate Kaunda and Makiwane agreed with Dr Banda, the Nyasaland leader, that I should represent them all on the steering committee, so I found myself playing a prominent role at the meeting, taking the chair at sessions and using every opportunity to win friends for my cause.

The main topic of the conference was not so much African liberation as African unity. This was Nkrumah's great dream, and we had to go along with our host – although most of us were more concerned with the freedom of our own territories than with his vision of the future. But I must admit that Nkrumah was one of the most inspiring orators I have ever heard, especially at that time in his career. Later I had grave doubts about his realism. I remember a meeting with him and Kenneth Kaunda some years later, at the time of the terrible civil war that followed the independence of the Belgian Congo, during which poor Lumumba was publicly humiliated and killed.

Soldiers from Ghana had been sent to form part of the United Nations peace-keeping force, and had done their job to everyone's admiration. Nkrumah was discussing that, when suddenly he said, almost casually, 'Of course, we feel that the Congo can one day be part of Ghana.' It seemed to me really strange that the leader of quite a small country could seriously consider taking over a much larger nation with no common language and several hundred kilometres away. As the words slipped out, Kaunda and I exchanged glances, and I could see that he was as disturbed as I was at this lack of realism.

Ghana was a revelation to me. I knew its history and geography, for Britain's African possessions were a special subject at school. I knew that its main crop was cocoa (though nobody at school had suggested to me that it took people to grow cocoa). Now I found that in the country they lived in round, thatched huts much like our own, and that in the cities they lived in slums which, although Ghana had been in contact with whites for hundreds of years longer than us, and although it was now independent, were far worse than anything in our regimented society. Accra was chaotic. (Later I discovered that it was not nearly as chaotic as Lagos, in Nigeria – the sheer confusion of west Africa is always baffling to us from the south.) But, much more important, Accra and all of Ghana was free. That was the main thing: that was what I wanted.

By far the most important thing that happened to me there was my new friendship with a young man from Uganda, John Kale, a brilliant organiser who helped me a great deal with my work on the steering committee. He was organising Joseph Kiwanuka's Uganda National Congress from an office in Cairo, and he introduced me to the leader of the Egyptian delegation, Dr Galal, and his deputy, Mohammed Mohammed Faiek. This was only two years after the Suez Canal war, when the British had mounted an attack on Egypt and been forced by world pressure to withdraw. Colonel Nasser, the Egyptian leader, was genuinely committed to national liberation in Africa, and Dr Galal invited me to travel on after the conference to meet Nasser himself. This I was happy to do.

I then committed an absurd political error. I knew very little about the Middle East beyond what I could see on the map. I reckoned that the government of Southern Rhodesia might get very upset if they found I had visited Egypt, a country with which Britain had no diplomatic relations since the Suez war. But I knew that Israel was on good terms with the British and the Southern Rhodesians, and I thought an Israeli visa in my passport would provide me with a good excuse for visiting that part of the world. So I visited the Israeli diplomatic mission in Ghana, said I hoped to visit their country, and had their visa stamped in my passport, although I had no real intention of going there. I did not need an Egyptian visa. With my passport thus marked I set off for the heart of the Arab world.

In order to get to Cairo I had to change aircraft at Tripoli, in Libya (then still ruled by King Idris, who was pro-Western but very strongly anti-Israeli). I landed there on Christmas Eve.

The Egyptian ambassador was not there to meet me, as I had expected, so I found myself the only accommodation I could afford, which was a room in a filthy little hotel, and waited. Next day being Christmas, the Egyptian ambassador was still not in his office, nor were any of his officials.

At Tripoli airport the immigration officer had given me a transit visa for a couple of days, and of course this had now run out. So I went to the immigration office to sort it out – and there they examined my passport, found the Israeli visa, and began to kick up a storm. They had a long discussion in Arabic, pointing at that wretched visa. I tried to explain that I came from Southern Rhodesia – they had never heard of it – and that I was going not to Israel but to Egypt, which they would not believe. They obviously thought I should be deported, and since I had a British passport they suggested sending me to Britain.

I insisted that the officials refer the matter to the chief of police. He turned out to be a very decent man who spoke good English and soon understood my problem. In no time at all the policemen were giving me coffee and picking up my bags from the terrible hotel to check me into a better one. But it shows what trouble a simple piece of ignorance like my Israeli visa can cause. Next day I met the Egyptian ambassador, and started off for Cairo in time for New Year 1959.

The official to whom my friend Dr Galal reported was the head of the Arab Socialist Union, Egypt's main political party; his name was Anwar Sadat. He was not remotely interested in Africa – indeed he gave the impression that he wished Egypt were part of Europe, so strong was his indifference to African problems. I tried to explain to him that I represented a colonised people, that the British were oppressing us, that we were part of a world-wide struggle against oppression. He was not in the least impressed.

Sadat said the British had just given Ghana independence, they would give their other colonies independence one day, so there was nothing to worry about. I replied that he was right, we would be independent one day, but meanwhile we needed the help of free countries. The people in the Egyptian Foreign Office understood very well, but not Sadat. Yet without his leave I was not going to be admitted to meet President Nasser. I was put in a horrible hotel, extremely cold in the middle of the Egyptian winter, and I was getting nowhere. Mohammed Faiek, who had been told to look after me and soon became a close friend, was deeply embarrassed.

One night, somewhere near despair, I switched on the radio to listen to the BBC. For once there was news from home. 'The African National Congress of Southern Rhodesia has been declared a banned organisation, and its leaders have been placed under arrest. Joshua Nkomo, president of the ANC, is still at large, and is thought to be in Egypt.' I was rescued by the BBC, which had publicly issued me with these credentials as an important man, dangerous to British interests. In the morning I was promptly summoned to the Foreign Office, most politely received and taken in to meet President Nasser himself.

Nasser, unlike Sadat, had an immediate grasp of the situation. My own reaction to the news of the banning of the ANC was that I should return home as soon as possible and do what I could to help. Nasser said I must stay in Egypt. The Southern Rhodesian government, he said, had obviously panicked. That was why they had locked up hundreds of my supporters. But if I went home they would quietly lock me up too, the whole crisis would die down and in a few months the world would forget about it. He invited me to stay in Cairo, in an office that he would provide, and tell the world about our case.

I moved into a more comfortable hotel, at Egyptian government expense, and opened up a small office in the building of the African Association in Zamalek, the smart district of Cairo. The association was the channel through which President Nasser gave support to liberation movements. Other offices in the building were occupied by Dr Moumie, of the Cameroons, whom I had got to know quite well in Accra, and by my friend John Kale of Uganda.

Kale was a man of great charm and talent. He showed me all the techniques needed for running a political office, and we exchanged ideas about the future. His only disadvantage as the organiser of a freedom movement was his terror of flying in aircraft. Tragically, it turned out to be fully justified. A few years later he was in a Soviet airliner bound for Moscow when it crashed, killing everybody aboard.

John Kale argued, and I came to agree, that the conflict between the British and the supporters of freedom for Africa was not about ideology, but about nationhood. Because the British perceived African advancement as being against their interests, the countries closely allied with Britain were obliged to act as though it were against their interests too. The Americans, in particular, had good historical reasons for supporting people wishing to liberate themselves from Britain. But their general pro-British stance, which had nothing to do with Africa as such, made them behave in a way contrary to African interests whatever their beliefs might be.

We had to get outside support for our liberation struggle, and if we could not get it from the West we would have to ask for it from the East. At the time the only thing I did to put this to the test was to call at the Cuban embassy, explain our problem and ask for their support. The Cubans were interested and sympathetic, but there was nothing they could do in practise to help us. Fidel Castro had taken power less than a year previously, and they had their own problems to sort out before those of other countries. But I was assured that Castro himself was committed to ending colonialism in Africa. This was a commitment which the Cubans have fully honoured. I am glad to think that I was the first person to try to make it a reality, and I have often reminded my friend President Castro of that.

But, sympathetic as its leader was, Egypt was a backwater. It was practically impossible to phone home from there. Even the mail was unreliable, and a letter would take two or three weeks at best to get to southern Africa. It was very difficult to make the wider outside contacts that I needed for my work, and it was absolutely impossible to have any influence over British policy from there. In the aftermath of the Suez fiasco, the British had no diplomatic representative in Cairo; their interests were looked after by a special section in the American embassy, and I had no contacts with them at all. Probably the Americans were prevented by respect for their British colleagues from trying to make any contact with me. Usually they are quite open about seeking people out and trying to influence them in America's favour. The Soviets and East Europeans, on the other hand, invariably wait for others to approach them and ask for help, as I did later.

So I decided that I had better go to the heart of the matter and start work in London itself. The Egyptians raised no objection – indeed they even gave me some money to live on for a time, and paid my air fare. So once again, in mid-1959, I set off for London.

By now I had become a bit of a celebrity, and I had many friends and allies. In London there were archives and libraries to consult, newspaper and radio journalists to meet, all sorts of valuable activities that had been impossible in Cairo. And there were a number of organisations ready and willing to offer help. There was the Reverend Michael Scott, backed up by Jane Simmonds, at the Africa Bureau. There was Commander Fox-Pitt at the Anti-Slavery Society. There was the Fabian Society and the Labour party, and there were many other individuals fully committed to the anti-colonial cause.

I made some solid friends in these days. A special one was Ian Mikardo, the Labour MP from East London. We spent several uncomfortable nights together, sitting and talking endlessly in railway waiting rooms when our meeting had gone on past the time of the last train. Later I struck up a friendship with another leading Labour personality, the wonderful Joan Lestor, whose only problem in appearing on an anti-imperial platform with me was her everlasting difficulty in pronouncing my name. These were great times, and great companionships.

But it was embarrassing to see that some devoted people would actually compete with each other to offer me help. Their organisations were positively jealous of each other. Each wanted to work with me and to have me make speeches at their own meetings: that way they could get publicity, increase their membership and gain the satisfaction of feeling they were useful. I say this without any critical intention towards people whose good-will and sincerity cannot possibly be in doubt – but their kindness was sometimes overwhelming to the point where it became a distraction. I became genuinely worried about that saintly man Michael Scott. So deep was his commitment to the welfare of others that he had forgotten his own welfare. He would dash out into the rain and cold, forgetting his overcoat on bitter winter days. I said to him one day: 'If you don't look after yourself you won't be able to look after the people you are committed to help.'

My British friends could not fully understand what I intended to do. They thought I had come to London as a traditional political exile, prepared for many years of patient waiting and planning before I went home to fight for independence by legal means. But I wanted quicker results than could be got in that way – and I longed to be home, with my wife and growing children, not living on another country's charity.

I was taken by kind people to register as an unemployed Commonwealth immigrant for my weekly dole from the National Assistance Board – and I found the process humiliating. They fitted me out with a heavy second-hand overcoat, which I needed in the English winter – and I hated the idea of wearing someone else's cast-off clothes. They generously found me somewhere to live, in the warden's house of a charity looking after deprived children in Bethnal Green, in the East End. I found the place interesting, and gladly discussed social work with my host the warden. But in someone else's house I could not carry on full-time with my political work.

One day I had had enough. I was too embarrassed to explain exactly what was wrong to my kind host, so I simply moved out of his house without saying anything – I even left behind the African blanket that had followed me everywhere on my travels, at home and abroad, and in which I had so often wrapped up to sleep for a few hours in some lonely and uncomfortable place. Now I was independent, and I worked all the harder for it. My independence was made possible by the remains of my gift of money from the Egyptian government.

At first I set up a home and office at 200 Gower Street, near the university. I contacted Kanyama Chiume, from Nyasaland, who was doing similar work to my own while his leader, Dr Banda, was locked up in jail at home. Because of the existence of the Central African Federation, we found we shared many problems, and had a better chance of getting our views across to the British press. The London papers had for some time been carrying a fair amount of news from Northern Rhodesia and from Nyasaland, but very little from Southern Rhodesia, and I was able to put the balance a little more fairly. Soon Chiume and I found that the rent in central London was too

5a. 1961: under constant watch by the police.   (*Parade*)

5b. 1962: a policeman orders Nkomo to disperse a meeting of the NDP. His words were: 'This is a police force, with the emphasis on force, not the Salvation Army.'

6. The home to which Nkomo was confined by government order in 1962. The picture, taken in 1983, shows on the left his cousin Sihle Nkomo, next to him is Smart Malaba, grandson of the community chief; then Abed Nkomo; and the women and children of the family, in whom the first signs of malnutrition are visible.   (*Nicholas Harman*)

... enjoy a private audience by a courageous journalist. L. to r.: Ruth Chinamano, Daniel Madzimbamuto, Joshua Nkomo, Josiah Chinamano, Joseph Msika and Stanislas Marembo.

8. 1965: the nationalist leaders summoned from prison to meet the British prime minister. *L. to r.*: Daniel Madzimbamuto, Josiah Chinamano, Harold Wilson, Joshua Nkomo and Joseph Msika.

high for our slender means and I moved out to a flat in Swiss Cottage, northwards on the underground line.

Later I moved further out again, to Golders Green, where I was joined by my old friend and colleague from the African National Congress, Enoch Dumbutshena, whom I had first met on the train going to Adams College in 1942. Enoch worked extremely hard on our problems, sitting up late into the night to do the office work – I said that he was the writer, I was the speaker, and so we shared the work. I registered as a law student at Lincoln's Inn, but I truly could not find time to do any worthwhile studying. Enoch managed to work full-time on nationalist business and to pass his bar exams too, and his success has given Zimbabwe a distinguished judge today.

Now I set to work seriously to contact diplomats and others from all the countries that might be able to help us in our struggle. Soon after setting up in Gower Street, I called on the Soviet embassy. I also pursued my American friendships.

I had remained in touch with the American friend I had made at the World Assembly of Youth in New Delhi, Frank Ferrari. He was working for the African-American Institute, one of the 'semi-governmental' organisations through which the United States government conducted so much of its international work at that time. His particular job was to create scholarships for Africans, arrange visits and lecture tours of the United States, and so on. I knew that he had greatly helped Tom Mboya, the Kenyan whom I so much admired.

Frank, I must emphasise, was also a genuine friend of mine, a person whom it was a pleasure to be with, quite apart from the help he was able to arrange. Through him the American Committee on Africa, which was run by a highly intelligent man called George Hauser, arranged a lecture tour of the United States for myself and Chiume. One new and welcome aspect of this was that we were actually paid for speaking to institutions and universities. The sponsoring organisation took a cut of the fees to cover their expenses in setting up the trip, but it was a useful source of income, and Chiume and I had no other.

The American audiences consisted mainly of students, and were full of interest in Africa and its colonial problems. They had a natural sympathy for the idea of national independence from Britain, and they were excited by the example of Ghana. They seemed to draw no parallels between our problems and their own racial difficulties, or with the issues of what later came to be called the civil rights campaign. But, although I visited almost half of the United States, I was not asked to go anywhere south of North Carolina. In 1960 the desegregation of the south still had a long way to go – perhaps they wanted to spare me embarrassment, or maybe they preferred me not to see the south as it was in those days.

On my travels I hardly saw the country, except out of the aircraft window. So I was delighted when, on my return to New York, one of the very few black people on the organising committee kindly asked me up to Harlem to talk to a political club – it was a society organised by a Mrs Francis, mainly to support the liberation of the Congo. George Hauser, the chief organiser of my tour, was anxious about this speaking engagement which he had not arranged, and I felt he was concerned that I might say something subversive. But I went anyway, and saw a completely different face of America. It seemed really offensive that people should live in such squalor in a city of magnificent skyscrapers. I spoke in a dingy hall in a district where most of the people spoke a sort of Spanish-English, and were from Puerto Rico. The contrast with downtown Manhattan was shocking.

The relationship with black Americans tends to be a bit awkward for African visitors. Naturally, being of African origin and looking like Africans, black Americans feel solidarity with us. Some of them go on to develop this into such an enthusiasm that they forget they are really Americans after all. Then, when Africans treat them as Americans, it leads to all sorts of disappointments. Many years later, the fact that President Carter had senior black people in his government and was anxious to get the black people's votes was helpful to us. But I was always interested in getting support from Americans whatever their colour.

The great opportunity opened up by that American trip was a meeting with ambassadors at the United Nations. It was my business to put Southern Rhodesia firmly on the UN agenda, but there was a difficulty which continued for many years thereafter. It was illustrated by the fact that Chiume and I were travelling together, both representing parties from within the same federation. Nyasaland, Chiume's country, was a British protectorate – clearly a 'dependent territory', and so of legitimate interest to the UN. Even the British, who did not like it, accepted that. But Southern Rhodesia, they said, was altogether different. Since 1923, said the British diplomats (with increasing embarrassment), Southern Rhodesia had been a 'self-governing colony'. Although Britain retained theoretical sovereignty over it, and although Britain had some residual constitutional responsibilities for its foreign affairs, there was nothing the British government could do about the Southern Rhodesian government's internal policies. It was therefore not a 'dependent' territory, and the UN had no right to inquire into it.

To any unbiased mind this was lunacy. That brilliant man L. K. Jha, the Indian chairman of the decolonisation committee who was so helpful and courteous to me on many occasions, once asked the British delegate, – 'Well, is this place a colony or isn't it?' The answer seemed to be both yes and no. It was 1962, with the federation already breaking up, before the UN was finally able to defeat the irrational objections of the British, and put the question of the independence of Southern Rhodesia on the agenda of its Fourth Committee.

The countries whose delegates were most helpful to me were Ghana (of course), and later Nigeria after they got their independence in 1960, as well as India, Tunisia and Egypt, where I had established good relations over a long period, and had personally visited the countries. It was at first very hard to make progress at the UN itself, where delegates obviously had to rely on instructions from their home governments.

I remember being invited to the home of Mr Bingham, the American ambassador, where his charming wife and daughter asked me all sorts of questions about my country and my work. The daughter became really excited by what I was saying, and turned to her father and asked: 'Surely you are going to vote for Mr Nkomo, aren't you, Daddy?' His answer was perfectly correct: 'I'd vote for him if the vote were mine, but unfortunately my vote belongs to the United States.' The much-respected Swedish ambassador, Mrs Myrdal, once sadly explained to me that her government's sympathy was entirely with us – but they had ties going back for centuries with the British, and with the best will in the world they could not break that loyalty for our sake. Even Golda Meir, when she was foreign minister of Israel, excused herself from giving us a crucial vote on the grounds that she could not afford to alienate the British – and anyway we had the Arab votes, so we could not have Israel's too.

I had at first high hopes that the Latin Americans would be on our side, with their anti-imperialist tradition. But I could not talk informally and make friends with Spanish-speakers, and they were completely ignorant of what our struggle was about or even where Southern Rhodesia was. One ambassador seemed to think that, since it was in Africa, it must be either in Egypt or in Kenya. And so I learned the realities of international diplomacy.

The cause I stood for needed friends who were not automatically committed, on other grounds, to supporting Great Britain because they would in turn need British support. And I needed to visit the capitals of those countries, to win the support not only of their diplomats but of their decision-makers. I have often been criticised for being too fond of travel, and for spending too little of my time at home. But that was not how I would have chosen to spend my life. It was the work I set myself, because I thought it was essential if my country was to get her freedom. In that I am sure I was right.

Chapter 9
Onto the World Stage

My American hosts were both kind and constructive, and I saved a little money from my lectures there. Then I moved on to Ghana, the Ghanaians gave me a ticket on to Guinea, the Guineans gave me one to Liberia, and the Liberians gave me one to Ethiopia. And so bit by bit I established contact with the leaders of the few independent nations in Africa. It was an exhausting business, relieved only by the knowledge that my meetings with the heads of those governments were building up a fund of good-will for my country's future. Let me tell a little bit of what it is like on this kind of journey.

I have never entirely overcome my nerves at that moment when the aircraft gathers speed for take-off: I am never entirely confident on landing until its wheels have stopped rolling. But that is the least of my worries on my travels. The real anxiety arises from never knowing how you will be received in the next country you are heading for, or where you will go after that. The telegrams and telexes go on ahead, but they are not always received, and if received are not always acted upon.

The best thing is if somebody meets the plane: then you know you will be looked after. But sometimes the plane is met by someone unhelpful – I have already described how Colonel Sadat in Egypt deliberately kept me away from President Nasser, because he was unsympathetic to African liberation movements. In Ghana I was once met by an official from Dr Gbedemah's finance ministry, only to discover that Gbedemah was doing his best to stop President Nkrumah from offering any more help to liberation movements, and it took a great deal of effort to get round his obstruction.

The worst is not to be met at all. Then there is nothing for it but to take a taxi to a cheap hotel, get on the telephone and try to establish the contact that has broken down. On my travels I very rarely had any money at all, except for a few carefully saved US dollar bills, in small denominations, that would be accepted almost anywhere for a taxi fare, airport taxes or similar unexpected but unavoidable charges. I once told Charles Njonjo of Kenya – he had been a friend of mine since Adams College days – that I had to sell my shoes to pay the Nairobi airport tax when leaving, and it was almost true.

As for those expensive hotels, the simple truth is that, as a government guest, you stay in the hotel where the government puts you. There is no choice about it – and not much comfort either in the long hours of lonely waiting and frustrated telephoning that are the usual way of passing a day. Governments usually pay for their guests' room and board, but not for any extras like drinks (though fortunately I do not drink) or taxi fares. It can be truly frustrating to be in a strange and interesting city with nothing to do but wait for an appointment, but also to have not a cent to spend on getting out to see it.

On that first African trip in 1960 I was especially grateful for the personal kindness of some of the leaders I met. President Tubman of Liberia most kindly gave me $5,000 in cash, which freed me from the usual tight constraints and helped me to live for several months in London thereafter. The emperor Haile Selassie did the most generous thing of all. I was summoned to see him, a very old, thin man surrounded by the most impressive staff in his great palace. I found him full of kindness. As usual, I explained my country's colonial problem.

The emperor promptly understood, and said so in a way that revealed the depth of his understanding. But then he explained that, in the days of his exile after the Italian invasion, the king of England had treated him with respect and sympathy, and the British government had seen to his safety throughout the Second World War. He was loyal to Africa, but he could not betray the debt that he owed to Britain. Instead, he asked about my personal life – the emperor understood what exile was like. I told him frankly of my distress at being separated for so long from my wife and young children. Haile Selassie's response was to authorise an air ticket from Salisbury to London for maFuyana and for Thandi, Ernest and Michael too. It is hard to express how grateful I was.

I flew down from Addis to Khartoum, and there I met my dear family again. MaFuyana was terribly thin: she had been living on the fringe of poverty at home while I was working abroad for my country, and she had obviously been under strain from constant observation by the police (who had, I must admit, never subjected her to any deliberate persecution). I have never been so glad to see anyone in my life. And so we returned together to London, where we were able for three months to live as normal a family life as is possible in exile.

I must at this point mention one other person whose kindness to my family has earned my everlasting gratitude. During my first visit to the United States, Frank Ferrari had introduced me to Arthur and Matilde Krim, who then became and have remained to this day among my truest friends. They have huge houses both in Manhattan and on Long Island. Whenever I go to the United States I manage to stay with them for a few days, if I can possibly get off work.

My daughter Regina (my father's daughter, whom I adopted after his death) was in effect educated by the Krims, who financed her through college in the States. When she got married in 1973 to a young Zimbabwean doctor, the Krims gave her away and stood her a magnificent wedding party. As recently as 1983, when I was once more forced into exile, my youngest daughter Louise wrote to me from New York to tell me of her distress. Arthur at once arranged for Louise to fly to London to be with me for three days. It is impossible to exaggerate the importance to me and my family of such complete generosity. Here I simply put it on record.

As the 1960s opened, things were changing fast in Southern Rhodesia, and for the worse. In 1958 the white politicians of the ruling United Federal Party had decided to get rid of a prime minister who claimed to believe in African progress (although he did little enough about it). The party caucus threw out Garfield Todd and brought in the hard-liner Edgar Whitehead, who at once began to try to crush the emerging African opposition.

On 26 February 1959, the Whitehead government had banned the African National Congress and arrested hundreds of its leaders – this was the news that secured my interview with President Nasser. Some, including my close colleagues James Chikerema and George Nyandoro, remained in prison for four years. As the year went on, the government increased its repression, using its powers to the full against all forms of dissent.

But one thing restrained the government of Southern Rhodesia from going as fast as it wished down the road to repression. Although the Conservative government in Britain was firmly committed to the support of the Central African Federation it had created, there was strong criticism of it in Britain. Moreover, the British government, on setting up the federation in 1953, had promised that its constitution would be reviewed in 1960. In mid-July 1959, they established a commission, chaired by Lord Monckton, to report on the constitutions of the federation and the three member countries.

The United Federal Party realised that if Monckton reported that the federation was moving in a more liberal direction, that would disarm their critics in Britain and make it easier to strengthen white rule. The Whitehead government therefore tried to remove the aspects of racial segregation which the federal prime minister, Sir Roy Welensky, described as 'pinpricks' – that is, policies that caused immediate resentment among Africans, but could be changed without reducing the fundamental power of the white electorate. This was not of much interest to the African nationalist movement, since we knew very well that nothing basic was going to change without an upheaval. But it did put some restraint on the government, and made our task a bit easier.

At the beginning of 1960 a group of people from the banned African National Congress met to form the new National Democratic Party. Its provisional constitution was almost identical with its predecessor's, and to underline the continuity I was elected president *in absentia*, while I pursued my work abroad.

Meanwhile Southern Rhodesia was going through an economic recession; unemployment and discontent spread among Africans, both in the cities and in the countryside. In July a new cycle of demonstrations by Africans, and repression by the police, broke out into violence. The Whitehead government introduced a new set of repressive laws into parliament, giving the government such arbitrary powers that the chief justice, Sir Robert Tredgold, resigned his office in protest, and the ex-prime minister, Garfield Todd, joined me in London to ask the British government to suspend the constitution of Southern Rhodesia and take back power from the men who were abusing it.

It was time for me to go home. I was invited as an official guest to the independence celebrations of Nigeria – a splendid event, signifying the arrival on the world scene of the first giant African nation, and for us showing clearly that the British were on the way out of our continent. That was on 1 October. From Lagos I flew on to Salisbury – by way of Rome, indicating the amazing lack of direct links between the different parts of Africa. That things had changed at home in my twenty-two months of absence I knew. But I did not know how much.

As I emerged into the sunlight on the steps at Salisbury airport, I looked down into an ocean of faces, all turned towards me, all shouting and laughing. It was the largest crowd ever seen up to that time in Southern Rhodesia, orderly, happy, confident that I embodied their future. The official police estimate was that 50,000 people were present at the airport that day. Some observers thought it many more.

For more than half a century the people of Southern Rhodesia had been told, until they came to believe it, that they were of no account in the world. Their own homeland, they said to each other and even to their children, was *Ilizwe laMakhiwa*, white man's country. They accepted as a fact that white people determined their fate – that their homes, their farms, their livestock and their jobs were held only by the leave of white officials. They were dejected and hopeless.

Abroad, I had not known how this had changed. The people had grown hungry for news of the campaign at the United Nations, and in the capitals of free African nations, signifying to them that the rest of the human race cared about their predicament, and was working out ways of changing it. I had been the focus of that campaign. Because I had been at liberty when my comrades were arrested, and had used my liberty to advance their cause, I now became the symbol and the leader of their aspirations. The vast throng at the airport had gathered to let me know that the people were behind me, and to urge me to carry on.

Of course I would have wished to stay in my own country, to enjoy at last the upsurge of popular feeling that my return unleashed. But there was once more work to be done abroad. Many of my old colleagues of the ANC were still locked up: they were needed to build its replacement, the NDP, into a strong political force. And in London, on 5 December, the British government was due to open the conference to review the federal constitution.

The African case at the conference was immensely strengthened by the publication, in mid-October, of the report of the Monckton commission of inquiry into political life within the federation. It was a damning document, falling only just short of proposing that the federation should be broken up. In particular it criticised the situation in Nyasaland, where Dr Banda was still in detention although he was clearly the legitimate spokesman for the vast majority of the people. The report did not (I need hardly say) propose any changes that would have been acceptable to the African people of Southern Rhodesia. But it put African opinion in the centre of the debate.

In this climate, the British government strongly urged Sir Edgar Whitehead to include some African spokesmen in the Southern Rhodesia delegation to the conference, and Whitehead unwillingly agreed. So once again I set off for London. The conference was, of course, useless. The British had no intention of doing anything other than hand back power to the settler electorate that had been allowed to run Southern Rhodesia since the 1920s. It was worth our while attending simply to show the world that that was happening.

The British minister who chaired the conference was Alan Lennox-Boyd, and he kept what seemed an almost appreciative eye on myself and my colleagues. Perhaps he hoped to persuade us to tell the world that the new constitution really was an advance towards interracial partnership. Both at the United Nations and within Britain there were friends of the Conservative party who would have been heartily relieved if that had happened. But our delegation – my main colleagues were Ndabaningi Sithole, T. G. Silundika and that brilliant lawyer Herbert Chitepo as legal adviser – remained solid in opposition to the whole principle of federation. We withdrew from the conference, and I dare say the British were relieved by that. But the federal review was never completed, and the federation was doomed.

But the constitutional labours continued, next for Southern Rhodesia. Our own national constitutional conference opened in Salisbury in the first week of February 1961, chaired by the secretary for commonwealth relations from London, Duncan Sandys. He was a smooth character and a son-in-law of Sir Winston Churchill. There were two main sticking-points. We insisted that any worthwhile constitution would have to outlaw the system of land tenure which excluded black Africans from the right to own property in the best half of the nation's farmland, and in the cities too. The British said the national parliament should deal with land questions, and they should not be covered by the constitution. We said this was meaningless: a parliament dominated by the white electorate could never legislate fairly for land, which our people cared deeply about, and on that we stuck firm.

The other obstacle to any agreement was the question of the voters' roll and the number of black members of parliament to be elected on it. The British proposed a small increase in African representation, but not enough to make any difference to the dominance of the white electorate. We said so, and refused to approve the final document.

Sandys then emerged from the conference and, according to waiting journalists, said that I and my colleagues had accepted its conclusions. This was a flat untruth, but Sandys's words were widely reported and believed. Later Sir Edgar Whitehead confirmed in London that I had not signed any document. In 1963, when I met Sandys at the Kenya independence celebrations, I asked him why he had said something so blatantly false. He replied blandly that if he had admitted that I had not signed, he would be seen to have presided over an unsuccessful conference, and that would have damaged his political career. So much for the word of an English politician.

Sandys's false claim may have seemed to him a harmless piece of deception. But it had damaging effects on my party, the NDP. It turned out later that my colleagues Chitepo and Silundika had done something very risky. They had written to Sandys privately, saying that they rejected the proposed

constitution but that nevertheless it might be made to work –
and this naturally undermined the solidarity of our side.

On the other hand some of our members exploited Sandys's
claim in order to attack me personally. Leopold Takawira had
failed to get elected to the NDP executive on its formation in
1960: as a consolation I had appointed him to the important job
as our resident representative in London. Hearing Sandys's
claim on the radio, he sent me a telegram urging me to disown
my signature. When I emphasised that I had not accepted or
signed the document, Takawira began claiming personal credit
for preventing Nkomo from selling out to the British. This was
the first sign of a campaign of lies directed at me from within
my own party.

But in reality the argument over the constitution was a
side-issue. As leader of the NDP I began the work of building
up the new party, travelling endlessly and speaking endlessly
the length and breadth of Southern Rhodesia. Steadily the
party's roots grew and spread throughout the country. Our
technique, once more, was to exploit every grievance, local or
even personal, that people might have against the
administration. The authorities did all they could to frustrate
us.

The police had bought a whole range of new equipment
since last I had campaigned in the villages. They had new
Land-Rovers, with windows wired against stone-throwing and
special wheels for crossing obstacles. In particular they had a
new and most efficient radio communications system. When we
slept in a house where they did not want us to be, they would
park a Land-Rover outside and turn its radio speaker up high
so that the crackling conversation of our police watchers kept
us awake throughout the night. We, the regular politicians,
were not especially worried by such threats. But it was hard on
those who gave us shelter to subject their households to the
menace of the police, and the howling of their dogs throughout
the night.

The government did not at first use its powers to ban us
outright from entering African areas of the country. Instead
the district commissioners put pressure on the local chiefs to use
their traditional authority to keep us out. In return I went to
the chiefs themselves and reminded them that they held their

authority by custom and descent, while the district administrators were only civil servants – servants of the chiefs as well as of the government. It was remarkable how even the most passive of the chiefs responded to this reminder that they, not the administrators, were the rightful rulers of their districts.

Then the government started to ban our meetings outright. So I stopped organising meetings – but I was always happy to be a guest at parties, and there from time to time I would make a speech from inside the house, through a window, or maybe from behind a reed partition, so that I was not legally part of the gathering. These events were very successful in raising both support and the funds that we needed – they were good parties, and an effective means of political education too.

A police tail always followed us about, and it became a pleasure to evade it. The young police officers did not know what was happening to them. One young white officer was really persuaded that I was a magician. While he was tailing me I jumped out of my car, leaving the police vehicle to follow it while I changed my clothes in an Indian friend's shop and emerged as a dusty old man walking down the road. Then another of our cars came by and picked me up. This car's radio was tuned to the police frequency, as they talked about how Nkomo had driven off and another of his cars had picked up a ragged old man.

Later that night, when the police team had finally caught up with me at my own house, I invited them in for a cup of tea and told them exactly what their conversation had been that afternoon. 'But how do you know all this?' asked the young officer.

'I was with you all the time, in your car. You cannot see me, I can be a cat or an ant and you will never find me,' I said – the poor boy believed it, and seemed really frightened.

The police had to handle us with restraint, and to stay strictly within their legal powers. They knew we had good lawyers, and that if they failed to stick by the rule-book they would get a rap over the knuckles from the courts. The Whitehead government had a special reason for wishing to seem moderate and strictly constitutional, now that the Central African Federation was obviously breaking up. Nyasaland was moving rapidly towards self-government, the prelude to full independence: Dr Banda, released from detention, became a minister in a new government on 12 September 1961, and from that moment on it was certain that the federation could not survive. All the Southern Rhodesian government could do about that was to try to ensure that when the break-up came they got as many of the assets as possible.

Whitehead and his colleagues were determined to inherit the federal air force and most of the federal army, and realised that the British Conservative government would find it easier to do them favours if they kept strictly within the rule of law.

On 26 July 1961, the Southern Rhodesian government held its referendum to approve the new constitution ensuring continued white rule. The official results showed that it was carried by 41,949 Yes votes to 21,848 Noes. The NDP had urged the few Africans with votes to boycott the government referendum, and organised its own poll. We set it up as fairly as possible, and asked as many journalists as we could to observe its conduct. The result of 584 Yes votes, 467,189 Noes – ten times as many African negatives as there had been European positive votes. Of course, it made no difference. But once again we demonstrated the absurdity of allowing a tiny, white-dominated electorate to make 'democratic' decisions against the will of an enormously larger disenfranchised population.

The government's response to our referendum was a total ban for three months on all political activity in the country. The ban was probably illegal, and anyway it made little difference to the way in which we conducted our campaign. The government's token liberalisation of 'pinprick' segregation proceeded with the admission of a few token Africans to municipal boards and councils. They reformed the liquor laws, allowing Africans with university degrees to buy strong drink (a change I personally was against, although some of my colleagues did persuade me to take out a permit and pass my supply on to them!). They opened, in theory, public swimming pools to all races. But this was all window-dressing, whose main effect was to annoy the government's hard-line white supporters. Everyone knew the crisis was coming.

Tanganyika's independence came on 9 December 1961, and naturally I was invited as a guest to represent the NDP. On independence day itself I was happily chatting to some colleagues from other African countries when Julius Nyerere, the head of the new government, came over to us covered in smiles. 'You should not be here – you don't represent anybody,' he said. Turning to our colleagues he explained, still in great good humour: 'His party has been banned – it no longer exists.' The news was less amusing to me than to my host.

I left Dar es Salaam at once for the short flight home. The NDP had indeed been banned. But the law under which it was proscribed said nothing about any other party. We at once decided to carry on exactly as before, under a new name but with the same membership and constitution. The name we chose was the Zimbabwe African People's Union. As Zapu, banned or not banned, we have gone on standing for freedom, justice and equality for everyone in our country, right up to the independence of Zimbabwe and ever since. The name Zimbabwe, of course, is that of the ancient stone court and palace built by the rulers of the nation before any non-African intruders had appeared within our land.

Chapter 10
The First Guns

The year 1962 began with the creation of Zapu and ended in armed confrontation with a new and even more frankly racist government of Southern Rhodesia. Of course I would have preferred the peaceful road to freedom that was open to practically all the other former British colonies in Africa. It had been just possible that British intervention, or pressure from the outside world, or even an outbreak of common sense among the settler community, might have created a hope of African advancement by peaceful means. But it was not to be. We were forced to fight.

Well before it actually began, I told a British minister in London exactly why we would be forced into the armed struggle. That was in mid-1961, after the Salisbury government's referendum of white people had approved a new constitution for Southern Rhodesia which entrenched white power, and my party's own unofficial African referendum had rejected it by an enormously larger majority. Since the British government was responsible for imposing the new constitution on its 'self-governing' colony, I went to London to present those results.

I was ushered in to the junior minister at the Commonwealth Relations office, the duke of Devonshire, a small man, sitting in an office so huge that it seemed quite a long journey from the door to his desk. The duke was polite and frank. He listened to my presentation of the African case, then said: 'Mr Nkomo, you must realise that Southern Rhodesia has a complicated, advanced economy. We could not possibly hand it over to be run by untrained hands.'

I answered him directly: 'If development in Southern Rhodesia is an obstacle to the political freedom of the black people there, then we shall have to destroy that development. In the war, if a bridge became a danger to your nation, you blew up that bridge – not that you do not think bridges a good thing, but because at that time that particular bridge was helping your enemy. So if factories in Southern Rhodesia are an obstacle to our advance, we shall have to blow up those factories.'

The duke was horrified. When I came out of the meeting I told the press what I had said, and it was printed in the papers in Southern Rhodesia. That was one of the statements the white people never forgave me for – but it was true, and I meant it. I had given warning, and when I reported all this to the central committee of my party they fully approved.

If fighting was inevitable, we needed all the outside help we could get. In February 1962 our international campaign took two important steps forward. In Addis Ababa at the beginning of the month, Kenneth Kaunda took the chair at a meeting of the Pan-African Freedom Movement for East, Central and Southern Africa. All the independent African nations, and guests from almost all the liberation movements, agreed to back our struggle and to start a freedom fund. That brought us political support, and some financial help, from sympathetic countries outside Africa too. Since the British were opposed to our stand, and the Americans lined up with the British, this in practice meant that we strengthened our contacts with the countries opposed to the Anglo-American alliance.

In late February the scene moved to the United Nations in New York. The trusteeship committee of the UN decided formally 'to consider whether the territory of Southern Rhodesia has attained a full measure of self-government'. The British objections to this were absurd. They agreed that the territory was not independent – indeed they could not claim it was, since they as the imperial power spoke for it on foreign policy. But they also claimed that it was self-governing – although they were responsible in law for the new constitution that would deny Africans the prospect of rapid political advancement.

To oppose this stupid argument I appeared in person before the committee. Another Southern Rhodesian who pleaded that the British should not impose the new constitution was Garfield Todd, the former missionary who had failed as prime minister to bring in more liberal policies: Todd wanted African progress at a rate much slower than I believed necessary – but he had the courage to stand up and defy the new hard-line white government, and I honour him for that.

The British ambassador to the UN, Sir Hugh Foot, grew increasingly embarrassed at having to put his government's ridiculous case. One day he was claiming credit for Britain because of the liberation of millions of people in its former colonies around the world. Mr Gromyko, the Soviet ambassador, jumped to his feet and said: 'Why do you claim credit for that? You should rather be claiming the blame for having colonised them in the first place.' Sir Hugh told me then that he would soon have to resign in protest against the instructions he was receiving from home – in fact he did so, but not until October.

Because of the alphabet, the three delegations of the United Kingdom, the United States and the Union of Soviet Socialist Republics all sat together, and it was easy to see the Russians laughing at the discomfort of the Americans when they heard some of the British arguments. The Americans' embarrassment was greatest just after Sir Hugh's resignation, when one day a seat with the British delegation was occupied by none other than Sir Edgar Whitehead, the prime minister of the colony that the British claimed was, in law, self-governing.

At home, in the early part of 1962, Whitehead's government was preparing for the elections due to be held in December under the new constitution. It needed to prove to its white critics that it was getting tougher with the African freedom campaigners, and it did so by tightening up its repressive legislation once again, and increasing police harassment of our leaders. Demonstrations in August in the big towns were met by police violence and turned into serious riots.

It was clear to us that the government would soon move to ban Zapu, as it had banned the ANC and the NDP before it: they could not leave us free to organise. The Zapu central committee got ready for the ban. It passed a resolution that no successor party would be organised this time, and that Zapu would remain the sole voice of nationalism in Southern Rhodesia until it became Zimbabwe. (Several of those who reached this agreement were soon to found a break-away party of their own.) The central committee also sent emissaries, including myself, to Egypt on important business, and began to prepare our members all over the country for the banning, which this time, since there would be no successor party, meant organising a clandestine movement. Now the police, no doubt suspecting our plans, began to play dirty tricks of the most dangerous kind. The worst incident looked like murder.

Samuel Parirenyatwa was the first Southern Rhodesian African to qualify as a doctor: in 1956 he returned from medical school in South Africa and was employed in a rural hospital in southern Matabeleland. His professional skill and his personal goodness made a deep impression on all who met him. His African patients trusted him more fully than they had ever trusted his European predecessors; the white farmers of his remote area were supposed to use their own racially segregated medical services, but soon came to rely on Dr Pari's excellent care. He was one of those people before whom artificial barriers just crumbled away: even in delicate matters like gynaecology, the white farmers' wives preferred to be treated by him than to travel the long distance into Bulawayo to see a white doctor. He was, in fact, by his skill and his very existence, a threat to the whole absurd and divisive system by which our country was governed. Needless to say he was a passionate supporter of the nationalist cause, and he rapidly rose to be a vice-president of our new Zapu party.

On 14 August 1962, Dr Pari was travelling to Bulawayo on party business in a car driven by Edward 'Danger' Sibanda. The car was recovered from under a train on a level-crossing: Dr Pari was dead, Edward Sibanda was taken from the wreckage to hospital with serious injuries. Sibanda was positive that he had not driven into the track of the train. His last memory was of being surrounded by white soldiers, and of losing consciousness: when he came to his senses he was in the car under the wheels of the train, and Dr Pari was dead. (Ironically enough, it was the same night that the only African who had been persuaded to accept a ministry in the government of the federation resigned, in protest against its lack of progress towards African rights: he was Jasper Savanhu, with whom I had gone to London in 1952 in the official delegation to the first federal conference.)

Dr Parirenyatwa's death stiffened our determination to fight. Developments elsewhere had made it possible for us, at last, to get the weapons we needed. In June a summit conference of the 'Casablanca group' of African nations (Ghana, Guinea, Mali,

Egypt, Morocco, Libya and the Algerian provisional revolutionary government) had agreed to set up a military command for African liberation under Egyptian leadership. The Zapu central committee had authorised me and two colleagues to get arms where we could – for security reasons we were exempted from the usual obligation to report to our colleagues. And so it was that, on 12 September 1962, I found myself in Cairo, packing rifles into long boxes together with my good friend Mohammed Faiek, whom I had first met in Ghana five years earlier.

We had not wanted the armed struggle – but we were under attack, and we had to defend our people. I must admit that our first efforts were amateurish. They included a session when Mohammed and I went out into the desert and fired off the guns so that I would be sure of knowing how they worked. Then I set off for home, literally carrying the weapons on me. They were twenty-four semi-automatic assault rifles, with magazines and ammunition, and a big bag of grenades. Mohammed Faiek took me to the airport and personally saw to it that the cases of rifles were loaded into the hold of the plane. I carried ammunition and grenades – unprimed, I checked that – as hand baggage, with a first-class ticket by Air France. The excess baggage charge was £300.

The flight was to Dar es Salaam, via Nairobi, and at Nairobi (which was still under British colonial rule) everyone had to leave the aircraft. I insisted on carrying my personal baggage with me into the transit lounge, refusing the crew's kind offer of help. The two bags were a tremendous weight, but I took the grenades in one hand and the ammunition in the other, so that they were nicely balanced, and pretended that carrying them was no effort at all. Fortunately they did not examine our bags when we were called to get back into the aircraft.

At Dar es Salaam arrangements had been made to divert the luggage past customs through the freight area. I was so relieved that I felt like a student coming out of a successful examination, and the heat of Dar felt cool to me after the strain. Later I made another trip to pick up yet more ammunition and grenades from Cairo. In these days of airline security it seems incredible, but I was able to load the lot into the Air France baggage hold with no questions asked. I was the only person on that aircraft who knew what it was carrying, and I was even more anxious than usual for the duration of that flight.

There was still the problem of transporting the arms out of Tanganyika and into Southern Rhodesia, which meant passing through Northern Rhodesia, still a British colony, although Kenneth Kaunda was now the dominating figure in the government and independence lay only a few months ahead. My colleague Joseph Msika personally took the arms across the border.

We received valuable cooperation in our smuggling operations from ministers in the Northern Rhodesian government, with Kaunda's knowledge and approval. George Lusinde, minister of home affairs in Tanganyika, himself made the arrangements for getting past the customs there, and Julius Nyerere knew what was going on.

So the armed struggle had taken its first steps when the government of Southern Rhodesia formerly rejected the possibility of progress by peaceful means. On 19 September 1962 it announced that Zapu was banned and its leaders restricted to live in the areas where they were born. The banning of the party was permanent, but the restriction orders were for three months starting on 20 September. The aim was obviously to keep us out of the way until after the elections, which were due on 14 December, I decided to return from Lusaka to Tanganyika, set up the contacts that would ensure a continuing flow of weapons, then go home myself to face restriction.

So that was what we did. Naturally enough all the journalists in Lusaka were camped outside my house waiting for interviews with the banned Nkomo, and the police were on the watch as well. So Patrick Kumbai, who is roughly my size, dressed in clothes like mine and drove out in a car. The police and the press chased off after him and I drove quietly out a little later in my own car and set off for Tanganyika. In Dar I made the usual calls on some friendly embassies, explained our position and asked for help in our fight. The Egyptians, of course, already knew what was going on through Mohammed Faiek. The Soviet Union and some of the eastern Europeans were understanding, but could give no immediate assistance.

Then I took the plane home and was met at the airport as a VIP. I got right out of the aircraft and into a car from the Special Branch of the police. They searched me thoroughly –

they were even tearing the rubber tube out of the inside of my fountain pen, until I shouted at the officer in charge and he quietened his men down. Then they put me into a light aircraft and flew me away. My friends in Salisbury had seen me get off the plane from Dar, but neither they nor I knew where I was going next. It turned out to be Bulawayo, where I was met by no less than three police cars. They put me in the middle one and drove off with the others in front and behind. After a while I realised they were heading out onto the road for Kezi district, where I was born.

The only relation I had there was my cousin Sihle Nkomo, the son of my father's late brother, Ndumiso. He had no idea I was coming until the police cars dropped me off at his home in the bush – there was not even a road to his village – and told me that I should stay there for three months and not move out of a five kilometre radius. My cousin came out and asked what was going on. 'They have brought me to stay with you. I am restricted here,' I said.

Sihle simply answered: 'Welcome.'

At first I looked forward to the chance of a little rest, but people soon found out where I was. My cousin's house became a Mecca. Friends came in from all over the country, often people I had never seen before, bringing messages and words of support, and asking for guidance on policy. Meetings were of course illegal. But the tea and coffee were on the boil all day long, and people brought gifts of food and cooked them up in different huts so that there would never be enough of a crowd in one place to constitute an illegal assembly. There was no shortage of work.

Naturally I was worried about what had happened to the weapons I had brought in to Lusaka, across the Northern Rhodesian border. Soon I got the worst possible news of them. I switched on the radio and the announcer had something dramatic to say. Illegal automatic weapons had been found in Southern Rhodesia: an African had been stopped on the road from Bulawayo to Shabani, and automatic weapons had been found in his car. The arrested man was a regional secretary of Zapu and one of our very best young people, Bobylock Manyonga. There must have been treachery within our party. Someone had evidently tipped off the police about his cargo.

Manyonga was heroic, claiming throughout that the guns had been planted in his car and that he knew nothing about them. He served fourteen years in prison for that, and I fear his life was ruined. The weapons, incidentally, were British-made, but since they came from Egyptian stocks they could be identified as not originating in Southern Rhodesia. What Manyonga never revealed was that his weapons training had been acquired on a short course in the Soviet Union, as the first of many who were to go there.

Manyonga's resistance to interrogation meant that the authorities had no evidence against anyone else in Zapu. For the three months of my restriction to my cousin's house I was able to talk to my visitors, carefully persuading suitable people that the time for peaceful protest was over, and we must get ready to fight. The result of the elections proved once again that I was right. Sir Edgar Whitehead had been prime minister of Southern Rhodesia only since 1958, but he represented the tradition of settler government that went right back to the first election won by his predecessor, Sir Godfrey Huggins, in 1933. These men and their supporters believed absolutely in white supremacy. But they were at heart paternalists, ready to be polite to Africans who accepted their inferior status.

The election was a triumph for a new, much tougher party of right-wing racists, the Rhodesian Front. There were 65 seats in parliament, 50 of them elected on the 'A' roll, on which white people, Indians and coloureds voted. The Rhodesian Front won 35 of them, Whitehead's United Federal Party only 15. Whitehead's people also won 14 of the 'B' roll seats for which the few eligible Africans were entitled to vote; the remaining one 'B' roll seat was won by a white man, Ahrn Palley.

Whitehead had banned our party and constantly repressed African hopes. Now he had been rejected by the white electorate as too moderate.

The new prime minister was Winston Field, a big farmer from Marandellas who had made his name in an organisation called the White Rhodesia Council. His aim was to make Southern Rhodesia more like South Africa, to build a defensive alliance with the South Africans and the Portuguese, and to abandon the thin façade of racial tolerance to which the white rulers had hitherto paid lip-service.

In some ways Field's election made our task easier. We no longer had to struggle to make clear to outsiders that the regime in our country really was different from those in the other colonies that the British were abandoning. African politics and white politics were now under leaderships with no illusions about the other. The fight was on.

Zapu needed to organise as fast as possible to meet the new situation. Immediately following the elections the three months of restriction to our home districts expired, and we were at liberty. But we knew it could not be for long. On my release from my cousin's house I at once began to travel again, speaking and organising the party. We gained important support when, after four years, James Chikerema and George Nyandoro were released from restriction in Gokwe. I travelled up to greet them as they came out, and together we took the train to Salisbury, where they had first made their reputations in the days of the bus boycott, and the riots that followed, in the early days of the Youth League in 1956.

There were supporters with cars to meet us at the station, but we decided we preferred to walk to the African township of Harare. As we went along people gathered behind us, turning our walk into a grand parade for which we had of course not obtained permission. Passing the police barracks as we entered Harare township, we found the road blocked by a line of armed police. The officer in charge approached us and warned us that we were leading an unauthorised procession. No, we protested, we were just walking home from the railway station, and it was not our responsibility if a lot of people had decided to walk behind us.

In the old days this argument would have had the policemen discussing among themselves the exact interpretation of the law. Now there was no such doubt. 'If you take one step further we shall shoot,' said the police commander – and we believed him. We got into the cars and rode home.

Until now our relations with the police had always been correct, even when they were strained. Once Field became prime minister all that changed. The harassment was constant, and tempers got hot on both sides. At Rusape one Saturday night I was eating, late, with Chikerema, Nyandoro and Maurice Nyagumbo, in a supporter's house after a meeting. We were tired, and so were the policemen detailed to watch us. The young officer in charge came rushing into the room where we were eating and officiously told us that we had no authorisation to spend the night in that township; we must finish our dinner and get out of there so that he could go off duty. Foolishly he had come in alone, leaving his black constables outside. Nyagumbo lost his temper and pulled the young chap down with a smash onto the plates on the table. Then Chikerema waded in and they gave the policeman a real beating. He was quite a mess when he went out to his men.

We were locked up, of course, and remanded in custody over the weekend. On Monday the magistrate granted us bail to appear a month later on charges of assault against the police. (One detail of the charge was that I had prodded the man with my 'stick of office' – which was just an ordinary walking stick, and with which I had not touched him anyway.) My very good friend and legal adviser Leo Baron, from Bulawayo, organised our defence brilliantly: as counsel for our defence he briefed Herbert Chitepo, who was now working by agreement with Zapu in Dar es Salaam as Director of Public Prosecutions for the Tanganyika government. Fortunately the policeman had no witnesses.

Our defence was that the police officer had accidentally fallen against the table when he rushed into the brightly lit room from the dark outside, and had regrettably become confused as a result of his fall. The policeman admitted that he had not identified himself before entering the room. The courts eventually had to rule that there was reasonable doubt about what had happened. Quite wrongly, we were discharged after an appeal. This did not make the police any more sweet-tempered.

In early 1963 there was still just one constraint on the actions of the Field government, which had vaguely promised its white supporters complete independence from Britain soon. The Central African Federation was still legally in existence, although Nyasaland had been allowed to hold free elections in February, which resulted in a government headed by Dr Banda; obviously it would soon secede from the federation. Field and his colleagues were determined that when the British shared out the federal assets, they would get the main share, so meanwhile they had to behave in a way acceptable to British political opinion.

This they managed well enough. In late June 1963 I attended but took no part in the conference at Victoria Falls on dividing up the federal property: R. A. Butler was the British minister who took the chair, and he obviously knew very little about what was really at stake. As a result, the British – who had vetoed a UN resolution urging them to take over the federal armed forces – decided that the blatantly racist government of Southern Rhodesia should inherit the entire fighting force of the Royal Rhodesian Air Force (including its modern jet fighters), the battalion of parachute commandos and the equivalent of two brigades of well-armed and well-trained soldiers, with strong light-armoured detachments. The two black-ruled countries of the federation got some transport aircraft but no warplanes, and the equivalent of one brigade of infantry between them. When the British later argued that they could not intervene militarily in Rhodesia because of the strength of its armed forces, I often reflected on who had ensured that its forces were so strong.

Chapter 11
Splitting Up

Winston Field's right-wing government was quietly preparing its new repressive legislation, and by March 1963 it had formidable powers. Zapu was banned. Our leaders were technically at liberty but our ability to run a political organisation was under close restraint. As the leading nationalist, I was banned from entering the tribal trust areas that covered half of the country's habitable land. In these areas the rising population, and the increasing severity of the district commissioners in limiting the livestock people could own and the crops they could grow, were creating a ferment of discontent. I was also banned from attending public meetings anywhere. My political activity was confined to the African townships attached to European settlements, where I met people by subterfuges, speaking from behind a partition, or from the window of a neighbouring house, under the pretext of a social gathering.

Repression created a new solidarity within the country: at home our people had never been more united. But tragically it was at this moment that divisions began to appear within our movement's organisation abroad. This problem of disunity has persisted right up until today.

The root of the problem lay in Dar es Salaam, the capital of Tanganyika, which because of its geographical location had to be the main base of our external organisation. The Pan-African Freedom Movement, Pafmecsa, sited its support organisation in Dar in 1962, and the Organisation of African Unity's liberation committee followed when it was set up in 1963. The city became the main headquarters for liberation movements for central and southern Africa – for Mozambique, South Africa and Namibia as well as for my own country. But being in Dar es Salaam meant being under the wing of President Julius Nyerere of Tanganyika, and that caused two sorts of problems.

Nyerere lacked confidence in the ability of Africans to rule themselves. He had actually requested the British to postpone the date for his own country's independence, only to find that Britain was determined to shed its responsibilities as fast as possible. Although his ministers – and especially his minister of home affairs, George (Job) Lusinde – had helped me get my illegal weapons through customs on their way from Egypt to Northern Rhodesia, Julius himself seemed to take the view that I and my colleagues supported the armed struggle because we were bloodthirsty. He insisted that he had won his own country's independence without fighting, and said that if we would not talk to the Southern Rhodesian government he would speak to his British friends on our behalf. In other words he entirely failed to understand the essence of our problem, which was that our country was ruled by a very different sort of colonial government.

Moreover, Nyerere had a special problem with me personally. He always sought to dominate the policies and the personalities of the liberation movements to which he gave hospitality. But my contacts with the outside world were older than his and independent of his patronage. Perhaps he saw me as a threat to the leadership he wished to assert. In any case, he has regularly taken positions opposed to mine, and backed my critics even when that damaged the cause of freedom in my country. This may have been reinforced by the influence of the Chinese advisers in whom he had great confidence.

A further problem arose with the growing exile membership of our party, which consisted largely of students at universities all over the world, but mainly in London and New York. The most influential of these was Leopold Takawira, our London representative – the man who had misrepresented my position after the abortive constitutional conference in 1961. Takawira (who died in prison in 1970) was a nervous character of great personal ambition. He had much influence over the younger students at the Catholic mission station where he grew up, the most notable of whom was Robert Mugabe, the shy intellectual who became publicity secretary of the National Democratic Party on his return from three years' teaching in Ghana, in 1960. Takawira had for several years in the 1950s earned his living as an official of the Capricorn Africa Society, which was organised by a former British officer, Colonel David Stirling. Its aim was to build up African elites prepared to take over government in cooperation with the rich white property owners. Takawira supported its scheme for allowing selected Africans to qualify gradually for a share in power: his follower, Mugabe, sent home newspaper articles in which he made unfavourable comparisons between the progress of Ghana under African rule and that of Southern Rhodesia under its racist regime. Such sophisticated and unrealistic ideas were current among the exiled intellectuals, and helped to undermine our party's unity.

But as repression grew and one by one we in the leadership were charged and tried with various offences, it became necessary to move out to Dar es Salaam. The journey was often risky, and many of us slipped quietly across the borders. A particular problem arose in the case of Robert Mugabe and his Ghanaian wife, Sally. They were both facing charges of subversion in the courts, so leaving the country meant jumping their bail: Robert was ordered to do so, but he refused to leave Sally behind. So they both fled into Botswana, and from there, with great trouble, I arranged for a light aircraft to carry them safely to Tanganyika without the fatigue of the roundabout overland journey.

My own departure was surprisingly easy. I was invited to a non-political event, to open a fund-raising fête run by the famous charitable self-help organisation, Jairos Jiri, with which I had long been associated. I told the people they should all support the charity, since in these days of mechanisation everyone was at risk of disablement through accidents involving cars or aircraft or machines. It was in fact a farewell speech.

That was in Barbourfields stadium, in Bulawayo. At the end of the meeting my friend William Sivako picked me up in a car and drove me out to Nyamandlovu station on the railway line about forty-eight kilometres northwards. The police suspected nothing. The train stopped, and I slipped quietly onto it. I had been welfare officer and general secretary of the railway union, so all the train crews knew me. They put me in a service coach, which the customs in those days never bothered about at the border, and I sat there quietly until the train pulled in at Lusaka in Northern Rhodesia.

Soon I was back in Dar es Salaam, reestablishing contact with my overseas friends and organising supplies of weapons for the coming struggle. The focus of my effort was of course at the United Nations, with its unrivalled opportunities for international contact. I visited the Soviet Union for the first time, and the Chinese People's Republic for the only time, and I made my way into the new world of the non-aligned nations.

But the most important event by far was the inaugural meeting of the Organisation of African Unity, over which the Emperor Haile Selassie presided in Addis Ababa in May 1963. North Africans and those south of the Sahara, French-speakers and English-speakers, progressives and conservatives, came together to dedicate themselves to the future of our continent. Enthusiasm was high, and Kwame Nkrumah's vision of unity swept everyone along. The OAU has by no means fulfilled all the hopes we then placed in it, but it was and still is a noble idea. Ironically it was during that inaugural meeting, when all our minds should have been on the single purpose of liberating Africa, that the divisions within our movement first came into the open.

The first indication I had that something was wrong came in Nairobi, on the way to Addis. My Egyptian friend Mohammed Faiek suddenly put a completely unexpected question: 'Is Zapu still one party? What tribe do you belong to?' I said I did not know what he meant. 'Are you an Ndebele?' asked Mohammed.

'Yes, that is what I speak, but what do you mean?' I asked.

Mohammed seemed surprisingly well-informed. He explained that he had been told that the Shonas were the majority tribe, and that there was a move by them to take over the leadership of the party. I explained that our tribal situation was not nearly as clear-cut as he seemed to think, and wondered where he had got these dangerous ideas from. Mohammed finished up with a warning: 'You watch out, there's a problem in your party.'

At the Addis Ababa meeting I found out what he meant, when Leopold Takawira and his friends launched their campaign against my leadership. They started in the full glare of publicity, in a way calculated to damage our cause as much as possible. The OAU offered us a splendid opportunity to gain the attention of the world's press, and our press conference was booked for 2 p.m. one day, the best time for the news media throughout Africa and Europe. Our publicity committee had agreed on a formal statement of the case for Zimbabwean independence, which I was to read before answering questions.

The typing and copying of the statement as a press hand-out was the responsibility of the publicity secretary, Robert Mugabe. I arrived with 1 ½ hours to spare to get ready and prepare the answers to likely questions – but by the time the journalists arrived, neither Mugabe nor the copies of the statement were available. I had to make some impromptu remarks and apologise for the lack of the press statement that had been promised. Mugabe's absence was clearly deliberate, done to embarrass me and to sabotage our chance of publicity. My friends confirmed this, asserting that he had fallen under the influence of his old mentor, Leopold Takawira. I regretted this all the more for being manifest in public.

Joseph Msika, then deputy treasurer of Zapu, had an even more disturbing experience. He saw one of our colleagues, Washington Malianga, nervously hiding away a printed document. Joseph asked to see it, Washington refused, so Joseph snatched it away and read it. He found it was a circular openly urging Zapu to bring the 'majority tribes' to the leadership of the party, and to get rid of '*Zimundebere*', which is a derogatory term in the Shona language for 'the old Ndebele man'. That meant me: the attack was a straight incitement to tribal feeling against me. Joseph gave the wretched document back to Malianga, who tore it up and pretended it had never existed.

At that time, in the villages of Zimbabwe, rivalry between the two main language groups barely existed. In the towns the two groups are so mixed that it did not occur to people to divide in this way. But the students at universities abroad had lost contact with the realities of life at home. They felt the need to create some artificial loyalty to a group, and they chose to exploit 'tribal' differences as a means of rallying that loyalty. White 'experts' on Rhodesia – missionaries, government employees, academics loyal to successive regimes – had for long emphasised and exaggerated such differences as a way of dividing the people. Now their work was bearing fruit, to damage our cause.

The leadership of Zapu had always been drawn without distinction from all the areas of the country: the central committee at that time – and indeed at all times – had and has a majority of Shona-speakers. Now I was accused of giving preference to Ndebele-speakers. Part of the false accusation stuck, and was exploited by people who wished to attack me for their own personal advantage. That is our country's tragedy.

An atmosphere of conspiracy grew up around our party, and the Southern Rhodesian government was quick to exploit it through its secret services. One of the most promising younger members of the Zapu central committee was Agrippa Mukahlera. He was approached by some strangers from home who seemed full of enthusiasm for our cause, and offered to help. Mukahlera, without checking on his new friends' identity, told them more than he should about our organisation. Then they disappeared and Mukahlera reported his conversations to the rest of us. We established that they were almost certainly spies sent from Salisbury to penetrate our organisation.

We soon cleared Mukahlera of anything but imprudence. But he felt deeply guilty, would not believe he had been cleared, and collapsed with mental strain. He was sent to hospital under sedation. One of our leading members in Dar was my old lawyer, Herbert Chitepo, now working as director of public prosecutions for the Tanganyika government – and he had now lined up with the group opposed to me. His wife Victoria visited the confused young man in hospital and told him I was playing tricks on him: he grew desperate and fled to her house, convinced that I was out to get him.

All I could do was to go round and try to sort it out in person. Herbert Chitepo was not at home. I found Victoria sitting with Dr Terence Ranger, a liberal-minded white man who had just been expelled from the university in Salisbury by the Field regime. Victoria walked straight out of the room, leaving Dr Ranger to make it clear I was not welcome in the house. Even our supporters were involved in our troubles, with their constant undercurrent of tribalism.

The far more genuine issue dividing the central committee at this time was that of the armed struggle to which I was myself firmly committed. Julius Nyerere, having at first characteristically wavered, now came down firmly with the opinion that the best way of dealing with the hard-line settler government in Salisbury was by polite talks with British officials. He combined this with a strong leaning towards the group in opposition to me, whose emerging leader was the Reverend Ndabaningi Sithole.

Julius called me in to State House and gave me a stern message. He said that my efforts to organise the armed struggle from Dar es Salaam were not practical. He would give Zapu office space and the chance for some of our people to organise politically. But my place, said Nyerere, was in Southern Rhodesia, organising my own people, and he would not have me in his capital.

I had to go home fast. This was embarrassing: I had become very friendly with the Yugoslav ambassador, who had even lent me one of his embassy's spare flats to work from. I was about to leave for his country, to meet President Tito, the leading figure of the non-aligned movement. There was nothing for it but to tell the Yugoslavs that something urgent had come up so that I must cancel my appointment with Tito. (On my request, the ambassador very kindly made the flat I was occupying available to Robert and Sally Mugabe, who, I felt, needed a good place to live for the sake of their new baby daughter.) Then I left for home, on President Nyerere's orders.

Maurice Nyagumbo and I set off by car for Northern Rhodesia, and back home by the same route I had followed on leaving – onto the train at a country stop south of Lusaka, across the frontier in the service coach, then off the train unobtrusively in Luveve, the western township of Bulawayo. I took a taxi home to my wife and children, who had no warning of my arrival. It was wonderful to be together again, if only for a while.

The strangest thing about the next few months was that, although I was harassed and followed everywhere by the police, they never picked me up. I was, of course, an expert on the nuances of what it was lawful to say and do under the rigid terms of the Law and Order Maintenance Act and all the rest of the oppressive legislation. Winston Field, the prime minister, was fiercely criticised by his supporters for allowing me so much freedom. But maybe he was more subtle than we gave him credit for, since the opposition within Zapu was tearing our party apart better than his police could have done.

Ndabaningi Sithole had now emerged clearly as leader of the dissidents. They kept trying, and failing, to organise a meeting of the central committee that would vote me out of office. Their aim was to hold such a meeting as far as possible from Southern Rhodesia itself, where my support among the people would have least effect. One appointment was set to take place in a remote house in the bush in Northern Rhodesia belonging to a rich liberal, Sir Stuart Gore-Brown: as I was leaving for it James Chikerema discovered a plot to kill or capture me there, so I did not go, and ordered the meeting to be cancelled. Early in August the Sithole group made it clear that they were on the brink of founding their own break-away party.

I had to act decisively, and I sought a democratic decision of our party to resolve our problems. I summoned a general congress to meet in one of the few possible places, the cooperative farm run by liberal white people a few kilometres out of Salisbury on the Bulawayo road, and known as Cold Comfort Farm. Although thinly disguised, for Zapu was still banned, this was to be a representative party congress. I telegraphed the Dar es Salaam office to summon its members home for the occasion, authorising air tickets for all of them. Thousands of the party faithful from all over the country came to Cold Comfort Farm, but a small group of the Dar es Salaam people chose not to come. Instead they held their own little meeting in Enos Nkala's home in Highfields, in Salisbury, and announced that they were setting up their own rival party called Zanu, the Zimbabwe African National Union.

The Zapu congress, on 10 and 11 August 1963, passed some decisive resolutions. It confirmed me as president – indeed, on James Chikerema's proposal, it voted to make me president for life. This I strongly disagreed with, and said so. I was far too young for such an honour, only forty-six, not a venerable old man. Anyway, I thought it wrong for the party to commit itself to a single president for the years ahead. But that was what they wanted, and I could hardly veto their decision.

The congress also reaffirmed the decision that while Zapu remained banned, no other party should be created to replace it – in the past we had created a succession of parties to get round banning orders, but this time there was to be no such easy way out. Meanwhile we needed some framework within which to carry on our work, so we invented an informal body called the People's Caretaker Council, not as a political party but as a social group to which people could lawfully admit to belonging.

Zanu, the opposition group, had split off for good. It had, of course, no members within Southern Rhodesia, and its self-chosen leadership was based over the border out of contact with the people. But in Dar es Salaam it had the support of President Nyerere, and the international backing that went along with that. Zanu's principal officials were Sithole as president, Takawira as vice-president, Mugabe as secretary-general and Moton Malianga as secretary for youth. Takawira and Malianga's brother Washington had been the main promoters of tribal propaganda against me. Their colleagues must have known what game they were playing, and they would have had to be very foolish not to understand the dangers for our country.

The next few months were frantic. Zanu was determined to make its mark by fair means or foul. Among my own supporters there was real anger at the Zanu leadership's betrayal of national solidarity. On each side there was violence against the other, leading in particular to a campaign of petrol-bombing in the townships that caused real distress. The government was obviously delighted at this split among its enemies, and did its best to foster confusion. I do not know how much of the actual violence was inflicted by government agents, but surprisingly well-printed posters began to appear overnight in sensitive areas, abusing me and encouraging the split.

Winston Field's government, knowingly or not, did their best to encourage the growth of the break-away party by restricting my movements. First they banned me from a forty-kilometre radius of the capital, Salisbury. The police picked me up on the road from Umtali one day, read me a banning order and escorted me forty kilometres out of town on the Bulawayo road. This was a severe blow, since so many routes both by rail and road passed through Salisbury. Then they banned me from all the tribal trust areas of the country, so that I was forbidden to visit the areas where the vast majority of our supporters lived. Then they prohibited the publication of my name in the newspapers, a ban that lasted a dozen years in an unsuccessful attempt to force the people to forget me.

But we of the Zapu leadership kept on travelling, using the back roads and appearing where the police did not expect us. I became expert at laying false trails. Once I was arrested for using a road that I genuinely did not know crossed the border of a tribal trust area. But the police revealed to the magistrate that they had been following me and had permitted me to cross the line that made my journey unlawful. Since they were thus accessories to my offence, I was acquitted.

Finally, despite my hard-won expertise in the details of the law, they found a charge that they thought they could make stick against me. I made a speech on lines that were familiar enough. I described the political structure of our country, saying that power was reserved by a group of fellows who collected our property and divided it up among themselves. I meant, of course, the government. I further stated that the government was chosen not by us, the people, but by a small group called the electorate who were concerned to maintain their wealth and privileges.

The law said that criticising the government was fair game, but that criticising white people was subversive. Since I was criticising the electorate, and that electorate consisted almost entirely of white people, the government decided that they could probably get a conviction. They charged me with subversion: I was convicted in the magistrates' court, appealed, was released on bail, and awaited what I was fairly sure would be a stiff term in prison.

But this government action was not enough for the hard-liners of the ruling Rhodesian Front. Winston Field had been elected leader on a vague promise to declare independence from Britain, but had not dared to carry out that threat. Early in April 1964, the party caucus met and sacked Field. He was replaced by another farmer, a former fighter-pilot who seemed really to believe in unilateral independence, and publicly talked a lot of nonsense about the excellent race relations of Southern Rhodesia. He was the former finance minister, Ian Douglas Smith. We were delighted. The cowboys had taken over the ranch. Now the fight could come into the open. Three days later I was arrested. That was on 16 April 1964. I became a free man again on 3 December 1974. Those were a long ten years.

Chapter 12
Prisoner

They arrested me late at night in the African township of the little settlement of Enkeldoorn, on the highway south of Salisbury. I was on my way to an ox-roast party planned by one of our supporters, Chiriseri, on his farm in a former European area, as near to Salisbury as I could get. On my roundabout way there, avoiding the areas from which I was banned, I stopped the night in Enkeldoorn. Even in that little place a social party and informal political gathering was planned for me – as usual I was to stay in the house overnight and speak to the people from there, in the intervals between the singing and dancing.

Suddenly the music died down and there came from the darkness the sound of car doors slamming, and the chatter of radios from the police vehicles. The people in the garden were ordered to lie flat on their faces, in case shooting started. A senior policeman's voice shouted: 'Nkomo, where are you? We have come to pick you up.' So it began. I told the people not to worry, I would be back, and climbed into the police truck with my few belongings. As the engine started up I could hear people crying.

The police pretended not to know where I was going. They took me to the little police post at Lalapansi, where a senior officer read me an order stating that I was to be detained at a place called Gonakudzingwa. But as far as anybody knew there was no such place. The police were perfectly polite, and after a while we worked out that it was part of the Gonarezhou Game Reserve, an area of wild country along the Mozambique border in the far south-east corner of the country – in fact about as remote as it could possibly be. 'My word,' I said – there seemed no other response. So I signed the necessary forms, collected my things, and once more climbed into the police truck.

First stop was Thornhill air force base, near Gweru, where there was not a black face to be seen. They had paid me the compliment of having all the African staff sent away while I passed through. Was I going alone, I asked? Nobody knew, but they made me some coffee and we drank it together and waited in the officers' mess for three hours. It is strange how the separation of the races broke down at times like that. At dawn a small plane arrived bringing my deputy, Josiah Chinamano, and his wife, Ruth.

Josiah is the most reliable of friends and a devoted patriot: Ruth Chinamano, a keen party activist, insisted that she was detained in her own right, not just as Josiah's wife. So I knew I was in good company. Then Joseph Msika came too, which made four of us. Two hours later, at about eight in the morning, they put us in a Dakota and we flew off towards the south-east in low cloud. It was not a happy trip. Somewhere near Fort Victoria the pilot pulled the plane sharply up into the sky and announced that he had just missed a small mountain, that he could not find the airstrip, and we were going back to Gweru.

That afternoon, when the clouds lifted, they flew us down to Nuanetsi Ranch, a huge European-owned place with vast herds of cattle and its own airstrip. I could see the African workers waving from behind their huts to show they were on our side. Then we were put into two jeeps and taken away to the game reserve.

I am told that the idea of hiding prisoners away in game reserves came from Sir Godfrey Huggins, the long-serving prime minister of Southern Rhodesia who later became Lord Malvern. It seems that he once met Dr Salazar, the old Portuguese dictator, and began to explain his country's native policy. Salazar was not much interested. Portugal, he said, did not have a native policy: the natives were just there, part of the African fauna like the elephants. Portugal did not have an elephant policy, so he did not see why it should have a native policy. Huggins answered that the British colonies did have an elephant policy, where they were herded into reserves for their own safety, and its policy for natives was much the same.

So here the four of us were, the first natives to be hidden away in the elephant reserve. After a while we were joined by Dan Madzimbamuto, Stanislas Marembo and Willie Musarurwa. The lions and elephants made sure we did not run away. Joseph and Stanislas had a habit of taking early morning walks until one morning they met a lion – a big male – on the

path, and they came flying home. One day we all took a walk to
the nearby police post, leaving the little camp deserted. When
we returned we found a herd of big wild elephants looking
thirstily at our water-tank. We took to our heels. Josiah
Chinamano was the first one back to the police post, and his
wife Ruth has never forgiven him for letting her lag behind.
The animals were dangerous, but not hostile by intent. They
were taking a walk or looking for water, just like us. It was their
jungle, not ours. But nobody was going to escape while they
were around.

In this forest where we found ourselves there was nothing
but about a dozen well-built prefabricated huts, lined in a sort
of plastic material, each with a sitting room and bedroom and a
little kitchen with a coal stove. There was running water at a
standpipe, and a man came every couple of days to run the
water-pump, which also supplied the toilets and showers. Apart
from that there was nobody about, as far as we could see. Just
beside the camp ran the Mozambique frontier fence. On our
side an area of ten hectares was marked out with white stones,
and that was our place of restriction. There was no road, but a
track led off into the bush in the direction of the railway line,
which passed nearby.

The only supervision was from a little frontier police post on
the railway line. It was called Vila Salazar, and where the
railway line ran over into Portuguese territory was one of their
frontier police posts, called Malvernia. The two old bosses had
given these names as compliments to each other, when the line
was first laid down from Lourenço Marques. Later in our
detention, when we heard on the radio how the British were
enforcing the embargo on oil imports to Southern Rhodesia,
we used to watch the rail tankers of petroleum trundling up
that line with the names of British companies written large on
their sides, and that taught us to despise the hypocritical lies of
the British government.

Those early days of our detention were marked by a series of
law-suits against the government, master-minded by my
wonderful lawyer and good friend Leo Baron of Bulawayo.
(Leo is now a judge of the High Court of Zimbabwe, a well-
deserved honour.) First we were confined to a mere ten hectares at Gonakudzingwa. Then that form of restriction was

declared unlawful. The government's response was to confine us to what they called the Sengwe tribal trust land, consisting of 650 square kilometres. In fact this meant that we stayed in the same place – but the railway halt at Vila Salazar was now included in our area, and visitors could come and go freely.

Next Leo lost the appeal against my sentence for subversion, and I was sent to serve six weeks' hard labour in Gweru prison: with remission, that meant I served a month. The prison authorities were very anxious that I should not come into contact with the ordinary prisoners, most of whom were our supporters, since they knew I would get them organised.

To make my confinement really solitary they put me by myself in the white prisoner's section of the jail. The only hard labour I got was cooking for myself, and it was real labour stoking up the huge coal stove meant for a whole wing of white criminals. The prison clothes were marked with a broad arrow, in the old British tradition, and the trousers were made of canvas so stiff that they stood up by themselves. Because I was in the white prisoners' wing they gave me white people's rations – a whole loaf of bread a day, a large tin of syrup a week, a little rice, sugar, salt, tea and beans. The bean ration was so small that I saved them up for days before it was worth cooking them – one day I counted them and there were just eighty-seven beans.

In protest I insisted that I was a black man and must get a black man's rations, even if I was in a white man's cell. I said I wanted *sadza*, the maize porridge that is our staple diet. I said my whole body is made of *sadza*, I could not live without it. So they gave it to me. That is the sort of little victory that keeps you going in solitary confinement. The other triumph of Gweru was that, as an ordinary prisoner, I was entitled to visits by my family. MaFuyana brought with her our new-born daughter, my beloved Louise Sehlule.

The government evidently found it convenient to have me out of the way in Gweru, because when the date came for my release they kept me there on a detention order, and Chinamano and several others were sent to join me in prison. Although Zanu prisoners were normally kept apart from Zapu people, the authorities mistakenly sent one of them to join us there. When some of my followers got a bit rough with him I took him into my own cell, where he would be safe. He was Edgar Tekere, later one of the least successful ministers in Robert Mugabe's first government.

But once again Leo Baron had been at work, and this time he got the courts to declare that detaining us in prison was unlawful. So back we went to Gonakudzingwa, or rather the Sengwe area of 650 square kilometres, with the lions and elephants to guard us. On our return we found that the government had constructed an extra camp alongside our original one.

Now many more people were sent to join us, as the Smith government cracked down hard on all opposition. We were allowed visitors, and anyone who wanted to come could do so by rail. Within a very short time there were four separate camps built within a few hundred metres of each other. The number of detainees fluctuated, but rose at one time to over 3,000 people. Their visitors began to flow in by the hundred, bringing their own food and prepared for a few days' stay.

Our prison became a centre for political education, both for us prisoners and for our visitors. The government had evidently not thought what the effect would be of putting us away in that remote place, almost without supervision. We took control of our own lives, set up our own camp government and ran it as a practical course in democratic administration. The camp was run by the central committee, whose members acted as the chairmen of specialised committees for education, reception, hospitality and so on. The committee secretaries ran the day-to-day business, carrying out policy and reporting back on the people's reactions to it.

The nearest local residents lived two days' walk away, along the railway line or the Mozambique boundary fence. They took to coming in, first out of curiosity, later because they became interested in what we were saying. There was a drought that year, and people for many kilometres around were short of water. Our pump provided plenty of that, so they moved in to take advantage of it. Many came across from the Portuguese side of the border to visit us and hear our message of freedom. The local language on both sides of the border is Shangani, which resembles Sindebele, so we had no problem talking to each other.

We even got our own Roneo machine and produced a

publication called the *Gonakudzingwa News,* which became extremely popular until it was finally banned. People would push and shove to get copies of these little papers, which were done up with a picture of me on the front, and greetings and thanks for coming in several languages. Our message was that the country belonged to all the people who lived there, and everyone had a right to a share in the work of governing it. The Portuguese authorities began to complain to the Smith government that we were spreading subversion on their border, and they asked that the camps be moved away to where they would not cause such a threat.

The few policemen at the Vila Salazar frontier post had to tolerate this. They soon grew relieved that we were keeping order with no need for any intervention from them. It was our strict policy to behave politely to all our guards, and to show them that we had nothing against white people as such, only against the system of government that denied the rights of black people.

By mid-1965 there were five separate detention camps within a radius of a few kilometres in that remote corner of the country. The largest was Camp 3, with a capacity of two or three thousand people. Camp 5 was exclusively for our Indian and coloured comrades. Obviously the authorities could not let us go on building up what was from their point of view a centre for subversion.

One morning we saw, out of the blue, a group of soldiers marching towards us. A large number of visitors were waiting for our mass meeting to begin, and obviously they were very frightened when the soldiers set up their machine guns and surrounded us. The officer in charge came over to the shelter where I was, with my senior colleagues, preparing to speak to the crowd. He said that the government had declared a state of emergency throughout our area, which meant that nobody might visit without authorisation. All those not restricted must leave at once, including those from the Mozambique side, who were by now living almost permanently with us. Large meetings were also prohibited. He also had orders to remove certain articles, including my fur hat and stick, which I duly handed over.

So that was that. The visitors who had come by truck and bus found their own way home on the forest trails. The rest were herded into barbed wire enclosures and put onto a train for transport away out of the forest, and the railway halt was declared closed. From now on the only access to our area was on foot from the nearest permitted road, about twenty-four kilometres away, through the forest full of dangerous animals and snakes. The flow of visitors shrank to a trickle: permits were hard to get, even for our legal advisers and our immediate families. Obviously the country was moving towards some sort of crisis.

Ian Smith was talking once more about declaring independence of Britain, and he promised that this would be put to the electorate in a general election. The electorate was the white-dominated one defined by the 1961 constitution: there was no way the tiny minority of black, Indian and coloured voters could influence its results, so we had declared a boycott of all voting. In November 1964 a referendum of this electorate had produced a large majority for 'independence based on the 1961 constitution'. (Only 64,000 people voted, out of a total population of more than 3 million: that was Smith's idea of democracy.) In May 1965 they held their general election, at which all fifty white seats (out of a total of sixty-five in parliament) were won by supporters of Smith's Rhodesian Front party. The unilateral declaration of independence was promised.

There was just one ground for hope. In 1964 Britain had elected a Labour government, which claimed to have the interests of oppressed people at heart, and which included some people whom I had known in my days in Britain to be of good-will. In October 1965 the British prime minister, Harold Wilson, flew to Southern Rhodesia in a final attempt to persuade Ian Smith not to break his links with Britain. The Labour government had laid down conditions that a Rhodesian government would have to meet in negotiations. They fell far short of what Zapu was by now demanding, so they were not in fact of great interest to us. But still, Wilson's visit, accompanied by the Commonwealth secretary, Arthur Bottomley, might embarrass Smith's repressive government.

In late October we were invited to visit Wilson in Salisbury. With four or five others I was flown to New Sarum airport and transferred by helicopter to a field near Government House.

Our guards were obviously very anxious lest we should be seen: they put us into the back of a soft-topped truck, pulled the flap down to hide us, and drove off. Then the truck just parked. It was dreadfully hot under the canvas, with no air coming in. I shouted to the man in charge that we were suffocating, but he paid no attention. My colleagues and I began banging on the walls of the truck until an angry policeman opened it up, and we ordered him to drive the truck somewhere out of the sun where we would not be boiled up.

The authorities clearly did not know when Wilson would want to see us. After a time they took us to the main police camp near Government House, where an area in the middle had been screened off with hessian for secrecy, and we were left to wait. Then we drove out by a devious route into the back entrance of Government House. Our Zanu counterparts were there too, we gathered; but we were sent for first by Wilson.

Harold Wilson began by assuring us that the British government was very concerned about the Smith government's objective of declaring independence. So why, we asked, had Arthur Bottomley said in Nairobi that the British would never use force to prevent an illegal declaration of independence? This statement alarmed us because it seemed an open invitation to Smith: it sounded as though the British government was simply saying, 'Go ahead'.

Wilson's reply was extremely long, but not convincing. He assured us that, if Rhodesia declared independence illegally, the British government would impose an economic embargo and ask the United Nations to see that other countries followed that example. He talked very dramatically about the effects of a petroleum embargo, the disastrous consequences for the country, and the difficulty it would have existing in a world isolated, unwanted and without friends.

I asked what would happen if they were without friends but carried on anyway? South Africa would help, and what would the British do about South Africa – put an embargo on them too? Wilson admitted that Britain could not afford to put an embargo on South Africa, nor to police the South African border against imports from the outside world. So I told Wilson that he was admitting there was nothing he could do about the threat of illegal independence. He asked us to wait until the following day, when his attorney-general would be there to spell out the legal definition of Britain's measures to quell a rebellion.

We waited overnight at the police camp, and next morning again we were brought to Government House to see the British prime minister and the attorney-general, Sir Elwyn Jones, who had arrived overnight. Wilson told us that in the event of an illegal declaration of independence Sir Humphrey would have the powers to run the country detailed in the document that his law officer would now read out to us. The man pulled out a sheet of paper and began reading a lot of formal language. But I was inside the room and the sun was shining in behind him through the paper as he read. I really believed that there was nothing written on the paper at all.

I did not tell Wilson that I and my colleagues believed his written 'guarantees' were simply a blank paper. But I was quite clear in my mind that Wilson was trying to fool us. We were taken back to our place of detention, certain that when Smith declared independence the British would do nothing effective about it.

A few days after our return, the government declared a state of emergency throughout the country. All our visits were stopped, the police guard on us was strengthened, and we were forbidden to move across into the other camps. One morning shortly after that a young man came to talk to us – a white lad, in the police – and said he was terribly frightened. He was sure the British were going to invade, he was afraid he would be caught up in the fighting, and he did not know what to do. Independence, he said, was going to be declared the next day.

Sure enough, next day we listened to Ian Smith as he read over the radio his unilateral declaration of independence. Within a few minutes a contingent of police came towards us and took everyone whose presence was not specifically authorised to the railway station. That was on 11 November 1965. We had been in restriction for almost nineteen months. Now there were to be no visits, no news of the outside world, no free association with the people in the neighbouring camps. We were shut away.

Of course I was excluded from active politics. But I had faith in our people's will to carry on the struggle. I knew the oppressive regime that governed us would in the end be forced to yield to the majority. I never lost hope, not for a moment. But all the same it was hard – hard especially to be separated from my wife and our growing children. For seven years I did not see my wife a single time. But her loyalty sustained me although we were apart, and helped me to keep the faith through the years that sometimes seemed endless.

Chapter 13
Left to Rot

Ian Smith's illegal government knew they could not break our spirit. They feared to kill us, since that would alienate the few friends they had in the world. They wanted us, and the cause we stood for, out of the way. So they shut us up to rot quietly, in Camp 5 of the Gonakudzingwa protected area, in Gonarezhou Game Reserve.

There were four of us at the start: Joseph Msika, Lazarus Nkala, Stanislas Marembo and myself. About four months later the guards discovered that Stanislas was missing: he had gone on a visit to Camp 2. The police, using tracker dogs found him, and he was taken away for detention in Gweru prison. So we three were together for the next nine years.

The objective was to cut us off from the world, to make it forget us and us forget it. But that is not so easy. The radios were our lifeline. One was built into the top of a little bedside medicine chest that I had made myself during the relatively relaxed initial period of restriction – a little Sanyo, using the same batteries as my pocket torch, so that I could buy replacements without difficulty. The other was hung on a pole fitted under the seat of our earth latrine, and the guards never found it there.

The other camps remained in occupation, a couple of kilometres away in the forest. The paths were patrolled not only by the usual wild beasts, but also by our own fierce-looking dogs. It was the dogs that enabled us to keep in touch with the other prisoners. Each camp put out food for the dogs at fixed, but different, times of the day, so they made a regular circuit of the camps. We fixed up little pouches behind their collars, so messages passed from one camp to another.

It was a tragedy for us when the police shot the dogs – but that was not because of the message system, which the guards never discovered. It was because of the names we had given the animals. There was Ian Smith, after the illegal prime minister, a female dog called Janet, after his wife, and an ugly beast called van der Byl. A big fat dog we called Dupont, after the pompous man who became president of their illegal state – and there were others named after other ministers. When the police came round to inspect us we would call 'Smith, Smith', and the dog would come running up to be patted. The police thought this lacking in respect, so they shot all the dogs with names. They called out the names we had given, the dogs came running, and were shot. They did not shoot poor Dupont; he was attacked by a leopard and lost his nerve, then got run over by a truck at Camp 5 and died. We gave him a state funeral.

Conditions in the camp were, I suppose, reasonably tolerable. The little barracks was clean enough, and we were responsible for our own cooking and cleaning. The food was the sort of plain diet given to African farm workers – plenty of *sadza* and some of the sort of low-grade beef that they called 'boys' meat', because it was especially for black servants. My colleagues insisted that I should not do menial work like cooking and cleaning, so I got very little exercise: with that and the diet consisting mainly of cereal, I put on a lot of weight, until a visiting doctor gave me tablets to cut my appetite. That slimmed me down a bit, and gave me the feeling of being extremely strong, so that I was able to do a lot of physical work, which cut my weight a bit more. I am sure the pills were bad for me, and after a while the doctor stopped them. I have never got my weight down near what it was before I was locked up.

In due course we improved our own diet by growing vegetables. The soil was so poor that practically nothing would grow in it without careful cultivation. The best thing was to ask leave to take a wheelbarrow out and collect the fine soil from ant-hills, and mix that with some dead leaves for humus. In that way we could make small, fertile beds for our green vegetables, which did us good. Apart from trouble with my teeth, the only sickness I got in that camp was a nasty fungus growth on my right foot, which did not get cured until I went to Vietnam in the late 1970s: a doctor there took one look at it and produced a tiny tube of ointment which cleared it up in a week.

In winter the camp was cold and in summer the heat was frightful. The shade trees had been cut down for a kilometre around the huts, for security, and the only shade was under our grass-roofed shelter. We used to move around it as the sun shifted, and hope for a breeze. The heat shimmered up from the open ground around us. One October, before the rains, the police made it even hotter by setting fire to the long grass. Black smuts fell out of the sky, making everything filthy.

Men's minds become obsessive in prison, full of absurd fantasies. In the other camps it was five years before any visits by women were allowed: in the small enclosure where we three were shut up it was seven years before we were allowed visits by our wives. Once we started an argument about whether women had eyelashes – it went on for weeks, and got really passionate. Then Lazarus had to go to hospital for some minor complaint and we said, 'Look now, make sure you see the nurses' eyes and tell us whether they have eyelashes or not.' For two days after he came back he just laughed and would not tell us, then on the third day he said, 'Yes, women really do have eyelashes.' It seems childish that grown-up people should have such an argument, but it happened.

When the men in the other camps were allowed visits by their wives and girlfriends, that created new problems. One camp was set aside for the visits. The woman would get her pass, arrive in the evening and stay overnight. In the morning a policeman would come to collect her man, lock him in a cell, then fetch the woman and lock her in with him. The visiting time was 2½ hours, strictly limited, and you can imagine what happened then. Quite a lot of women got pregnant in the cells. They hated it. During that time, while the pair were confused about meeting again after so long, the woman would tell her man all the things that were going on in his home – the house was in bad condition, her boss had died and she had no job, their daughter was pregnant by some wild man; all the worries of five years of marriage packed into 2½ hours.

After that the camp chief would call the man in to his office and ask what his wife had said, suggesting that he might like to promise good behaviour and go home. There was one lad who could not sleep for three weeks after his wife had been on a visit: the others would watch him and drift off to sleep, and when they woke he was still sitting there smoking. One night he boiled some rice late, and ate, then about 3 a.m. he left with some policemen. He must have talked. We never saw him again. But all those ten years and more, with around 3,000 people in the camps, there was only that case of one of our people defecting.

Even the mildest people grew tense in prison. One day my two friends, Joseph and Lazarus, got so angry with each other about some trivial thing that I took their knives away, just in case they did each other harm. Another time, in the early darkness of a very hot night, we heard a loud noise of fighting from the nearest of the other camps. It went on for some time, and then the sky lit up as the thatched roofs of the shelters caught fire. Then came the sound of gunfire, and sudden silence.

We in our separate enclosure were desperately worried. I said to Joseph Msika: 'If our people are actually fighting each other, that could be the end of our struggle.' After an hour, two of them turned up outside our fence and told us what had happened. There had been a long disagreement about who would do certain jobs in the camp: we had agreed that the elderly detainees – people in their sixties and seventies – should be excused from some jobs, notably from cleaning toilets. Some of the young chaps said this was unfair, others accepted it, and so a division of opinion had developed in the camp. This had turned into open fighting and burning of property, until the police came and fired into the air over the people's heads and stopped it.

The row died down as suddenly as it had started: perhaps the violence had done people good in some way. But the remarkable thing was the effect on the senior police officer in charge of the camps. I had seen him, of course, but only on routine business: we had never talked. This time he came to see me, and said: 'I am very sad today, and I come to you, Nkomo, as leader of these people. I am here guarding you not because it is a pleasure, but because it is my job. Many of us white people are carrying on with our jobs because we believe at the end of it all there will be peace in this country. You don't know what is in our minds. We know that in the end you will succeed and you will run this country. But after the violence last night I wonder whether after all this suffering you will be able to work together. If you cannot work together it is not just you, the black people, who will suffer. We whites too will suffer.

And because I am not sure, after last night, that you will be able to come through and work together I wonder whether it is worth remaining in this country after all.'

This was a passionate statement, and it revealed a great deal that I had not known. It showed that there were white men even among our guards who really understood what we were there for – that we were not just fighting against white people, or for our own black people, but because of our conviction that in the end we would all have to live together in Zimbabwe. I was comforted to know that he realised that, and very sad to think that the night of violence had disappointed him so much that he thought of leaving.

So I appealed to him not to go, not to abandon our country. I told him violence like that does happen: it is not the end of the world. It was fortunate that he had been in charge, since with another officer the bullets might not have been in the air, and there would be bodies on the ground. It would be a tragedy if he left: he was exactly the sort of person we wanted to stay with us after independence, for we were fighting not against white people but against an oppressive system, oppressive not only to those who are oppressed but to the oppressors too. I appealed to him not to resign from the cause in which we both believed, and to stay and work for the country which one day we would share. He said in the end that he would stay. But I never saw him again.

I have mentioned that there were people of Indian descent and coloured citizens in that camp, fellow-members of our party and colleagues in our cause. I know that we did have some white people on our side – my friend Leo Baron, my lawyer, spent a long time in solitary confinement, but apart from us. Garfield Todd, the ex-prime minister, was detained because he was on our side, and I respect him for it. We did what we could to show that our fight was not a racial one, against the whites, but for all the people of the country. From white supporters outside we received precious help.

No praise can be too high for the Defence and Aid Fund in London. I knew its chairman, that devoted Christian Canon John Collins, from my days in London, and it was through his work that many of our prisoners' families were able to hold together. With no man in the house and the difficulty our relations had in finding work, many wives and children would have starved without the small donations of money that Defence and Aid were able to send. My own wife maFuyana was saved from destitution by a grant from Canon Collins personally that helped her for a whole year. What the society provided was not political support but personal care: it was important that families could feel they had someone to turn to in an emergency. The Amnesty International scheme for supporting prisoners of conscience had the same effect, and was beyond any price.

For the prisoners themselves the most welcome name on the bottom of a letter was often that of Mrs Phyllis Altman, the Defence and Aid education officer. She organised books and study materials that were deeply appreciated. Lazarus Nkala was only one of those who took a degree from Gonakudzingwa: I began to study for one in economics, but became distracted after a while, I am afraid. One colleague in another camp qualified as a watchmaker thanks to Mrs Altman's support, and now has a prosperous business. Many others did likewise.

Officials of the Red Cross visited us regularly, and did their best to make our conditions more humane. Sometimes we would put a case to them, and they would go away and negotiate for it, and a year later the thing would be changed in the way we had suggested, although we had forgotten they were doing anything; patiently they would work away and get it done. One of those Red Cross people said something to me that really stuck in my mind: he felt I should know it.

He said: 'Do not think I believe you are living well here. This is a terrible place. I do not know how you survive. But I travel and see the conditions of detainees in all sorts of other African countries – I can't give you names, of course – where people live and are fed like beasts. In most African countries – most, not all – conditions are far, far worse than here. In South Africa the physical conditions are bare but adequate: what is evil there is the way the Afrikaners regard their prisoners, not as people but as monkeys or other animals. In the black African countries some guards do treat the prisoners as human beings, but the physical conditions are dreadful; it is the governments that treat the prisoners cruelly, far more cruelly than you are treated here.'

This made a deep impression on me. I resolved that, when Zimbabwe was free, I would fight to see that it never allowed such conditions to prevail. But I do not know whether I can succeed. Several leading Zanu people, including some now in the Zimbabwe government, were in detention or in prison at the same time as thousands of us in Zapu. The terms we served in prison damaged us and disrupted our families. All of us in public life in Zimbabwe know what prison is like. There is no excuse for ex-prisoners, if the prisons they now control are not humane.

But I fear they are not.

Most prison days passed without any event at all. Nothing happened. There were the three of us, with our small daily duties, and otherwise nothing at all to do. There cannot be many active politicians who have spent so much time studying the birds and snakes and lizards that were our only visitors. There was a certain kind of snake that eats lizards, waiting for hours motionless until the lizard moves within its range and it can strike. But the lizard has its own defence. It knows the snake will only attack a moving target. So when the snake strikes, the lizard sheds its tail like lightning. The tail keeps wriggling on the ground. But the lizard itself stays stock still. The snake eats the tail, the lizard itself survives.

The ants build beautiful, intricate nests, with every ant moving in order to its own place along its own pathway. There was a wonderful ants' nest right beside my sitting room, in the corner out of the way, and it gave me hours of pleasure and interest. After we had served seven years the minister for law and order, Mr Lardner-Burke, came to visit us. I suppose he wanted to see when our spirits would break. He was wearing very highly polished shoes. He saw the ants' nest and ground the heel of his shining shoe down on it, destroying the beautiful, organised home that the ants had built.

We had regular visits from the doctor, and there was a well-stocked dispensary for the camps (although it seemed to have more medicine for animals than for people, and we called our visits there trips to the vet). But my teeth got worse and worse until the camp doctor said I must go to a properly equipped surgery to have them seen to. They put me in a closed truck and drove me to hospital in absolute secrecy. I peeked out through the canvas cover in Fort Victoria and for the first time saw women wearing mini-skirts. I found that pretty shocking.

The hospital authorities did their best to keep all the African staff away from me, to preserve the secret. But of course it was not really possible. The nurses and hospital staff were mostly black, and black and white people worked together in a perfectly friendly way – although the whites got the best paid jobs.

When I was waiting for the dentist, an African nurse came in with a cup of coffee. She at once knew who I was and became very nervous, especially as a young white policeman was standing watching me. I thought all this was ridiculous so I asked the girl if she would bring the man a coffee too, and told the chap to sit down. They both got even more nervous: I suppose they only felt safe as long as they kept the rules. But after a while the policeman and I became friendly. He told me his superiors had warned him that I was some sort of fierce wild beast: he was quite confused to find me happy to have a chat while I waited for my teeth to be fixed.

There was something very odd about that visit to the dentist. On my arrival they took me not to the hospital but to a police cell, and there a doctor took my blood pressure and examined me. I wondered why this was not done at the hospital. Then I was told that I would be spending the night in the police camp, so I went to bed and fell asleep. In my sleep in the guarded cell I had a dream. My father appeared and spoke to me. 'They will give you whisky,' he said. 'You must not drink the whisky.' This was very strange; I had never drunk whisky or any strong liquor, and I would certainly not be tempted now.

Next day at the hospital the doctors examined my teeth, then presented me with a form to sign, saying I agreed to accept a general anaesthetic. Somehow I knew that was what my father had meant when he told me not take the whisky. I refused outright to sign their form, saying that a tooth operation could perfectly well be done with a local anaesthetic. The doctor was confused. He said he must go and consult the others. 'The other doctors? Why have they not examined me too then?' I asked. He got even more embarrassed, mumbling something about 'people from Salisbury', and went away.

I kept insisting that I would not sign the anaesthetic form, and without it the doctor would not put me to sleep. After a while they gave me a little local anaesthetic in my gum, sat me in the dentist's chair and pulled the sore tooth out. It hardly took five minutes. I really do not believe Smith's people would have been so stupid as to try to kill me in hospital. But it seems quite possible that they thought I would be willing to talk under one of the drugs they give as a general anaesthetic. My father's warning made sure I did not accept it.

So the years passed. The three of us – Msika, Nkala and Nkomo – were truly isolated from the world, in the heart of the game reserve. After the first seven years we were allowed family visits, lasting one hour every three months, and that was our only outside contact. Listening to the radio was like looking through a telescope at a planet far beyond our reach. We learned how to interpret the censored news of the Rhodesian and South African broadcasting services: whenever they told of a victory against the 'terrorists' we knew that the armed struggle was intensifying, and I knew the work I had begun was gathering pace. Indeed this biased information was often more revealing than the supposedly objective news of the BBC and the West German station, Deutsche Welle.

Our great encouragement was the news of the growing insurgency just over the border in 'Portuguese' Mozambique. I was greatly saddened to hear of the murder by a parcel bomb of that great man Eduardo Mondlane, the first president of their nationalist movement Frelimo: I had helped to persuade him to return from his good job at the United Nations, in New York, to join his people's struggle, and I deeply regretted the loss of this friend and brother.

It had been clear from the start that the British were going to do nothing effective about the open rebellion of their white subjects in Rhodesia. The only sensible suggestion from a British political leader came immediately after Smith's illegal declaration of independence, when the Liberal leader, Jeremy Thorpe, suggested cutting off the supply lines by bombing the railway lines from Mozambique and South Africa, well away from the civilian population. Since we were living alongside just such a railway line we knew that the idea was perfectly practical

– but Thorpe was ridiculed for even suggesting it, and that showed that the British had no will to put down the rebellion. The trains of petroleum tankers from Lourenço Marques into Rhodesia came right past the camp, and we could see ourselves that the economic sanctions were a farce.

Since the Rhodesian government was illegal, our detention was also unlawful. But the British did not lift a finger to free us. After Harold Wilson's second abortive meeting with Ian Smith on a warship, he sent his minister of state, George Thomson, to Rhodesia on what was meant to be a fact-finding mission. Thomson was accompanied by the Commonwealth Office minister, Maurice Foley, whom I had known since we first met in India in 1958, and whom I regarded as a personal friend. I was taken to meet them at New Sarum airfield. Our two conversations were embarrassing – more so, perhaps, because Foley was someone in whom I had hoped to be able to trust.

The British government was evidently looking for a way out of its promise that there should be no independence before majority rule: that meant free elections before any constitutional change. The two ministers explained Britain's difficulties, which I understood perfectly well and regarded as secondary to the obligation to bring freedom to my people. I was not going to help the British evade their clear responsibilities, and I said so. The two ministers seemed thoroughly frightened of being in the hands of Ian Smith's security forces, and I had very little respect for them. There was nothing useful we could say to each other. So in November 1968 my friend Foley flew back to Britain, and I returned to another six years of imprisonment.

The British Conservative government elected in 1970 made even more open attempts to do a deal with Smith, but they wanted it fixed up so as not to look like a surrender, which meant putting on a show of consulting African leaders. In November 1971, therefore, I was sent for from Salisbury to meet the British foreign secretary, Sir Alec Douglas-Home. He had reached an agreement with Smith that gave both sides pretty much what they wanted – for Smith, a free hand to run the country, and for Britain, an appearance of legality for their recognition of the regime.

I at first protested that if Home wanted to meet leaders of

African opinion he should talk to the whole Zapu central committee, not just me alone. But Smith's people insisted that it should be just me, the central committee accepted that, and I went. I was flown up to Salisbury and put into a little combi truck with its windows painted over and newspaper across the windscreen, so as to prevent anyone looking in. Instead of the usual seats they had put a sofa in the truck on a red carpet – I thought I was becoming pretty important these days. The press guessed something was going on when they saw this strange vehicle. One of the papers published a photo of it looking as though there was no passenger and no driver either, that was the kind of tight security we were under.

The meeting was on the lawn at Marimba House, the British representative's residence. Home met me on the lawn. His attitude was contemptuous: he kept his hat on the whole time, which may have been understandable for a visitor from the English winter, but was hardly polite. He simply told me that he had now come to an agreement with Smith, there would be a commission to inquire whether it was acceptable to the African people, and I would be free to give evidence to the commission. I told the foreign secretary that the British government was merely trying to legalise the Smith regime, which was an insult to the black people. If there was to be an agreement it must be negotiated by those of us who represented the African population. 'The people have completely forgotten you,' said Home. 'They no longer recognise you: you do not represent anybody now. What we have done is reasonable, and if you do not accept it you will be left out.' I told him that the African people would never accept this deal, and asked to be taken away. There was no point in arguing with a man who simply wanted to get Rhodesia off his plate.

Home and his advisers just did not understand that we insisted on running our own lives. Nor for that matter did Smith, or he would never have agreed to what he must have thought was a mere formality. To save the face of the British, Smith had agreed that, although I and the other African leaders should remain in prison, there should be a 'test' of African opinion on the proposed constitutional changes, to be conducted by a commission of inquiry headed by a British judge, Lord Pearce. Africans should be free to present their views to Lord Pearce, and Smith must have thought that the Africans' views would be the same as his own.

By now I had established ways of communicating with the outside world, sometimes by messages smuggled out in the spines of books, sometimes through the cooperation of our sympathisers among the black policemen who were guarding us. In preparation for the Pearce commission, I communicated with Garfield Todd, to ensure that his opposition would be expressed in terms similar to ours. I also got in touch with Josiah Chinamano, who had by now been released, in order to set up a front organisation to coordinate African opposition. On his suggestion we approached a well-known churchman, the Methodist Bishop Abel Muzorewa. He seemed an ideal candidate for the treasurership of the new body, which we decided to call the African National Council – if a bishop cannot raise money, who can?

It was soon suggested that, since the bishop was a political novice, while Josiah was closely identified with me, the council's appeal could be broadened if the bishop became chairman while Josiah acted as treasurer. I readily agreed, and this was the start of poor Abel Muzorewa's illusion that he had become a political leader.

Smith and the British government must have believed that Lord Pearce would do as they wanted and report that the Smith-Home deal was acceptable to African opinion, and then all would be over. They were badly mistaken. From his first public meeting, the judge was left in no doubt that the vast majority of Africans entirely rejected the handing over of power to the tiny white electorate. We three colleagues were taken to meet Lord Pearce at Nuanetsi Ranch. We left him quite clear about the people's rejection of the plan, but we felt he hardly needed to be told that: he seemed a stern, sensible man whom it would be very hard to fool. It was a replay of the Monckton commission of inquiry into African opinion in the old Central African Federation, back in 1960. Pearce reported that African opinion was heavily against the deal. Home's complacent scheme was shattered, and Smith was left in limbo.

The collapse of Portuguese power in Mozambique changed everything. As late as March 1974, Ian Smith had stated that he was confident the Portuguese would hold on against the rising tide of insurgency. But their control of Mozambique territory was fading every day, and only a month later came the *coup d'état* in Portugal itself. The new government was a group of soldiers who knew from experience that their army was too weak to hold the African people down.

The first effect on us, right up against the Mozambique border, was a much stricter guard on our camp. They built watchtowers and a high wire fence around us, with a swept track outside to show the footprints of anyone crossing. A strong paramilitary support unit was brought in to guard us, with black troops under white officers. This made our contacts with the outside world much easier. Many of the black policemen made it plain at once that they were on our side, some even being members of my party. We were cautious about establishing the first contacts, since we well knew the use the Rhodesian government made of spies.

The policemen carried messages in and out, opening up communications at last with our fighting men. They told how their patrols, if their white officers did not accompany them, held friendly meetings with their supposed enemies, sitting quietly in the shade smoking cigarettes instead of chasing each other through the bush. Our people did not have to climb the fence or jump over the security strip: the policemen would open the gates when the time was right and let us walk in and out.

Clearly the Rhodesian security forces were eaten away from inside by our supporters. One young man told me of his great fear that he might be wounded, and that one day he would have to explain to his son how he was injured in the liberation war – but fighting on the wrong side, for Smith. We had to persuade some of the lads to stay in uniform because they could serve us better from where they were than by deserting and joining our fighters. Victory, at last, seemed in sight.

Chapter 14
The Taste of Freedom

After ten years, the Gonakudzingwa restriction area had grown familiar. We had not grown fond of the place, not at all, but so many of the objects around us had been made by our own hands – the vegetable garden we had made of compost and the sifted dust of ant-hills, even trees that we had planted and seen grow almost to maturity. Formally, my property was just a cup and plate and a little bag of sugar. In reality I had my wood-working tools, and tables and benches and chairs that I had made, and literally dozens of stools that I had prepared for visitors, if ever we were allowed visitors. But the collapse of Portuguese rule in Mozambique meant that we could no longer be safely kept right up against the border. In June 1974 our ten years of confinement in that place were at last over.

As usual, the guards gave us advance warning of the move. When they came to get us we were ready to go, and the decision had been made to leave all the clutter behind. Some of my colleagues were moved to various maximum security prisons around the country. My own new home was the prison at Buffalo Range, in a flat, low-lying area of irrigated land occupied by huge white-owned company farms – kilometres and kilometres of sugar-cane lay all around us. We lost the privilege of running our own lives, cooking for ourselves and making our own time-table. From now on I was locked in alone behind a series of heavy doors from four o'clock every afternoon to eight the next morning. The prison was set up on a bit of high ground with a clear field of fire all round it – it was the sort of thing you dream of if you dream of prison. On arrival I was searched and they took my personal belongings, even my watch. On leaving Gonakudzingwa I had removed my faithful little radio from the medicine cabinet where I had kept it hidden all those years, and I flatly refused to hand it over. The man just looked at me and I put it in my overcoat pocket – it was cold in that place, in midwinter.

Then I understood that the people in charge were

frightened of us. We had been defined as dangerous people, and anyway they knew very well that one day we were going to be running the country. There were three cells in a row for us three, Msika, Nkala and myself. I chose the middle one. There was no glazed window, just an opening high up with thick wire-netting over it. When it rained, the water came pouring in, and when they burned off the cane-fields before the harvest the cells were full of smoke and bits of charred leaves. The sheets we were given were more like loin cloths, about a metre wide, and for my size that was far too narrow. Even keeping clean was an ordeal. There was no hot water at first, in the winter-time, and the showers did not even have a rose to make the water spray down. The food from the big prison pots was terrible. But all the discomfort did not make much difference to our spirits: prison is prison – it is being shut up that is the worst.

Yet even prisons can become humane. On weekends the senior staff, who were all white, went off duty. We soon found that the African jailers were mostly members of Zapu. They would come in and we would talk together about the future. They brought messages in and passed our letters out without going through the official censor.

Best of all, the neighbouring cells were for women prisoners, and there were four or five very nice young women guards. By that time I had been sent a little record player, and they brought in some modern dance records, and we had a very pleasant little party almost every weekend. The senior medical orderly of the prison was an African, and he joined us. He was very worried that we might think he was collaborating with the enemy, but we reassured him that any health worker in the country was more than welcome, and we certainly were not going to chase him away simply because he had taken that particular medical job rather than another one.

The staff kept us in touch with the world outside. But still my radio remained our lifeline. Although we were not allowed to talk from cell to cell, I managed to pass on the news to my two neighbours as soon as I got it. We invented a very simple code, substituting false names for real ones, and we managed to have discussions at breakfast time. The breakfasts had been revolting at first, but after we complained the authorities allowed us a great block of cheese to provide some nourishment after being locked up for sixteen hours. So breakfast became cheese-time, and the best moment of the day.

One cheese-time we had been extremely worried by the Rhodesian radio's announcement that a meeting would take place that day between Ian Smith and Bishop Muzorewa, whom we called Muzangara in our little code. We knew Muzorewa was beginning to believe he was the chosen leader of the nation, although in fact he was merely appointed by us as a mild and respectable figure to be the figurehead of the African National Council while we remained behind bars. We were very anxious that he might make some sort of deal, claiming to speak for us, which would help Smith. That evening I listened to the radio with anxiety and at last the news came across that the meeting had ended with no agreement. I shouted, 'No, he has said no,' and I could hear Msika and Nkala clapping in their cells, for joy that the war would go on.

It seems terrible now to have been happy that the fighting and killing would go on in our country outside our prison. But we knew that, if the fighting stopped before we had made real progress, that could mean years more of subjection for our people – and years more of imprisonment for us, too. I heard the announcements of the casualties in such and such a battle – so many soldiers killed, so many 'communist terrorists', as they called our forces. And I could be sure that when they said two of our people were dead there were probably several innocent bystanders killed too. It made us more than ever determined never to compromise with our enemy.

Then one night I had a visit. It was not a dream, I am sure of that. There was a woman in my cell. She called me by name: 'Joshua,' she said.

I said, 'Who are you?'

She did not answer. She just said: 'I have come to tell you it is all over now. Get out of here.' Again I asked her who she was. Again she gave her message. Then she disappeared. There were at least four doors to pass through before you came to my cell, and the door of the cell was 150 millimetres of African teak, the strongest wood there is. There was a steel plate opposite the lock, to prevent anyone getting at it from the inside. In the morning the doors were unlocked, and a big piece of wood had been knocked out of the door beside the steel plate. I told my two friends of the vision and emphasised that I was certain it was not a dream. They insisted that I must have been dreaming. But there was this big chunk of wood on the ground, missing from the solid door.

When the sun was overhead, Msika and I went to our cells for the cool; Nkala had gone to the prison office where he was writing exam papers for his degree. The prison superintendent himself came to my door, and knocked before he came in, which told me something special was going on. He said someone wanted to see me in his office – it was Special Branch, he told me when I asked.

When I got there a young man was waiting, very well dressed and well groomed, not like the usual sort of policeman. I sat down: he stood, and casually put his foot on the chair as he began to talk.

'Now look, sonny,' I said, 'don't talk to me with your foot on the chair. Sit down, or I am getting out of here. I won't accept that sort of behaviour.' He sat down. I knew it was serious business. His message was that I was wanted in Salisbury the following day. 'By whom?' I asked. He said he did not know, he was just a messenger, but I was to be ready in the morning. I insisted, of course, on consulting my colleagues, who approved my going alone.

After so long in prison clothes, my concern was to be decently dressed, I only had one suit, sent in by a friend, and one safari suit. Both had grown pretty tight since I had put on so much weight from prison living. So I had the warders bring them, mended up a few loose stitches and made myself as respectable as I could. Next morning I was taken to the Buffalo Range airport – and what did I see but Ian Smith's personal Dakota waiting for me, with his own pilot, steward and air hostess. This plane was really the command post from which Smith ran the country when he was travelling about, and they had sent it to fetch me. So away we flew to New Sarum air force base, and into the officers' mess, where they left me alone to wait for a visitor, whom they did not know. I did not trust those fellows one inch, and I thought that perhaps at last this was the time they would do me some harm. I made up my mind that if they did get violent I would fight as hard as I could; they would not expect me to fight.

9a. 1974: the Lusaka agreement of unity between the Zimbabwe nationalist parties was signed on 7 December. Seated, *l. to r.*, are the Rev. Ndabaningi Sithole, Bishop Abel Muzorewa, Joshua Nkomo and James Chikerema. Standing, *left*, is President Kaunda of Zambia. (*Zambia Information Services*)

9b. 1975, December: leaving the office of the illegal prime minister, Ian Smith, after talks (which failed) to persuade him to hand over power to the nationalist parties. *L. to r.*: John Nkomo, Josiah Chinamano, Joshua Nkomo, Daniel Madzimbamuto, Clement Muchachi and Chief Mangwende. (*Zimbabwe Ministry of Information*)

10. 1975, August: the Victoria Falls conference, on a train suspended between Zambia and Rhodesia, led to stalemate. On the left are Ian Smith and P. K. van der Byl; on the right, looking up, is Prime Minister B. J. Vorster of South Africa. At the end of the table, in clerical collar, is Bishop Abel Muzorewa of the ANC delegation. (*Zimbabwe Publishing House, Harare*)

11a. 1978: with President Castro in Cuba – practice with the AK 47.

11b. 1978: wearing a Soviet army cap to inspect Zipra troops during training in the bush in Zambia.

12. The front-line presidents, in 1980, whose support was vital to the liberation forces. *L.to r.*: President Kenneth Kaunda of Zambia, President Samora Machel of Mozambique and President Julius Nyerere of Tanzania. (*Zimbabwe Ministry of Information*)

The door opened and in walked Mark Chona. I knew him well in the old days in Lusaka – his brother Mainza Chona, the lawyer, was a special friend of mine – and I was astonished to see him. All I could say was: 'Hey, Chona, where do you come from?' But it was a very emotional greeting. Then we sat down and I started to wonder. 'What's going on – have you sold out?' I asked. He answered that he was sent by my old friend Kenneth Kaunda. So I said, 'Let's get out of here and talk business.'

We went and sat in the shade under a tree. We had chatted a bit about my health, and how I had put on weight in prison. Then he said that my friend – he meant Kenneth Kaunda – might see me in person, that he, Chona, had just come to see how I was and how I felt. I told him it was pretty rough in prison but I was ready to stay there for as long as was necessary, until things began really to change. 'Don't worry,' I said, 'we can go on for another ten years if need be.' With that he left, and they took me back to prison.

My friends could not believe what had happened – meeting a senior man, a personal emissary from President Kaunda, on Salisbury air force base when Zambia and Rhodesia were as near as nothing at war. I reminded them about my night visitor, and insisted that something big was going on. But there was nothing at all we could do: we had supper and went to bed in our cells. Next morning there was the same procedure with the well-dressed Special Branch man, warning me that I would be wanted again the following morning. This time I insisted on taking a colleague. Nkala was still sitting his exams, so Msika and I flew up in Smith's personal plane to New Sarum air base, and out to a tent by the runway. I half expected it to be Chona again, but it was someone very different. There were two middle-aged white men in the tent, with security men in the background. One I did not know, but he looked like a senior politician. The other was the most senior civil servant in the Rhodesian government, the secretary to Smith's cabinet, Jack Gaylard – the man whom everybody agreed was a brilliant manipulator, and who really kept the illegal regime running.

Gaylard said he wanted to see me because there were big things afoot, and first they wanted to find out my thinking on a couple of things. What did I think of the fighting that was going on? And was I ready to make some other arrangements? I said I could not possibly answer until I knew what those other arrangements might be. Gaylard said that as a civil servant he could not say what they were. Someone else would explain that. After a while the prime minister, Ian Smith, was escorted in.

This was the man we had been fighting against for all these years. I knew his face so well from the newspaper photographs. I imagine he knew mine just as well, but since my name was banned from the local press he must have relied on the pictures in their intelligence files. It seemed unreal to be face to face at last. Because of the wound he suffered as a Second World War pilot his facial expression was rather immobile and stiff, and I had the impression of a man striving to be master of the situation, looking me straight in the eye and acting the prime minister. I do not pretend it was a friendly meeting. But there was business to be done.

Smith said that some of my friends had been contacting him, saying they thought it was time for talks. Perhaps it was, but before he could talk to us we had to say that we would stop terrorism: on that condition talks might begin. I lost my temper. I told him that he was asking me to stop terrorism, when the biggest of all the terrorists was himself.

I had been trying for twenty years to talk to successive governments about independence for the people of this country, and they would never talk to us. Two days after he came to power, Smith had thrown me and my colleagues into prison, locked us up in various places, and never spoken to us. That was why the people of Zimbabwe had started the fighting, in response to his terror. We were driven to fighting by his actions, and now he asks us to stop fighting before he will talk to us. Did he think we were organising the fighting from his prisons or was it the people themselves who were organising it? If that was his line, he could send for his Dakota and take us back to jail.

Joseph Msika tried to cool things down. 'Don't lose your temper, let me talk to him,' he told me, and started speaking in a calm way: 'Mr Smith, if you want to talk meaningfully to us as leaders of our people, well, that can be considered, but if you come and use provocative words as you have done you must appreciate that my leader . . .' and so on.

So Smith replied: 'Don't talk nonsense, you are the terrorists and you have got to stop it.'

It was Joseph's turn to lose his temper. 'You talk!' he said. 'Who do you think you are? You go to hell!'

I told him I thought I was cooler than him after all, and that the best thing we could do was abandon these talks, for they were hopeless. Smith was talking as the victor to the vanquished, calling us terrorists, and there was no point in going on with that.

Joseph and I got out of that tent; Smith waited for a few minutes talking to his men, then drove off without a sign to us, leaving us alongside the tarmac to wait for the plane. But before our aircraft came another landed, a little Lear jet, and out got Mark Chona from Zambia. He came over to us and said he was on his way from President Kaunda to see Smith, to make sure Smith stuck by the terms of reference agreed between the two. We told him what Smith had said to us, and he agreed that if that was what he said the whole thing was off, since Smith had agreed to talk to us as leaders, not as terrorists. If Smith continued to claim that we were terrorists, Kaunda would definitely not go ahead with the talks. We went off to Buffalo Range prison in the Dakota, the whole peace initiative having apparently come to nothing.

A week later the business came back to life. The three of us from Buffalo Range were picked up in a plane, and the first people we saw waiting at the airstrip were Bishop Muzorewa and Dr Elliot Gabellah from the African National Council. The plane, we learned, was taking us not to Salisbury but to Lusaka, the Zambian capital, as the guests in State House of the president, Kenneth Kaunda. We were told that another plane was flying up from Kwekwe prison, bringing the Zanu leaders. We were all to meet in the greatest secrecy, with Presidents Nyerere of Tanzania and Machel of Mozambique, to discuss an initiative in which – we did not entirely understand this part – the South African government was also involved.

All this was a great deal to take in without warning. The comfort of that first night in State House was overwhelming. For ten years I had been in prison, sleeping on a hard board. Now I was in a very soft bed with snow-white sheets. I was very, very uncomfortable in that comfort. But I did not for a moment regret having missed such things for all that time. Now we seemed to be on the way forward, and that was the reward.

Next morning we gathered for our meeting with the presidents of the black nations of Southern Africa who were in the front line of the struggle against racism. Julius Nyerere walked in off his plane and greeted us all, and the first question he asked was: 'Where's Ndabaningi?' The Zanu team, surprisingly enough, did not include Sithole, whom we all regarded as president of that party. Instead there were its secretary-general, Robert Mugabe, and its secretary for youth and culture, Moton Malianga. It turned out that five members of the Zanu central committee had been kept together in prison and allowed to hold meetings there. This tiny group, without consulting their members or their colleagues, had decided to depose Sithole as their president: Mugabe and Malianga were acting as their spokesmen.

The presidents obviously could not accept these two relatively unknown people as valid spokesmen for Zanu, so they were sent off to wait in their rooms while the business of the meeting was tackled. We were told that there was a possibility of arranging talks with Ian Smith. The South Africans had persuaded him to talk to us, so what did we think?

I told the meeting of my fruitless meeting with Smith, and said that more years of fighting might possibly force something more useful out of him. President Kaunda assured me that he had been in office for many years without ever wavering in his support for us, and that would certainly never change; but although he could not guarantee it, he thought there was a chance that talks might get something out of Smith. We had already lost enough good people in the war. The decision was ours, but the presidents were for talking.

The front-line presidents were clearly disturbed at the evidence of quarreling within Zanu: President Machel even accused Mugabe and Malianga of having 'conducted a *coup d'état* in prison'. They were also unclear about the role of Bishop Muzorewa, not having understood that his ANC was really a front organisation set up on our initiative: the bishop agreed that this was so, and that was helpful. So the meeting was a useful one, and we left well satisfied. I was especially pleased that Julius Nyerere apologised for having sent me home, eleven years before, to face certain imprisonment. 'Joshua,' he said, 'I must admit that at the time I did not understand the nature of your problems. I really apologise.' So we returned to Buffalo Range.

Life began to move forwards again, after the lonely prison years. In Lusaka we were able to meet our old friends Jason Moyo and George Silundika, who, together with Edward Ndlovu and Sikwili Moyo, had been leading the external wing of Zapu and organising the armed struggle while we were in detention: it was an emotional meeting. Then a couple of weeks later we left prison for Lusaka once again.

The same aircraft picked up my team from Buffalo Range, then Sithole's team from Kwekwe – with Sithole himself in charge this time, on the front-line presidents' insistence. Muzorewa, who had never been imprisoned, was picked up from Salisbury.

In Lusaka we again met with the front-line presidents, and this time the talks did not go well. There was agreement that we should talk to Smith, on terms which committed neither side to any specific future action. But there was complete disagreement on the composition of a united nationalist front to negotiate with Smith. On this the nationalists were unable to agree, and so the meeting broke up without a conclusion.

The front-line presidents were very much disappointed by our failure to unite. President Nyerere spoke very firmly. He insisted that only after full talks with Smith could it be established that he really would not agree to majority rule. Unless that could be proven, said Nyerere, Tanzania would no longer be available as a base from which we sent young people to fight and die.

On this sour note the presidents went home, leaving President Kaunda as host to the African National Council, Zapu and Zanu. He provided a room in which the leaders of the three organisations met to thrash out their problems. One of our first decisions was to invite James Chikerema to join us. That brought together all the four nationalist organisations with some degree of genuine existence.

There was Zapu, with myself as its uncontested leader. Zanu was led by Ndabaningi Sithole, but with a big question over his leadership. James Chikerema, my impetuous old colleague, had set up his own militant organisation Frolizi, the Front for the Liberation of Zimbabwe: it had a small fighting force of men drawn from both Zapu and Zanu armies, but as far as we knew it had no party members. And there was Abel Muzorewa as president of the African National Council, which I knew was a front organisation set up under my patronage, although Muzorewa was starting to think of it as a great national movement.

Around the table on 7 December 1974 in Lusaka, all four organisations solemnly agreed to unite on the following terms. The ANC, as the compromise body, was recognised as the unifying force. Under Muzorewa's chairmanship the presidents of Zapu, Zanu and Frolizi – that is, myself, Sithole and Chikerema – with three members of each of the organisations, would form a new executive. That executive would do any negotiating necessary, with Smith or others. Within four months the executive would also prepare a constitution for a new ANC, and then call a congress to elect a leadership to represent the united people of Zimbabwe.

The Lusaka agreement* was to be the charter for reuniting the nationalist forces. Tragically, it was never carried out. My own party, Zapu, was the only component of the African National Council to fulfil its terms. The agreement specified that Zapu, Zanu and Frolizi would merge their 'organs and structures' into the ANC. But in reality neither Zanu nor Frolizi had any organs or structures. As political bodies they simply did not exist. Their leaders left the country rather than face up to this, as did Bishop Muzorewa, whose delusions of national leadership were gathering about him. The Lusaka agreement came to nothing largely because the leaders of the other nationalist movements feared that if elections were held I would emerge as leader. Our lack of unity prolonged the war for another six years, and led to many tens of thousands of deaths.

All the front-line presidents were solidly behind the cause of independence and majority rule for Zimbabwe. They wanted to help bring unity among the Zimbabweans, because they thought our unity would bring peace closer. As patriots they were all too well aware of the economic damage being inflicted on their own countries by the disruption of the whole southern

* See Appendix A, p.253.

African region. Its communications were developed by the colonial powers to suit their own interests, and three of the major countries – Zambia, Botswana and Zimbabwe itself – are landlocked. Trouble in any one country damaged the others and was readily exploited by South Africa.

But with the Portuguese cleared out of Mozambique, the South Africans were ready for a new deal. Through intermediaries they had approached President Kaunda of Zambia, asking him to use his influence on the Zimbabwean nationalists while they used their influence on Ian Smith. It seemed that Prime Minister Vorster might be able to persuade Smith to agree to a formula by which the fighting in Zimbabwe would be stopped and we would get real majority rule within five years. While there was even a shadow of a chance of freedom in five years without more killing, I pursued it.

But first, after the decade in prison, I had to pick up the loose ends of my own life. It was agreed that John Nkomo and Simon Muzenda should represent the newly united ANC in Lusaka. I flew down to Salisbury and on to Bulawayo. It was all unexpected: very few knew I was coming, and there was no time to give warning of my return. But despite that there was a good turn-out to greet me with excitement. There was pushing and shouting, with people almost unable to believe that I was back. I hardly had time to greet my beloved wife, and she was frightened that somebody would be crushed to death in the confusion.

Bulawayo had grown while I had been away, with new industries and new people moving in from the countryside to live in new townships on the edge of the city. I was almost a stranger. The shock of my release, and the strain of the negotiations in Lusaka, caught up with me – I was so unused to crowds and new companions that I could hardly speak. I just went home and collapsed into bed, exhausted.

For two weeks I sat there and shook hands with all the people who had come to wish me well. It was a pleasure, and the start of our party election campaign too. Soon it was time to travel to Maputo for the first time, for the formal independence celebrations of Mozambique. I had been an honoured guest at so many independence celebrations, and now at last it looked as though our own turn was coming soon.

Chapter 15
Peace Deferred

The conference that might have brought peace in 1975 was a strange business altogether. It was arranged, as I have explained, by two parties not directly concerned in the confrontation for Zimbabwe, the governments of Zambia and of South Africa, with private business interests as the go-between. It had to be held on neutral ground: Smith would not agree to come to Zambia, and we could not go into Rhodesia as long as Smith's regime claimed that some of us were criminals and terrorists. The decision was taken to hold the meeting on 25 and 26 August 1975, right on the frontier between the two countries, on the railway bridge that crosses the Zambezi at the Victoria Falls, where Zambia and Zimbabwe are linked.

A white line was drawn across the bridge to mark the exact border, and a carriage was placed so that its centre was exactly on the line, which was then extended so as to bisect a long table running down the middle of the carriage. On the Rhodesian end sat Smith and his team – P.K. van der Byl, my prison visitor Lardner-Burke and the rest. At our end were the nationalist delegations, led by myself, Ndabaningi Sithole, James Chikerema and Bishop Abel Muzorewa. At our end of the train was President Kaunda of Zambia, at Smith's end were Prime Minister Vorster of South Africa, and his sinister security chief, General van den Bergh. The coaches were supplied by South African Railways (who tactlessly called them the 'White Train'). The bar at our end was generously stocked, and some supporters of the nationalist delegations spent far too much time in that area.

We had clearly agreed that Bishop Muzorewa would do the talking for the nationalist side. He had no experience as a negotiator, and made a real mess of his case: at lunch on the first day it was agreed that Sithole, Chikerema and I would intervene to support him when he was unable to stand up to Smith's arguments. Ian Smith was if anything an even worse bargainer. Vorster and the South Africans had shoved him to the negotiating table: he could not refuse to go, but he was not prepared to give anything away, let alone agree to bring majority rule soon.

The first day the talks made no progress at all. Neither side moved an inch, and it was well past midnight when things looked like breaking down for good. President Kaunda came in and got it started again, or at least he persuaded us to agree to meet again the following day. We went back behind our white line, they went back behind theirs, and we slept on it.

Next day we met again and returned to our own ends of the bridge for lunch. At the times for refreshment the tea and coffee came in to each side from their own ends of the train – nothing came across the line, not even ideas. We argued that any conference on a long-term settlement should take place within our country. Smith would not agree to meet our full leadership teams there. He said he would never talk to terrorists, nor allow people charged with terrorist offences to enter territory he controlled without being arrested. That was what broke the conference up.

President Kaunda took immense risks in the attempt to make the conference succeed. He even invited Vorster over onto Zambian territory and welcomed him there. It was hard for an African president to shake hands with a politician whose hands were stained with black people's blood, but Kenneth did it, because he was truly dedicated to peace and the Zimbabwean cause. Yet the South Africans could not persuade Smith to deliver on the promises they thought he had given them, whatever they were. The Victoria Falls conference was a complete waste of time.

It was time to review the military set-up that had developed during the prison years. Zapu's military wing was the Zimbabwe People's Revolutionary Army, Zipra.* Zanu's was the Zimbabwe African National Liberation Army, Zanla. Chikerema's Frolizi was neither a party nor an army but a collection of Zapu and Zanu defectors; its fighting men were drawn mainly from Zipra

---

* Zipra's supreme body was the War Council: with myself as chairman the members were Akim Ndlovu, Lookout Masuku, Alfred Mangena, Dumiso Dabengwa and Samuel Munodawafa.

militants. The bishop had no army at all, but while he was acting as interim president of the African National Council that we had agreed to set up at Lusaka, I allowed him the title of commander-in-chief of Zipra. (It was during this period that he visited some of my soldiers in Zambia, and someone gave him a light machine gun to look at: he was photographed waving this thing around, and so was born the dream of Muzorewa, the great jungle fighter.)

It was unfortunate that there was no single national army. But military unity could not come until we had a unified political direction, and that was the aim of the Lusaka agreement, to hold elections for the leadership of the nationalist movement. The agreement was that these elections should be held at a national congress bringing together all the parties making up the African National Council. But it was impossible to hold such a congress, since both Bishop Muzorewa and the Reverend Ndabaningi Sithole had decided to leave the country. Rather than leave the national movement without any leadership, Zapu decided to go ahead and hold its own congress on 26-27 September 1975. The congress elected a new leadership, and once again Zimbabwean nationalism had a genuine voice, the ANC Zimbabwe.*

Once the congress was over, Ian Smith renewed his approaches to me. Before I would talk to him there were some points to be cleared up. The Victoria Falls bridge conference had broken down over his refusal to agree that our exiles take part in a conference within Southern Rhodesia – was he now prepared to let them travel in and out unharmed? We had not discussed majority rule at Victoria Falls – was he now prepared to talk about that? We had favourable answers to both preliminary inquiries, and an initial meeting took place on 31 October, leading to a declaration of intent to negotiate a settlement, signed by Smith and myself on 1 December 1975.† The conference began in earnest on 11 December in Salisbury.

---

* The officers elected at the congress were: President, Joshua Nkomo; Vice-president, Josiah Chinamano; General Secretary, Joseph Msika; Treasurer, Amon Jirira; National Chairman, Samuel Munodawafa; National Vice-chairman, William Khona.

† See Appendix B, p.254.

I had, of course, kept the front-line presidents fully informed of all the preparations. President Kaunda sent an observer on behalf of all the presidents, who sat in throughout the conference. President Nyerere provided one of our team of six legal advisers, Roland Brown. As Nyerere had forcefully stated to us at the Lusaka meeting a year previously, this was the crucial test of whether Smith would in fact accept majority rule.

From our side, we went to great lengths to offer conditions that the Rhodesian regime might find acceptable. We offered 'safeguards' for white people, including some seats reserved for white people in parliament, which we detested. But Smith and his colleagues would not budge an inch away from their position that white people, elected on racially defined electoral rolls, should retain a majority in parliament. We advocated strictly non-racial criteria for electing the majority of MPs, and this Smith declined to contemplate.

I proposed that our ideas should be put to a referendum in which all of the people of Southern Rhodesia would be free to choose their future constitution. Smith said no. He would not even agree to put it to the vote. He said: 'Nkomo, I represent white people. As a white man I know your ideas are nonsense. We cannot vote on such a proposal.' I asked him not to turn something down without putting it to the people. I said: 'Look, imagine you accept our proposal for a referendum in which all the people, black and white, can vote. If the white people do as you think and vote against, that is their responsibility, not yours. What the white people say is their decision, not yours. I believe that if given the chance they would accept majority rule, rather than continue with the war and the international isolation they have today. Let them decide.'

Smith believed that when he rejected my proposal he was speaking for all the white people in the country. I know he was tired of the war, and I believe the ordinary white people were even more tired of it. But he would not even let them vote. He thus bears the personal responsibility for five more terrible years of war, during which the chances of reconciliation between black and white people became fewer every day. Smith simply could not give the possibility of a non-racial Zimbabwe a chance. The talks collapsed on 'the single and fundamental issue of majority rule now'. Smith could not accept that, because he was racist to the bone.

In talking to Smith I took a big personal risk. President Kaunda was criticised for doing business with the South Africans to bring about the Victoria Falls talks, although some of his loudest critics were the quietest when he did so to free us from prison. I am still criticised for trying to negotiate with Smith. I hated what the man personally stood for. I longed for majority rule in Zimbabwe, and justice for my people. I wanted those things with as little killing as possible, and with as little bitterness as possible between the white people and the black people who had an equal right to live in the new nation of Zimbabwe. I knew all too well that fierce fighting would mean grave problems at the end of the war. But now it had to start again, and I was to do my share.

The period of failed negotiations had a high price for the nationalist side. Smith's army and police took advantage of the lull in the fighting to strengthen their position. There was a great propaganda campaign to persuade people that Zapu had no army: the bishop's supporters invented the slogan 'heavy-heavy', referring to the time when he had trouble lifting the sub-machine gun and implying that he was the leader of many armed soldiers. This did not worry me – I knew Zipra was there.

My fellow nationalists in Zanu were growing ever more bitterly divided among themselves. Even while we were holding the talks with the front-line presidents after our release from detention, their quarrels had broken out into violence: some of the party leaders were abducted by their own army, Zanla, and had been released only after prompt action by the Zambian police.

One prominent casualty of their in-fighting was my old friend and lawyer, Herbert Chitepo. He had done great service as a defender of nationalists before the Rhodesian courts; then he was seconded by us to serve as Director of Public Prosecutions for Julius Nyerere's government in Tanzania, and in Dar es Salaam he grew remote from his own people. He yielded to the temptation, so common among the Zanu leadership, to exploit tribalism in his own interest. In March 1975 a bomb exploded under his car outside his home in

Lusaka, killing him outright. An international commission of inquiry into his murder later established that he, as a member of the Nyika tribe of the Shona-speaking group, had been killed by rivals in the Karanga group within his own party.

This tragedy reflected the divisions that had developed within Zanu. I well remember Bishop Muzorewa, a Shona-speaker, returning horrified from a visit to Lusaka at this time. He said that he had seen tribalism at its worst, not between Shona and Ndebele, but among Shona-speakers divided into their own sub-groups. It was an unpleasant period which has left its mark deeply on Zanu to this day.

The front-line presidents had now clearly decided, following the failure of all efforts to talk constructively with Ian Smith, to give full backing to the military preparations that had slowed down during the talks. The presidents – Kaunda and Nyerere, Seretse Khama of Botswana, Machel of Mozambique and Neto of Angola – considered that the nationalist cause would be better served by a unified army command, responding to a political leadership. They therefore requested President Nyerere as their chairman to call a meeting of Zimbabwe organisations in Dar to try to help bring this about.

Those present were myself, Ndabaningi Sithole and Abel Muzorewa, with Alfred Mangena, the commander of Zipra, who later died tragically in a clash with the enemy, and Rex Nhongo, commander of Zanla. Julius Nyerere, as chairman of the meeting, began by asking the political leaders whether their movement had a military wing. In my case it was easy: I said Zipra was Zapu's army, Mangena agreed, and that was that. Julius then asked the bishop whether he had an army: Muzorewa said he did have one, but at present it was in Mozambique and included within Zanla. 'You have no army, Bishop,' said Julius.

Then Nyerere asked Sithole whether he had an army. Sithole said Zanla was his army, but it had deserted him. 'Reverend, that is what is called a coup,' said President Nyerere, so Sithole was out of the running. Nyerere turned to Nhongo, the Zanla commander, and asked him who was his political leader. Nhongo answered that his army had rejected Sithole and at present had no political leadership. Nyerere asked me to persuade the Zanla commanders to produce a name acceptable to them.

Later, Nhongo gave me a piece of paper. On it was written the name of Robert Mugabe. He had recently been expelled from Zambia for making extremely derogatory remarks about President Kaunda, and had spent several months confined by order of President Machel to a house in the small town of Quelimane, in Mozambique, along with his unpredictable friend Edgar Tekere. I asked Nhongo what he thought Mugabe's capacity should be. 'Our political spokesman,' he said. I handed the paper to President Nyerere.

My next task was to consult some Zanu central committee members who were detained in Zambia in connection with the Chitepo murder. President Kaunda gave me leave to talk to the three who were detained in Kabwe prison. Henry Hamadziripi, Rugare Gumbo and Kumbirai Kangai agreed with Nhongo's nomination of Mugabe as spokesman. I then asked to see Josiah Tongogara, who was actually in Lusaka prison facing charges arising out of the murder. Tongogara supported his colleagues. I reported to the presidents that Mugabe seemed to be the acceptable available spokesman. I then requested the release from detention of the three Zanla officers implicated in the death of Chitepo. Kaunda agreed, although Tongogara's release had to await the judgment of the courts (he was later acquitted because the evidence against him was held to be inadmissible). That was how I brought Robert Mugabe to the leadership of his party and secured the release of the colleagues who supported him.

The next stage was the formation of an embryo political leadership for the entire Zimbabwean nationalist movement. Under the name of the Patriotic Front, Mugabe and I began to meet and to try to work out joint policies. Progress was slow: Zanla and Zipra had never been further apart. Zanla units had mutinied in Zambia and a Zambian officer was shot dead: the guilty soldiers were expelled to Tanzania. Our Zipra trainees were sent to the training camps in Tanzania, and terrible consequences followed. Under Nyerere's influence, there were considerable numbers of Chinese instructors in the camps. Our young men were perfectly willing to accept their military instruction, but objected strongly to the political line, which was violently hostile to me personally and my followers. Many of our cadres were rounded up and detained. Some were tortured. At Mgagao an unknown but considerable number of our soldiers were shot. At Morogoro over a hundred young Zapu fighters died at the hands of the Zanla soldiers.

President Nyerere's only sign of regret was to allow some of our people to visit the sites of the massacres and re-bury the bodies, which had been thrown into a mass grave. Some were terribly mangled. President Kaunda insisted that a commission of inquiry be set up to investigate the killings: President Nyerere prevented it from ever meeting. Thereafter our people understandably resisted orders that they be sent to Tanzania for training.

Now Zipra became concentrated in Zambia, Zanla in Mozambique. This geographical split had grave political consequences. In earlier stages of the war, all military operations were based in Zambia: it was the only liberated country to share a frontier with Southern Rhodesia, and therefore the only possible operational base. But it was a hard base from which to operate. The frontier is along the valley of the Zambezi river, swelled from the early 1960s onwards by the creation of Lake Kariba behind its huge dam. The river valley was a strong first line of defence for the Rhodesians. Then, south of the river, lie ravines and high bare hills, then a wide expanse of open bush with semi-desert set with a maze of land mines. It was thirty days' journey, often against strong opposition, before a soldier moving south from Zambia could be in action against significant Rhodesian targets – and thirty days back once he had used his ammunition.

But after the liberation of Mozambique in 1974, that country opened up as an alternative way into Rhodesia. That border is mostly forest and mountains with good cover from the air – excellent guerilla country. Zanla, now that it was based in Tanzania and Mozambique, had relatively easy access to Rhodesia, and easy targets in front of it in the form of isolated white-owned farms. Zipra, from Zambia, still had the tough Zambezi country to cross.

These tactical realities led to different behaviour by the two armies within Rhodesia. Our forces, travelling out of Zambia, had to move in small parties and win the absolute trust of the sparse population of the areas they passed through. Zanla forces were able to penetrate the easier frontier facing them in much larger numbers, often in groups of up to a hundred. This in itself imposed much greater demands on the civilian population whose areas they crossed, especially when the visiting soldiers demanded meat and chickens from their hosts. They adopted a policy of forced political indoctrination of the local population – in Shona they called it *pungwe*, meaning compulsory all-night mass meetings. Zanla, in fact, operated as a political force, while Zipra had to behave in a strictly military way.

The extra danger was that the Rhodesian side of the Zambia and Botswana borders is inhabited by people most of whom are Sindebele-speaking. Zipra operated in and drew its recruits from these people. But the people living along the Mozambique border are mostly Shona-speaking. So Zanla increasingly became a Shona-speaking army and Zipra a Sindebele-speaking army. Thus the military realities reinforced the tribalistic tendencies which the Zanu leaders were openly fostering.

Zanu and Zanla had the further advantage of far better propaganda than ours. The Zambian government supported the Zimbabwe liberation struggle. The Tanzanian government supported Zanu as a party, and President Nyerere's skilful public relations advisers ensured that the work was well done. Even in prison I had listened with excitement to the broadcasts from Dar es Salaam, with recordings that really sounded as though they were made on the battlefield. Zapu's broadcasts were put out at the wrong time of day by Radio Zambia, and were sometimes unimaginative. (What did I hear to boost the morale of our boys in the bush but that dreadful song: 'Mona Lisa, Mona Lisa, man has called you.') In fact, talking after the war to those who fought against us, I heard that their wives and girlfriends worried much more if the fighting was on a Zipra front than on a Zanla one.

Chapter 16
Running an Army

Now, with full-scale war facing us all, I had to learn to be a military commander. I was immensely proud of my men; it was my task to see that they got the backing they deserved. I carefully left the day-to-day command of the men to our own senior soldiers. But I regularly visited the training camps and bases to explain just what was going on, and to raise morale. When negotiations broke down, I went to the soldiers and said I had done what I could, it was up to them now. I emphasised that they were not fighting to do me a favour, nor I them: we were in it together for our country. I was doing my best to keep them supplied with material to fight with, and to see it was fairly distributed. It was up to them to put those supplies to good use.

Our lads often came from poor homes, where blankets and clothes were highly prized possessions. I had to make sure they understood that such things were for military use, not for giving to girlfriends. The boys had no money: naturally they were tempted to sell off a blanket or a pair of boots to buy a present for a girl or to get some tobacco or a smoke of *dagga*, which is what we call marijuana. They were all volunteers who had chosen to leave home to fight: they had to be motivated, not ordered about.

We had more volunteers than we could feed, clothe and arm. There were allegations, particularly from Western journalists visiting our transit camps in Botswana, that we were kidnapping young people from the schools to turn them into fighters. In fact we tried hard to persuade them to stay and finish their studies, but they would not. Botswana, with its long, open border with South Africa, was terribly vulnerable to attack, and President Seretse Khama could not allow guerilla camps there. We had to charter aircraft to lift our refugees out of Botswana into Zambia – I am afraid we still owe the Zambian government several million dollars for the help they gave with that.

The generosity of the Zambian government and people was extraordinary. The establishment of one of our camps obviously put those who lived near it at risk of a Rhodesian raid, but there were never any objections. At one point towards the end of the war, transport difficulties, caused largely by South African disruption of traffic, led to a genuine shortage of food throughout Zambia. In our camps the people were going hungry, and our officers reported to me that morale was suffering badly. Without a regular ration of the *sadza* that was their staple diet, our young men might get out of control.

I went straight to President Kaunda and told him of the danger. He knew his own people were short of food, that discontent was growing and production suffering. But he picked up the telephone and gave an order. For the coming week all supplies of food for the civilian market were to be diverted to the Zimbabwean camps, in consultation with my staff. It is hard to imagine a greater act of generosity by a national leader, prepared to put his own popularity at risk for the sake of a cause that he believed in. But he had his people behind him: when the situation was explained to them, they accepted it willingly, and never failed in their support for the cause of Zimbabwe.

One of our special problems was that many thousands of young girl refugees insisted on volunteering to fight. We could not possibly find a place for them all. It was not the girls' fault, but the presence of young women in a camp of young male soldiers caused tremendous trouble. I remembered the story of King David, who lusted after his officer's wife, and sent the man into a dangerous spot to get killed: and we had to be careful not to have our young men rushed off to bring back Smith's beard on a charger for their girlfriends. Fortunately we had splendid women to face the challenge of organising the girls. Mai Nyamurowa and Thenjiwe Lesabe did a wonderful job – backed by generous help from international organisations – in setting up the Victory Camp school outside Lusaka for many of our young girls, where they got a better education than they would have done at home. Some we did train to use weapons and employed as camp guards, but they were a tiny minority.

The one thing I regret about our volunteers was that their

military discipline became almost too strong. Our tactic was to move in small groups against the enemy, so each man had to be ready to take over command as soon as the man above him had been knocked out of the fight: I always emphasised that to the lads when I spoke to them before going out on operations. But the discipline was so strong that individual soldiers would not answer me direct: they always waited for the most senior person present to answer, and refused to speak on their own initiative even to their commander-in-chief.

My only training for the role of a commander-in-chief was that of a social worker. I tried to approach the job dispassionately, realising that everyone in an army has a role to play. Even visiting the wounded I tried not to appear upset if I saw a fine young man who had lost an arm or a leg: I just said it was a soldier's job to suffer for his nation. I worried and worked to solve their individual problems – how to get artificial limbs, how to readapt to family life after a wound. But I never allowed myself to show distress. If the wounded men became demanding, ordering the nurses around or insisting on special treatment, I always told them to respect their colleagues, that everyone had a necessary place in the national struggle; getting wounded did not win any privileges when everyone was doing his best.

Most of our fighting was with small-arms and simple weapons. The AK rifle became every young man's dream – stubby and reliable, it was far better than the long Nato rifle carried by the Rhodesian forces. Transporting heavy weapons through the Rhodesian air cover was terribly risky, and it was rare that we brought off conspicuous triumphs like the rocketing of the oil storage tanks in Salisbury and in Bulawayo – the Salisbury tanks burned for a week, a symbol of our success, but the Bulawayo reserve was unfortunately empty when Zipra hit it.

But our success against the Rhodesian Air Force was far greater than they allowed to be known at the time. We could not claim the credit that we deserved, because we needed to keep secret the fact that we had been given some Soviet surface-to-air missiles, Sam-7s. We deployed them first in defence of our camps in Zambia, and caught the enemy by surprise. The first time we used them we knocked down two of their strike aircraft, the second time we got four. In all we shot down almost thirty of their planes and helicopters: the Rhodesian minister of defence was forced to resign, and they replaced the losses only by importing second-hand Hawker Hunters from Israel, with South African help. One of the Smith government's great propaganda successes was in covering up the extent of the damage we had done them. The only times they would admit to losses of aircraft were when we brought down passenger planes, which we did on two occasions. These tragic incidents need explaining.

The Rhodesians used their civil airliners equally for carrying passengers and for carrying troops. The first time we shot one down was immediately after Smith's troops had carried out a particularly brutal attack on the camps at Chimoio, in Mozambique, where well over a thousand of our young people died. Rhodesian television had shown pictures of Viscount aircraft in Air Rhodesia markings ferrying in their paratroopers for the attack. And a plane carrying armed soldiers is surely a legitimate target in a war.

Of course it was not our policy to shoot down civil airliners: if we had wanted to we could have done so often, but we carefully refrained from that. What happened was that we identified one of the same aircraft that had been shown on television loaded with troops. It landed at Victoria Falls, where we knew paratroops were stationed, and as it took off we shot it down with a Sam missile. Forty-eight people, most of them holidaymakers, died in the crash; eight survived. Ten of those who died were said to have been shot on the ground after escaping from the wreck. It was a tragic mistake. I felt it personally. One man was killed with his mother and father and his wife and children – the whole family wiped out. Their name was Gulab, Zimbabweans of Indian origin. Mr Gulab was a good friend of mine, who often fixed me up with airline tickets in ways that avoided alerting the police. I regret his loss very much.

The Rhodesian propaganda people at once claimed that our anti-aircraft team had killed ten survivors on the ground. This was obviously untrue, since the plane fell well away from the firing-point. Some of our Zipra boys did approach the crash site, and did help the eight survivors to get to safety, bringing them water and looking after them. I truly have no idea how the ten died. I do not believe they were killed by our people: I hope not.

I then made an error of a different kind. The following day the BBC telephoned me for a comment on the shooting-down. I told them as much of the truth as I knew. Then, fairly enough in the circumstances, they asked me what weapon the plane had been brought down with. Clearly I could not say it was a Sam-7: it was a secret that we had such things. To turn the question aside, I answered that we had brought it down by throwing stones, and as I said so I laughed a bit. I was not laughing at the deaths of all those civilians, but at the evasive answer. The laugh was remembered, rather than my regret at those unnecessary deaths.

In retaliation for the first Viscount disaster, the Rhodesians mounted a savage raid on our Freedom Camp, just north of Lusaka. It was not a military training camp, but a genuine refugee camp for young boys. Most of the 351 who died were just youngsters.

Later we again brought down one of Air Rhodesia's Viscounts, with serious loss of life. This time too civilians died because the Rhodesians used the same aircraft for civilian and for military purposes. Our intelligence people in Salisbury had identified the Rhodesian army commander, General Walls, getting into a Viscount plane. The same aircraft was identified landing at Wankie, at Victoria Falls and at Kariba: General Walls was reported to be still on board. After take-off from Kariba, the plane passed our Sam emplacement on the hill: the missile team identified the plane by its number, fired and brought it down. Shortly afterwards another Viscount took off and flew past our missile crew, who did not fire because our spies had not identified it as carrying a military target. General Walls had changed planes, and was aboard the second.

Walls and his staff officers were clearly a legitimate target. A few years later, when I was a minister and he was commanding our post-independence army, I asked him why he had swapped planes. He just laughed. We talked about the time when his troops raided my home in Lusaka and killed four people in the house, while I eluded them. We had each tried to kill the other, and in both attempts innocent people had been killed by mistake. It was that kind of war. I still wonder whether Walls had switched aircraft because they had intercepted our radio talk and knew it was a likely target. We, of course, could not say publicly that Walls was our target; we could not admit either that we had a sophisticated radio link, or that we had spies in all the civil airports of Rhodesia.

One other attempt to shoot down a civil airliner was unsuccessful. The target was P.W. Botha, the South African defence minister, who was flying in to Victoria Falls. That very day some South African soldiers who were operating in the area were killed by our men on Rhodesian territory. Botha was a legitimate target – but the missile malfunctioned, and missed his aircraft. He left in a hurry, without performing his task of inaugurating a swimming-pool for the troops.

The worst thing about the war was the callousness it bred. It is true, and I regret it, that atrocities were committed by people on our side, by Zipra fighters as well as by Zanla men. Some of those killed were isolated white farmers and their families who happened to be in the way. Some were African chiefs who may have collaborated with the Smith regime, but who had little alternative if their own families and their people were to survive. It was not our policy to kill such people. But armed men, alone or in small groups, may come to disregard the importance of human life. It was necessary to fight a guerilla war, and in such a war terrible things are bound to happen.

One killing that I especially regret was that of Bishop Adolf Schmitt of Bulawayo. The bishop was retired, and was a very old personal friend of mine – he had in fact blessed my marriage to maFuyana, an event complicated by her insistence on remaining a Catholic, while I insisted on remaining a Methodist, so that we had a registry office wedding and two blessings by clergymen. A lone killer murdered the bishop, one of his priests, Father Possent, an old friend of my family, and a nun: the story illustrates the confusion to which the guerilla war gave rise.

The killer was found by our people, alone, on the Zambian shore of the Zambezi, which he had apparently crossed by swimming. He said he had been fired on from both banks while crossing, and that he had got across the river after escaping from a cell in Victoria Falls prison, where he was wearing leg-irons and manacles: his wrists did indeed have what appeared to be the marks of irons. We investigated, and found that he had previously been in a Rhodesian prison. This he admitted, claiming that he had escaped once, stolen a weapon, murdered the priests, then been arrested again and once more escaped to join us.

This was an unconvincing story. We detained the man in Mboroma camp, where we kept those whom we regarded as accomplices of the Smith regime. Then Smith's forces raided Mboroma. Some of the detainees were heard to say: 'Our friends have come, folks, let's go.' With the murderer among them they ran to a helicopter and were whisked back into Rhodesia. It is a fact that the Smith regime did its worst to turn the Catholic church against us, though whether they, or their freelance agents, went so far as to murder the bishop is impossible to prove. On other occasions Smith's undercover troops, the Selous Scouts, certainly killed priests and missionaries in order to put the blame on our nationalist guerillas.

The Rhodesian intelligence service was remarkably well informed, and their forces were capable of extremely precise actions, such as the raid on my own home in Lusaka, which they carried out in trucks painted in the colours of the Zambian army, so that they could make their approach undetected. This makes me think that some of their worst atrocities were deliberate, not accidental. For example, they raided Mkushi camp north of Lusaka, entirely occupied by girl refugees with absolutely no military connection at all. They called the girls out of hiding, lined them up and told Jane Gumbo, the head of the camp, to fire on her own pupils: she refused, and was herself shot. The white soldiers, who seem to have been mercenaries rather than Rhodesians, massacred ninety-one girls: the black troops under their command helped large numbers of girls to escape, and came close to mutinying against their orders.

All of us who lived through that war became hardened by it. Those who died were our close friends: nowhere was safe. J.Z. Moyo was the man who came nearest to negotiating unity between the Zipra and Zanla armies. He was very close to me indeed. One day in January 1977 he received, in Lusaka, a parcel mailed from Botswana and addressed in the handwriting of one of his closest friends. He opened it and it exploded, killing him. I got the news while I was giving a press conference in Iraq, at the airport on my way to Yugoslavia. I just carried on. Death became a remote, impersonal fact. That was the atmosphere in which, when the war at last ended, we had to create a new and peaceful state in Zimbabwe. We have not succeeded in that, so far.

Jason Moyo's death forced me back almost full-time into the life of a military commander. As a vice-president of Zapu and the senior man directly concerned with Zipra, he had provided a crucial link between the direction of the political and military wings of our movement. With him gone, I had to fill his place. Until then I had concentrated on the task of arranging the party's contacts with the outside world, to obtain the support and supplies without which our forces could not operate, and to consolidate the international backing that was indispensable for our diplomatic and our military success.

In relation to the Western nations, our aim had been more to prevent them acting against our interests than to win the support that I knew they would not give us. Britain still had legal sovereignty over its rebel colony of Southern Rhodesia, but we had no reason to think that the British government would do anything effective to end the rebellion or to promote democracy in our country. The United States was locked into its alliance with Britain and would do nothing useful without British prompting, which was unlikely to come; nor, for that matter, would any country in the North Atlantic alliance. There was, however, a real danger that those countries might damage us severely if they recognised some arrangement for perpetuating minority rule in Rhodesia.

After the failure of my talks with Smith early in 1976, the Americans made a brief intervention in our area. The secretary of state, Henry Kissinger, decided he would use his magic to bring peace to southern Africa. In April 1976 he made a fleeting visit to the region, touring several countries in as many days. In Lusaka he asked President Kaunda to arrange for me to call on him, which I did.

I spent about seven minutes with Kissinger. He spoke in

short sentences in a dull, flat voice, like a businessman doing a quick deal. It was more like talking to a robot than to a person. First he would say something, then withdraw it and say something else, then add a further point to that, so by the end I only knew that whatever he wanted it was not what I wanted. He struck me as clever, of course, but unpleasant and untrustworthy.

On the same trip Kissinger saw Ian Smith in South Africa. Smith seems to have understood Kissinger to have offered a guarantee that the majority would not be allowed to take over in Rhodesia, although there would be some surface changes to disguise the deal. Smith seems further to have understood from Kissinger that this package had been sold to the front-line states and to the British. Smith became angry when the Americans did not stand by this package. He was a bad negotiator and not at all a clever man, but on this occasion I suspect that Kissinger, not he, was responsible for the confusion. Kissinger's southern Africa proposals were not really concerned with African problems at all, but with super-power politics. I think he would have been happiest if the whole region had settled down as a ring of satellite Bantustans dependent upon South Africa. His ideas were of no interest to us.

The next stage of international diplomacy was the conference of all parties convened by the British in Geneva in October 1976. Smith was not really interested in negotiating. He seemed to think that the conference would merely ratify what Kissinger had led him to believe was a deal involving the surrender of the nationalists. Bishop Muzorewa, as usual, did not appear to understand what was going on. On the nationalist side we had problems of our own.

The Patriotic Front, set up to coordinate the strategic activities of Zapu and Zanu earlier in the year, was not really up to the strain of negotiating as a single body. Robert Mugabe, having first been nominated by Zanla as their political spokesman, was then nominated president of Zanu in a general sharing-out of jobs among the thirty members of its central committee. He lacked both experience and self-confidence.

The personality in the Zanu delegation who impressed me most favourably was their military member, Josiah Tongogara.

I had met him in connection with the events after Herbert Chitepo's murder, when I visited him in prison to find out whether he agreed to the choice of Robert Mugabe as Zanu spokesman. Despite the reputation he acquired during the Chitepo affair, I realised in Geneva that he was a man of solid good-will with a real desire for Zimbabwean unity.

There was a curious episode when, without warning to the rest of us, the Zanu team was joined by the Zanla commander, Rex Nhongo, and a few other military officers. I had the impression that they were still not satisfied with the political leadership of their party, to whom they theoretically looked for orders. Nhongo is a decent military type, and his presence was if anything a steadying influence on the Zanu delegation. But it was not clear who had authority.

The talks were not helped towards success by the British choice of chairman. He was the Labour politician Ivor Richard, the British representative at the United Nations. Since the British at the UN had constantly vetoed every helpful proposal anyone made for Rhodesia, this was not exactly a recommendation. Richard was a cold person, uneasy in private talks and formal meetings alike, and he made no useful contribution. The conference was doomed. Shortly before Christmas everyone went home and the talks were never reconvened.

Chapter 17

World Traveller

Once again in the mid-1970s I resumed the circuit of capital cities that was necessary to win international support for our cause. My base was in Lusaka, but I did not really have a home. As the war intensified, I could no longer safely leave my wife either in Zimbabwe or in any neighbouring country. Our agents in the Rhodesian police intercepted threats to kidnap her, so she left to take up residence in East Berlin, where the government of the German Democratic Republic had generously offered her a flat. I no longer had to worry about her safety, but I certainly missed her company. The family was scattered. One son and both of my daughters were in the United States. The other boy went first to military academy in Cuba, then moved to Angola to work with our trainees there.

Perhaps this is the place to describe the life of a political nomad in the long years while I established and maintained relations with the supporters without whose help the struggle could not have continued. It was in Egypt in 1958 that I first saw the need for such support. The only significant contact I was able to make there was with the Cuban embassy: in the long run that turned out to have been an excellent choice, but at that time the infant socialist government of Cuba could give us good-will but no concrete help.

In London shortly afterwards I first approached the Soviet authorities for what was to be their decisive help, extended faithfully over many years. I telephoned their embassy and spoke to an official. He asked me what my business was, and I tried to explain about our struggle for independence. 'But do you have an embassy here?' the man asked – hardly a sensible question to put to someone who was complaining that he was subject to British rule. But he made an appointment for me to see another official, so I went round in person to state my case again. The man I spoke to appeared unable to discuss the matter. Later I found that Soviet diplomats invariably refer an unexpected problem at once to Moscow, without making any comment.

The Soviet Union and other east European countries work methodically through an elaborate committee system, and when I first came in contact with them tended to move slowly because they had had very little personal contact with Africa. The exceptions are the East Germans, who have a tradition of imperial involvement in Africa, and have some specialists who know a good deal about it. The Germans are a warm people anyway, as their kindness to maFuyana while she was their guest in Berlin showed: perhaps their traditional interest in Africa played a part in this too.

From my first contact in London my relations with the Soviet Union steadily developed, especially through New York, where Mr Gromyko as head of their UN delegation was always interested in decolonisation questions. (They noted that the 'free world' stopped supporting freedom when it came to southern Africa.) My first visit to Moscow itself was made in 1961 from my base in Dar es Salaam. I was received very formally by a section of the central committee of the Communist party, who made detailed notes of everything I said.

They were at first extremely sceptical of my request for help: they said they had liberated their own country without outside support, and asked why we could not follow their example. I had to explain that the days when a revolution could be achieved with a few rifles were over, and that the Rhodesians had been deliberately armed by the British to preserve their economic interests in that part of the world. They came round only very slowly.

I must emphasise that the Soviets never offered me help. Each time I asked for it I had to give good reasons and explain in detail what I wanted. Some people in the West pretend that anyone wanting to start a revolution need only go to Moscow and they will open up the armoury. It was not at all like that in my case. Once the party officials had decided that I and my party deserved support, they stood faithfully by the decision. Since their personalities do not change regularly, as in Western countries, their policies are more reliable.

Once the policy of support was decided, I was passed on to a military committee, and to it I had to justify every detail of my request. If I said we had 500 men, so we wanted 500 of their basic AK rifles, they would say no, 500 men means so many rifles, so

many light machine guns, so many mortars or anti-tank roc-
kets, and I would end up with only about 300 AKs. (This was
a problem, since our soldiers were proud of those little guns,
and everyone wanted one.) The Soviets never seemed to have
enough even of their simple infantry weapons: there would
always be a delay while they checked their stocks and worked
out the details. Only after I had studied the way armies are run
was I able to deal as an equal with the Soviet military people.
They were always reluctant to give anything away.

The Soviet Union provided training as well as weapons. They
did not train our combat soldiers directly, but trained our
people to do the training. Even so, the vast majority even of our
instructors who were trained in other African countries were
trained by other Africans – notably in Algeria, which was
extremely generous. Those who went to Cuba were trained by
Cubans.

Only for the most complex tasks were Zipra people sent to the
Soviet Union itself for training. By the end of the war we had tank
crews, and even the complete flying and maintenance staff for a
squadron of combat aircraft, who had passed out of
Soviet training schools. The real purpose of this advanced
training was to provide qualified fighting men to take over the
Zimbabwean armed forces after independence, if we were
attacked by South Africa, which seemed quite possible. Our
highly trained personnel never had the chance to use their
skills in combat. It is most unfortunate that no place for these
qualified people has been found in the Zimbabwe armed forces
since independence, and I am afraid that this expensive
training programme turned out to be a waste.

The most high-level occasion I ever attended in Moscow was
on the sixtieth anniversary of the October Revolution, in 1977,
when the heads of fraternal delegations were invited to watch
the formal proceedings of the Supreme Soviet. At the reception
afterwards, I briefly met the late President Breznev. Mr
Andropov, their present leader, I also met at a reception, but as
head of their security service, the KGB, he was chairman of the
committee dealing with the training of security operatives, and
I had extensive correspondence with him about that. The
former Soviet ambassador in Lusaka, Mr Solodonokov, was
reputed to be associated with the KGB. He was a very nice

fellow, and we got on very well on the personal level. Moreover, he was entirely professional about his work, and if you discussed a request with him you could be sure that it would soon get onto the agenda of the right committee in Moscow, and the decision would come back without too much delay.

In all my discussions, the Soviets never asked for any undertaking about our policies after independence. They were solidly on the side of our national independence, and that was all. Moreover, there was never any question of sending combat troops, or even advisers, from the Soviet Union or any other country to help us fight our war. A few Ghanaian specialist instructors served in our training camps in Tanzania, and were very much appreciated as professionals. We once had two Cuban security people on the spot to help train our headquarters security personnel. Apart from that, all the people at our bases and in our fighting units were Zimbabwean. It is our country, and if blood was to be shed it should be our blood. We did not ask for that sort of help, and we were never offered it.

The case of Angola, incidentally, is entirely different from ours. Angola, as a sovereign and independent nation, was attacked by South Africa. President Neto, as head of state, asked for and received Cuban help to resist external aggression.

The real difference between Western interests in Africa and those of the Soviet Union is that, when asked to leave, the Soviet Union has always left. At the request of the governments of those countries, there has at various times been a Soviet presence in Egypt, in Somalia and in Guinea. When the peoples of those countries asked the Soviets to leave, they went and left nothing behind. But you can go around the City of London and go around Harare now, and look at the names on the company boards, and you might as well have stayed in the one place. I do not say it is a bad thing that the British have stayed on to do business in countries in which they have abandoned a political role. But it is a fact that African countries' links with the former colonial powers have gone on; but where the Soviets have been asked to leave, or when they complete a contract, they have gone.

The very first non-African country that I asked for help was Cuba, in 1958. Since then I have developed an ever deeper admiration for that country and its leader, Fidel Castro. When I visited his country in 1977, I was deeply impressed by the way in which he has given himself to his people. I saw how he travelled about with no escort, stopping and talking freely with people on the road, taking no precautions at all. It showed that the people trusted him as much as he trusted them.

We travelled all around Cuba, by bus, by car, by plane and finally in a small boat to a little hide-away where he went to think things out in peace. It was a little island with a cottage right on a windy beach, which at first sight seemed very uncomfortable. The cottage consisted of a kitchen and just one room. I could not imagine where I was going to sleep, but Fidel made up the bed for me himself (which proved to be very comfortable) and went off to sleep in the little boat we had come in. In the morning we took the boat round to the Bay of Pigs and saw where the Americans had tried to invade, and how they were repulsed. Then he went snorkel fishing and caught fish for our lunch, which he cooked himself. The boat's crew stayed on board and the president did everything with his own hands, even the cleaning up. He did not do it to show off – obviously it was the way he liked to live.

The housing projects and the cooperative farming in Cuba seemed to me to work excellently, but the best thing of all was the schooling. They had centres to which young people came for a couple of weeks' break from their ordinary education. They had lectures and sports, and sessions in flight simulators, and all sorts of experiences that helped them to develop their own skills and personalities, and build up a sense of solidarity among young people from all over the country. I saw three of these places, and they seemed to me to match the spirit that Fidel had himself, and that he wanted everyone in Cuba to have the chance of sharing.

Fidel Castro is a man completely committed to the fight against oppression. He believes in that for Cuba, and he believes in that for Africa, although it is so far off. I do not know what the ordinary people in Cuba think of it, but I have met their soldiers in Angola, and I believe they are there because they have chosen to be there. The training they gave our soldiers was better and more realistic than that offered by almost any other country, and I am deeply grateful for it.

I believe it must be their own ideological weakness that makes the Western countries so frightened of the Cuban presence in Africa. It is perfectly normal for countries that agree with each other to offer each other help. The Americans help the west Europeans and nobody is surprised by that. But if any country friendly with the Soviet Union helps someone else, that is immediately denounced as Soviet imperialism.

Having Cubans, or Russians, or anyone else, in an African country does not mean that the country is being taken over. We had the British in our country for ninety years: we learned English in our schools, and we read Shakespeare and Dickens. But that did not make us British. We remained Africans. If we have Cubans in our countries for a few years that does not make us into Cubans – it certainly does not make us into Russians. The Americans must think the Soviets have something very powerful to teach us if they think we can be converted by a few military advisers: that is what I mean by ideological weakness. Africa can survive plenty more invasions, and beat them back if necessary, before it loses its identity.

Personally I am sorry to have had so few contacts with the People's Republic of China. My only trip there was in 1962, and it was a mystery tour. I was on my own and my timetable was tight. I flew from London by way of Moscow to Peking, planning to fly on from there to Hong Kong to catch the plane for Los Angeles and New York, where I was to address the UN decolonisation committee.

In Peking I first met several committees of officials. I had the impression I was being examined to see if I was worth introducing to someone very senior. At each meeting there was green tea to drink, unsweetened, in little cups without handles: I did not like the taste, but it left my mouth feeling clean and good for a long while after. I had, of course, the usual failures with chopsticks. I felt I was in a very powerful and strange culture, determined to preserve its own difference from others. People were reluctant to speak English. One eminent professor had a long conversation with me through an interpreter, which gradually got more and more interesting. As we reached a

Bishop Abel Muzorewa, Lord Carrington, Sir Ian Gilmour, Joshua Nkomo and Robert Mugabe. *(Popperfoto)*

14. 1980: Zimbabwe's first Cabinet under majority rule. (*Zimbabwe Ministry of Information*)

15a. Mrs Joshua Nkomo: maFuyana.

15b. The Nkomo children. *L. to r.*: Ernest Thuthani; Thandiwe; Louise Sehlule; Michael Sibangilizwe.

16. 1983: at home with the people in Makokoba market, Bulawayo. (*Nicholas Harman*)

specially intriguing point he suddenly began to speak perfect English. It turned out that he had been at Oxford. What I respected was that he did not at first try to put himself on my level by talking so that I could understand him directly, preferring to speak his own language so that he could be completely in control of the situation.

After my examination by the committees, I felt I must have done fairly well when I was invited to lunch in the Great Hall of the People – a place of tremendous impressiveness – by no less than Chou Enlai himself. He was a simple, soft-spoken person, appearing deeply interested in our subject. Instead of talking in ideological statements, he was entirely pragmatic, frankly approaching the problem through the facts. I left by the local plane for Hong Kong, feeling happy that contact had been established.

The aircraft stopped twice, and at the third stop we were told to take our hand luggage and go to the transit lounge. There they announced that the flight could not continue, since the runway at the next airport was flooded by heavy rain. I asked whether we could go on by train, and the answer was no.

We went into town, where as far as I had known nobody was expecting us. We were greeted with elaborate arrangements, a rousing welcome from the mayor and his staff, and a formal dinner. Next morning I again asked if we could fly on: they said even the roads were blocked, and it was regrettably necessary for us to stay. I am afraid I do not even remember the name of the town, which was on the Yellow river – we were shown a great new bridge and given lunch in a restaurant projecting over the water. Suddenly the young man who was acting as guide announced that a message had come to say that the airport was still closed, so it would not be possible to move that night. There was no telephone, he had no radio, and I would certainly have seen a messenger if one had come. I was worried, and asked to go back to the hotel.

At the hotel they told us that the plane would in fact leave that night. Then they took us to the station and put us on the train. We travelled the whole night and well into the following day. As the train went along, someone came into our compartment and spoke to the guide: of course I had no idea what was said. The guide passed on the message that we would have to disembark at the next station, since the rain had swept the line away for several kilometres. I could only laugh.

When we came to the station we got off the train, while the other passengers stayed on board and continued their journey. The explanation was that this was a town with suitable accommodation for distinguished foreigners. We were taken to the town hall, where there was another formal reception waiting, with choirs and dancers and a big ceremonial. The party went on till after midnight. By now I was sure there were no floods, but there was nothing to do but be patient.

Next morning the farce continued. We got back onto a train and continued down the line. They said it had been repaired. Yesterday it was swept away; today they had repaired it. We pulled into a huge port city at a station surrounded by water. It must have been Canton, but I had no idea where I was, having no map and being unable to read any signs. I looked round for the guide, but he was gone, and I never saw him again. A new guide took us to the hotel to pass another night.

Now I began to insist that I must leave. I was due at the United Nations and I must catch my plane at Hong Kong. Once more we waited until the afternoon, for another train that took us 125 kilometres to the border somewhere near Hong Kong. There were two guides by now, but when we changed trains they left my bags lying on the platform, and if I had not seen them lying there they would have been left behind. And so, despite everything, I caught the plane and made my way to New York.

It was an extraordinary way to treat a guest whom they must have hoped to impress. Their behaviour was impossible to understand. I suppose they wanted me to see some of their developments, and indeed they were impressive. But I got an even deeper impression of the problems they faced. The areas of cultivated land were immense, but then the poverty was immense too, on a scale that a visitor could barely grasp. Everything was formal yet muddled: even going round the museums was an ordeal, as we were passed from one guide to another and told one story after another about Chairman Mao.

I can hardly believe that they have now got rid of the idea that Chairman Mao's little red book contains the answer to every problem. The whole thing was naive and emotional, but maybe it did them good to have a methodical way of tackling their difficulties, so long as they had faith in it. Personally I learned one lesson from the little red book. Chairman Mao said that it is essential to consult the masses; but when the people are asked for their suggestions and bring them, then it is up to the leadership to decide what actually needs to be done. The important thing is to carry the people with you, to take account of their thinking, and to assure them that the solution has been built out of the bricks that they have provided. The final decision is the leader's, but his policy will work best if the people who have to carry it out truly believe they have had a hand in making it. That is wisdom.

I must not give the impression that the Zimbabwean national movement got help only from socialist countries. Western governments, as I have explained, insisted that their alliance with Britain prevented them from supplying the weapons we needed. But my many visits to Western countries convinced me that their people were much more favourable to our cause than their governments. Many non-governmental organisations (which often got their main funds from governments) gave us invaluable humanitarian assistance. The Friedrich Ebert Foundation of West Germany was extremely helpful, and the Bonn government backed it up. We had strong humanitarian support from the Netherlands, and I believe that Sweden, especially through its official agency, SIDA, was the most generous of all donors of food and clothing for our refugees.

Most important of all were the heavy Western contributions to the United Nations multilateral programmes which enabled tens of thousands of refugees from the Smith regime's oppression to survive in neighbouring countries. The biggest contributions to the UN High Commission for Refugees came from the United States, with great British support too. The high commissioner, Poul Hartling, took a close personal interest in our problems. The chairman of our refugee committee, Stephen Nkomo, worked closely with him to create the Victory Camp school outside Lusaka, which housed and gave an education to upwards of 8,000 girls. This was a tremendous enterprise, of great value. The education programmes for our young people depended very largely on Western countries' generosity: the Commonwealth Secretariat's special fund was of great value, and the British were large donors to that.

From the United States, which I visited regularly for my work at the UN, I received more personal kindnesses than official ones. I have already mentioned my friends Arthur and Matilde Krim, whose support to my family over many years was beyond thanks. I felt, too, the natural solidarity of many black Americans for Africa. But the fact that they are black does not make them less American, members of a culture which is very different from that of their ancestors.

On one occasion I was able to see at first hand the difficulties that black Americans have faced. This was in May 1979, when Morehouse College in Atlanta, Georgia, did me the great honour of conferring on me the honorary degree of Doctor of Laws. On my early visits to the United States I had been discouraged by my hosts from visiting the southern states, for obvious reasons. The great strides made since then towards racial justice had, they told me, changed all that, and a warm welcome was prepared for me in Atlanta, the capital of what they called the New South.

Unfortunately the reputation of an African freedom-fighter was more than the defenders of the Old South could stand, and the Ku Klux Klan turned out in force to greet me. I saw little of the demonstration, and I am sure it would not have bothered me. But the resulting security precautions, and the political turmoil that surrounded them, meant that the mayor of Atlanta felt it desirable to attend an engagement elsewhere, and I was hustled in and out of the degree ceremony in an almost surreptitious way. The honour conferred on me was not diminished, but the occasion was certainly tarnished.

My own position was clear. I was prepared to accept support for the Zimbabwean cause wherever it came from, provided it was not in exchange for future commitments. Newspapermen used regularly to ask me where my funds came from, and I would reply that I would be glad to take anything they offered, and be photographed taking it, to help Zimbabwe. One generous personal contributor was the British-based international businessman, Tiny Rowland, the man whose contacts both with the South African government and with President Kaunda facilitated my release, and that of the other nationalist leaders, from detention in 1974.

Tiny Rowland was, and still is, the chief executive of one of the larger multinational companies operating in Africa, Lonrho. His company's interest in bringing peace to southern Africa was obvious. It had mines or farms or other businesses in practically every country of the region, and in particular it owned the oil pipeline from the Mozambique port of Beira to Salisbury, which could not operate as long as United Nations sanctions were in force against the illegal regime in Rhodesia.

I knew this when I was introduced to Rowland in Lusaka by President Kaunda shortly after my release from detention, and naturally I was wary of the implications. At no time did I have any dealings with Lonrho as a company. My relations were purely with Tiny Rowland as an individual, his with Joshua Nkomo. This was understood from our brief first meeting.

We met again shortly afterwards in Botswana. He described his business interests. I remarked that some multinational companies were making a lot of money out of the Smith regime, and I asked him whose side he was on. He said he was on the side of his friend President Kaunda: 'I run my business in Zimbabwe, and if you people take over the country and run it in what you believe to be the interest of the people, I accept that.' He said that if I had problems and needed help, he would see what he could do for me personally.

Critics have grossly exaggerated Tiny Rowland's influence, saying, for example, that he was behind President Kaunda's campaign for peace and dialogue. This is grossly unfair. It was landlocked Zambia that bore the brunt of the struggle, and paid the heaviest economic price, when Mozambique and Angola were fighting for independence, and when Zimbabwe was fighting for its freedom. Of course Zambia had a real interest in peace – and President Kaunda is, moreover, a man who hates bloodshed. To imply that he was under the influence of the head of a private company is absurd: Kaunda is head of an independent state, and his power is vastly greater than any private businessman's.

As I got to know Tiny I came to trust him. His charming wife Josie is Zimbabwean-born, and Tiny has become one of us. I began to regard him as a son-in-law, what we call the *mkwenyana*, one of the family by marriage. He made generous contributions to me.

His most important contribution was airline tickets. I was constantly travelling, usually with two or three assistants: all I had to do was to ring up Tiny's office and the tickets would be ready. I was travelling between Belgrade and Moscow, or New York and Havana, on tickets provided by this great capitalist. He knew where we were going, but we never discussed it. The help was personal, not political, which was why I could take it. I used it for my country, not for myself, but Tiny never asked.

Rowland did not appear to want anything in return, or to be planning for me to take high office after independence. He once said that, since I had worked so hard and had had such tough times, he would help me to rest if that was what I wanted. He said he had a business in Mexico where he had more personal control than in his Lonrho activities, and if I was interested in coming in with him in Acapulco, I could have an easy life there and welcome. I said my duties would not end until Zimbabwe was free, and that if I had business interests they would be in Zimbabwe.

It was never a secret that I was being helped by Tiny Rowland: it is less well known that he helped several other prominent people in my country's public life, both by contributing to their travel and secretarial costs and by sorting out some personal financial problems. It is for those others to say who they are, not for me. His generosity could have brought me considerable personal wealth, inside or outside Zimbabwe. If that had been the case, I do not think Robert Mugabe's government would have charged me with the offence of trying to export the sum of $300 in Zimbabwean currency. That was hardly a rich man's crime. Nor would I have arrived penniless in London when I left my country under threat of death in 1983 – when, once more, Tiny Rowland came to my aid at a difficult time.

This is not a list of my friends: that would make a book on its own, for I have been blessed in my companions. But I want to tell of three African leaders who have made their mark on my life. The first is the Emperor Haile Selassie, the old man who by tradition ruled his people in God's name, and who was surrounded by court officials who behaved as though they were bound by the Almighty to obey him. You could tell that the emperor realised all that was out of date, but he was powerless to change it. The palace lions devoured whole carcasses of oxen while at the palace gates the people were starving. His regime was indefensible, but the man himself was kind. The difference between the ancient African regime of the emperor and the alien regimes of the colonial powers was not in the gulf between the rulers and the ruled: the colonial governors lived far above the standard of the common people, and so did the emperor. Yet his palace was not set apart in some remote suburb, but opened straight into the crowded slums of his capital. I think he understood in his heart the real problems of Africa, and I believe that was why, towards the end of his reign, he encouraged the growth of the Organisation of African Unity, and presided over its opening session. I was struck at the time by the difference between his regime and those that most of his fellow-rulers were trying to develop. His death marked the end of an era. I only wish he had been allowed to die in peace, maybe in exile, but free at least of the revenge of the rulers who succeeded him.

One of the first of the new generation of African rulers was Colonel Gadafi, of Libya, who generously helped us in the last stages of our war of liberation. He, too, came to power as the successor of an outworn monarchy, and I believe his style of government is intended more than anything to give his people the self-confidence and sense of national identity that they were never able to have before. Some of his policies are strange – it is not useful, for instance, to insist that all writing in the country be in Arabic when your pilots and mechanics are having to service jet aircraft with instruction manuals in European letters. But asserting that Arabic is a great international language is an honourable thing to do, and I understand why he does it.

I was driven out into the desert to meet Colonel Gadafi in 1975 or 1976. He was sitting on a mat, with camels nearby, beside an ancient castle, as his troops paraded past in their modern armoured vehicles. Through an interpreter I explained our problems to him, and his reply was to ask me how many men we wanted to train. When I said two thousand, he agreed at once; as soon as our troops were ready he sent aircraft down to Zambia and flew them up to Libya – he did not have enough long-range planes of his own, so he hired Bulgarian ones, and our men were given uniforms, weapons and a full training in how to use them. That was the promptest and most generous help we ever received with our military efforts.

Another African leader whom I greatly admire is General Obasanjo, the Nigerian who did something unheard of on our continent. He held absolute power in his country as head of state from 1976, when he succeeded his predecessor who had been murdered in an abortive *coup d'état*, until 1979. In that year the general peacefully and willingly handed over power to a new, democratically elected government.

Obasanjo, who thus set an example to the entire continent, is also a most kind and straightforward man. Once Robert Mugabe and I went to Nigeria, but we were unable to agree on a joint negotiating position. As our conversations dragged fruitlessly on, General Obasanjo told us firmly that it was impossible to run a campaign under two co-leaders. What Zimbabwe needed, he said, was a single, decisive man in charge. 'My suggestion to you two,' said the general, 'is that I lend you a pair of pistols and send you out into the field. There you fight it out fairly, in a duel, and the one who comes back in here is the one who will run the nationalist movement. That is the way to bring down your illegal government.' All this was said with such good humour and conviction that Robert and I both laughed heartily together. I was grateful for the laughter, but sorry that our disagreements continued just the same.

Chapter 18
To the Bitter End

The last and bitterest stages of the Zimbabwe liberation war were entirely unnecessary. By 1977 Ian Smith's regime was doomed. The Portuguese hold in Mozambique and Angola had vanished. Even Smith's South African backers were urging him to settle. But still he went on fighting. Militarily he was losing ground as the nationalist forces penetrated deeper into the country. Politically, he tried to set up an internal deal which would preserve the power of the white minority but give his friends in the outside world some justification for claiming that Rhodesia was now multiracial and could therefore be recognised.

Smith's chosen ally in this attempt to fool the world was Bishop Abel Muzorewa, who with the creation of the Patriotic Front had lost his position as compromise spokesman for the two main nationalist groups. Smith also manoeuvred into his corner the more significant figure of Ndabaningi Sithole, who was bitter at the way he had been ousted from the leadership of Zanu. Some old African chiefs, salaried employees of the government, were also included in Smith's multiracial charade. In March 1978, the bishop, Sithole, Chief Jeremiah Chirau and the illegal prime minister signed an agreement for a one-year transition period leading to a new constitution for what they called Zimbabwe-Rhodesia. African co-ministers were brought into several key government ministries – but not, of course, into those running the war, which was intensified behind this cloak of respectability. It was vital that governments outside Rhodesia should understand that this was a fraud. International recognition would have greatly strengthened Smith's hand.

After the failure of the British-sponsored Geneva conference, the next significant international negotiations took place in Malta early in 1978, involving the Patriotic Front, the British and American governments and General Prem Chand, the United Nations military representative. Both British and American policies were becoming a little more realistic, since the men in charge of them had changed. Dr David Owen, the new British foreign secretary, was at least energetic, rejecting the usual British official attitude that there was nothing useful to be done about Rhodesia. He had visited southern Africa early in 1977, immediately after tours of the front-line states by Presidents Podgorny of the USSR and Castro of Cuba, and was working closely with the new Carter administration in the United States.

Carter's new secretary of state was Cyrus Vance, with a strong public commitment to human rights, and American policy towards Africa was in the hands of the black American Andrew Young, ambassador to the UN, who was emotionally sympathetic to our cause. The Malta talks, reconvened in April in Dar es Salaam, were looking for a way of ensuring a period of peaceful transition in which elections could be held as a precondition of independence under majority rule. We hoped that the UN could be involved in supervising that period, and General Chand introduced us to the complicated security arrangements that would be necessary, including in particular the 'three-in-a-jeep' formula by which UN supervisory personnel would keep the peace jointly with security people from Smith's forces and the Patriotic Front.

The discussions did not involve the Smith regime, and had no practical effect. Short of supplying weapons to the nationalist armies, or imposing an effective embargo on Smith's South African suppliers, there was perhaps nothing positive the Western governments could do to bring down the illegal regime. I had the impression that both Owen and Young would have liked to do more than they were allowed to by their governments: at one point in Malta, Owen, who was much more experienced than Young, had to remind his American colleague that he was expressing his nation's policies, not his personal inclinations.

The most important result was that Owen assured us that the British government would take no steps to recognise any new government in Rhodesia until a conference had been held involving all parties to the conflict. This assurance helped to restrain the Conservative government, elected in 1979, from recognising the puppet government of Bishop Muzorewa.

It was at this moment, I believe, that Ian Smith's resolution cracked. I had always believed it would, and my international contacts began to confirm it. Messages reached me that he was ready to surrender. I did nothing until the same message arrived by way of President Kaunda. The one thing I was determined to avoid was being manoeuvred into any deal which could be misinterpreted as a secret bargain between myself and Smith. If there were to be talks, I insisted that the front-line presidents should be involved, and that Zanu should play its full part. But I knew the suspicious nature of the Zanu leadership, which was far from being under Robert Mugabe's control. I feared that if I myself broached the subject to them, they would suspect that I was playing a trick, and denounce me for seeking to join in Smith's so-called 'internal settlement'.

Despite this risk, I agreed to talk to Smith, face to face. In absolute secrecy we met in State House, Lusaka, as the guests of Kenneth Kaunda. I found Smith a tired man, a battered man. He told me he wanted to surrender power, to hand the whole thing over; I am convinced that he knew the game was up, that the time had come to concede defeat. But I could not on my own accept his offer. I told him that the important thing was his agreement to surrender power. But I also stated that the mechanics of the surrender was not something he could discuss with me alone. I had to bring in Robert Mugabe, my colleague in the Patriotic Front: it was to the PF that power must be surrendered, not to Joshua Nkomo or Zapu. Smith was critical of me: he asked President Kaunda why I was acting like that, did I not have the authority to settle? Kenneth, of course, supported my position that I could not finish the conflict on my own; it was the Patriotic Front that mattered.

I needed to convince Robert Mugabe, and his principal backer, Julius Nyerere, that it was worth talking to Smith, and I needed to do so through an intermediary who could not possibly be suspected of trying to advance my own or any other sectarian interest. I therefore, in close consultation with Kenneth Kaunda, decided to ask the Nigerian government for help. The then military government of Nigeria, headed by General Obasanjo and with Brigadier Joe Garba as the head of the foreign ministry, had already shown in many ways their commitment to liberation for Zimbabwe: I believed that a proposal from them would be sure of acceptance by Mugabe and Nyerere.

I therefore spoke to Brigadier Garba in London, assuring him of my information that Smith wished to hand over power, and informing him that I would do no business with Smith unless Robert Mugabe was fully involved. Garba discussed my proposition with General Obasanjo, who agreed to help and asked Robert to visit him in Nigeria. Robert understood and accepted the proposal for joint talks with Smith: all that was necessary was the agreement of Julius Nyerere and of Samora Machel, the president of Mozambique.

Once again State House in Lusaka was the venue for a meeting: there were present all five front-line presidents, Brigadier Garba, Robert Mugabe and myself. Mugabe himself had specifically agreed to take part in the new surrender discussions with Smith. But once more Nyerere's suspicions of me were too much for him. He said that this was a Nkomo thing, and he could not advise that Mugabe let himself in for it. Lacking unanimity, the talks could not go ahead. Smith was prepared to travel up to Lusaka as soon as our preliminary talks were complete. He was notified that his presence was not useful, and so the hope ended.

The Nigerians, understandably enough, withdrew from the whole business. They said they had, at our request, promoted the initiative and got the meeting going. But if there was quibbling and jealousy in southern Africa, that was beyond them and there was nothing more they could do to help. I told Julius Nyerere to his face that he was a saboteur, that he had thrown away the certainty of a quick surrender by the Smith regime. He replied that I was wrong.

Smith, who naturally did not know the details of our internal differences, may have had it in mind to hand over power to Nkomo. But neither with him, nor with the Zambians, nor with the Nigerians, had I ever given any indication of accepting that. The offer I wished to accept was of a hand-over to the Zimbabwean nationalist movement in the Patriotic Front, which would then decide how to organise to accept it. Nyerere, as I have said, had for long shown an extraordinary personal resentment of me. Perhaps he feared that a quick settlement might have brought me to power in a free Zimbabwe. To avoid that risk he condemned my country to three more years of civil war.

Immediately after the fiasco of the talks that came to

nothing, our Zapu anti-aircraft team brought down the first of the civilian Viscount aircraft. Brutal reprisal raids followed, killing hundreds of boys and girls who, as the Red Cross and the UN High Commission for Refugees confirmed, were civilian trainees, not military personnel. The Rhodesian propaganda services lied about the raids, even arranging corpses with weapons alongside them for the international press to photograph.

Bishop Muzorewa was by now firmly locked into the Rhodesian government structure, not actually running anything but in a position where he had to take responsibility. I cannot imagine how his conscience allowed him to take a share in the atrocities committed by the increasingly desperate army and secret forces. I suppose he thought that he would get his reward when Smith made him prime minister.

Smith's election came in April 1979. All the powers of Smith's army were out to ensure that Africans went to the polls and voted as they were told. The Patriotic Front parties of course put up no candidates. Under the reign of terror, a turnout of 64 per cent was claimed, and Muzorewa won his expected huge majority under the new constitution, which kept the real power in white hands.

The only genuine change that Muzorewa's temporary victory seemed likely to bring was in Britain's attitude. A general election was coming up. The Labour party had fully accepted that the constitution of 'Zimbabwe-Rhodesia' was a cheat, and had refused to send observers to the elections held under it. But the Conservatives sent their own observers, as Smith's guests: their leader was Lord Boyd, who had been involved in Rhodesian affairs since I had met him as Alan Lennox-Boyd during the negotiations to break up the Central African Federation in 1963.

The British election immediately followed the Rhodesian one: Margaret Thatcher and the Conservatives were elected, and promptly received Lord Boyd's report saying that Muzorewa had won fairly. Mrs Thatcher began to drop hints that her party would meet its election promise to recognise the Smith-Muzorewa regime: British recognition might well have meant that international sanctions against the regime would crumble. Once again I began an urgent round of international travel to muster support.

Nigeria, in particular, came to our help by cutting British firms out of the bidding for some big contracts, warning that there would be no new orders until the British government clarified its attitude. The best chance of checking Mrs Thatcher's progress towards recognition would come in Lusaka in July, where President Kaunda would be host to the two-yearly summit meeting of Commonwealth heads of government. This was a forum in which the Zimbabwe liberation movement had many advantages.

The Commonwealth summits, bringing together Britain with a large number of countries that had won independence from British rule, had a natural interest in the Rhodesian affair. As far back as 1966 they had set up a committee to support UN sanctions against the illegal regime, and had begun a successful scheme for helping with the eduction of our refugees. In 1975, soon after my release, I had visited (along with Muzorewa, Sithole and Chikerema) their summit in Jamaica: I stayed on after my colleagues had left, and was allowed to speak to an informal session of the summit meeting. As well as the Commonwealth African leaders, who were all of course on our side, I was assured of support by the then prime minister of Jamaica, Michael Manley, by Forbes Burnham of Guyana, and by Pierre Trudeau of Canada. The Commonwealth secretary-general, Sonny Ramphal, well understood the importance of our stand. India had supported majority rule ever since their representative in Salisbury had introduced me to Kenneth Kaunda, back in the 1950s. Countries as remote as Malaysia and Australia had come to recognise our problems through their Commonwealth connections.

This international backing was important now that the presence of Muzorewa as the nominal head of the Zimbabwe-Rhodesia government was leading some well-meaning but ignorant outside observers to ask what more we wanted, now that there was a black man in office in Salisbury. It was being argued that we should go home and try to change things internally – which I knew was impossible, since the change in power was a sham. But as far as the Commonwealth summit was concerned, our only worry was with its least experienced member, Margaret Thatcher – and, since Britain was still theoretically the colonial power for Rhodesia, she was the one who mattered.

At the Lusaka conference itself the heads of government met with no outsiders present, so I had to stay very much in the background, trusting our friends to convey the necessary messages. We owe a lot to Michael Manley of Jamaica and – perhaps more surprisingly – to Malcolm Fraser, then prime minister of Australia, whose political background had much in common with Mrs Thatcher's own. She had visited Australia immediately before the conference, and there she had publicly said she doubted whether the British House of Commons would continue with economic sanctions against Rhodesia when they came up for renewal in November. Fraser undoubtedly did a great deal to persuade her that this would damage Britain's own interests and reputation.

But the real persuader was Kenneth Kaunda himself. It is impossible to talk to him and fail to be won over by his sincerity. It was at the official conference ball, when he danced with Margaret Thatcher and you could see them both smiling in genuine friendship, that I began to believe that even this British prime minister would come to see the reality – that the only road to political stability in southern Africa led through the establishment of a genuinely democratic government in Zimbabwe. In that spirit the British agreed in Lusaka to accept, at last, the constitutional responsibility they had for so long ignored. A constitutional conference would be held of all the parties to the conflict to prepare for genuinely free elections and independence under a negotiated constitution.

It was necessary to keep up the pressure on Britain, and to keep open the possibility of a UN involvement in the transition to majority rule. I travelled to Havana for the non-aligned summit conference, where I was able to make much closer contacts with Third World leaders than had been possible at the Commonwealth meeting, and to address the full conference. But even there the pressure on us to reach a settlement was intense. The front-line states were being ruined by the war, to South Africa's advantage. Everyone was sick of the killing.

Then, at last, it was time to leave for the Lancaster House talks at which the war was to be ended and the new independence constitution at last agreed. On every possible occasion in the past, the British government had dodged its political responsibilities towards our people, while insisting on their own constitutional supremacy. The Conservative party was openly hostile to our cause, and Mrs Thatcher was obviously playing a devious game with her own supporters. The foreign secretary, Lord Carrington, who was to chair the conference, had the usual links with old-style imperialism in southern Africa, through his past directorship of the vast multinational company, Rio Tinto Zinc. Even if these people were prepared to hand over power to the people of Zimbabwe, we suspected they wanted to do so on terms that would make it impossible to govern as decisively as was necessary in a country at the end of fifteen years of civil war.

The British wanted a constitution which would 'safeguard' the political power of the white Zimbabweans, and thus preserve the resentment against them that they had earned by their past conduct. They wanted a constitution on the so-called 'Westminster model', with a ceremonial head of state and an executive prime minister – exactly the pattern that had been rejected as unsuitable by most African states. We wanted an electoral system with no racial bias, and a strong executive presidency. On both points we reluctantly gave ground to British arguments. The pressure on us to accept the second best was intense: the alternative was to continue a war of which everyone was sick, and to accept that if this attempt at a settlement failed, the British would probably wash their hands of the whole affair.

The most hopeful aspect of the Lancaster House proceedings was the cooperation that built up between Robert Mugabe and myself as leaders of the two wings of the Patriotic Front. Every morning and lunchtime our two delegations sat down together and agreed on our position. The working problems were minimal. Socially, though, the two delegations lived quite separately. Zapu had the advantage of having rooms at reduced rates in the Metropole Hotel, and was provided with offices and secretarial help that were finally used by both parties. The Zanu delegation, who were receiving exactly the same lodging allowances as us, moved into flats where they looked after themselves. I am afraid it looked as though any money they saved in this way was spent on whisky.

Our relationships with the white delegates from the

Rhodesian Front party were dominated by the knowledge that we were still at war, that as we talked people were fighting and dying. There was no friendship between us; there could not be. Ian Smith himself seemed a beaten man, hardly speaking. The most forceful personality from the white Rhodesian Front party was the finance minister, David Smith (who was no relation). But as time went on, in the coffee breaks, we began to grumble together about the English weather and exchange occasional smiles. That, at least, was progress.

It was harder to make human contact with Bishop Muzorewa's team. The bishop seemed to have decided that his only chance of political survival lay in sticking fast by the hard-line whites. He talked like an old-time settler, impatient with the talking, threatening to break off and go home, where, he said: 'After all, I have a country to run.' It was upsetting to hear a black man identify so strongly with the Smith regime that he referred to our guerillas as 'terrorists' – while the soldiers serving under him as 'prime minister' were conducting those savage raids on our civilian camps across the border.

Lord Carrington as chairman arranged the conference as far as possible so as to avoid direct confrontations between the two sides. Before each plenary session he would organise separate meetings, first with the other side and then with the Patriotic Front. This meant that we would find ourselves confronted with some deal worked out between Carrington and Muzorewa, and when we argued against it we would be told that altering the terms would mean the conference breaking down. By dealing with each side separately, Lord Carrington put himself at the centre of a spider's web, of which he alone could pull the strings. One day, in good spirits, I told him I was going to call him Spider: he managed to laugh, but I think he was angry.

The British and the Rhodesians had many common interests, which they used the conference to preserve. Even after the fifteen years of illegal independence, British companies still had as large a stake in the country as the local whites – not just in mines, manufacturing and service businesses, but also in land, which was the great point of argument. We said that the new constitution of Zimbabwe should permit the government to expropriate farmland if it was not being properly used. The British said fine, so long as we paid the full market price. But we knew that vast acreages were lying idle, unused and therefore without a market price, in the areas formerly reserved for white ownership. To buy areas adequate for resettling the many land-hungry African farmers who had been confined within the former tribal trust areas would be beyond the financial ability of the new state.

What we wanted was an arrangement like that made for Kenya at independence, whereby the British government itself would compensate farmers whose land was taken over in the interest of efficiency and food production. The British argued that the settlers in Rhodesia had been independent for a long time, and Britain could not now take responsibility for them. We replied that we did not regard the white farmers as settlers: as far as we were concerned they were Zimbabweans, and financial arrangements should be made to see that their Zimbabwean land was properly used.

This was the one point at which the Americans were helpful. They said they could not use their taxpayers' money to compensate inefficient landowners for not using land. But, if the British would help to buy the land, American funds could be used to develop it. Neither the British nor the Americans would tell us how much they would put up, but the principle was a useful one.

Behind the scenes a time-bomb was ticking away, and nobody but myself and senior Zapu colleagues knew of its nature. A year previously, Zapu and Zipra, in the closest secrecy, had decided that the war must be ended, the agony could not be allowed to drag on. We had set in motion what we called the 'turning-point' strategy, for a transformation of the war from a guerilla operation into a full-scale conflict in which we would match the Smith regime's armour and air cover with armour and air cover of our own. We had requested the Soviet Union to accelerate the training of our aircrews in that country, and to make available sophisticated modern aircraft which could strike on equal terms against Rhodesian strategic installations, communications and fuel supplies. We had also asked them to speed up delivery of tanks, armoured cars and personnel carriers, and to intensify the training of their crews in the USSR.

Without air cover we knew we could not conduct successful

ground operations against the Rhodesian army. Our plan was therefore to mount a lightning ground strike across the Zambezi, in order to seize the airfields at Victoria Falls and at Makuti, using armoured vehicles and amphibian transports. The airfields, once acquired, would enable our aircraft to fly in and operate freely from our own soil, putting us on a level with Smith's armed forces. (For security reasons, the plan was not coordinated with the Zanla army – but we assumed that when our attack began, Zanla would at once press into renewed guerilla activity, engaging large numbers of Rhodesian troops on the eastern front.)

The Soviet authorities had responded to our request, and we were assured that the training of our aircrews could be completed a year in advance, in time for the end of 1979. Some tanks and armoured vehicles had already been moved with their crews into Zambia. Arrangements were under way for the necessary supplies of fuel and ammunition and all the other complex logistical matters involved in running an intensive modern war. All this was well advanced when I and my senior colleagues became involved in the intricate constitutional discussions at Lancaster House. The suspense arose from the fact that operational decisions would have to be made well ahead of the actual military operations – the necessary movements of men and materials, involving huge distances and vast quantities of hardware, could not be altered or even modified overnight. Once we said go, we would have to go – but meanwhile there was the chance of final victory by negotiation.

Of course none of this could be even hinted at in our discussions in London. The moment at which we most nearly decided to launch our plan – which would have been irreversible – was when Rhodesian aircraft methodically bombed several strategic bridges within Zambia that would have been absolutely necessary if our tanks and armoured vehicles were to move into position to strike against the airfields across the Zambezi. I was positive that the only way the Rhodesians could have known of the significance of those particular bridges was by detailed knowledge of our plans. Such knowledge could only have reached them in one way, and that was through information collected by British intelligence in London. (In particular I was not certain that our communications were secure, despite the careful code procedures we followed.)

At this point Margaret Thatcher called publicly on both sides to issue orders that the fighting should be scaled down in order to allow the peace talks to proceed. I protested vigorously at this, saying that the only escalation of the conflict had been the Rhodesian attacks on the Zambian bridges: I added that these were deplorable attacks on civilian targets in a country not involved in the fighting. Zipra's forces, I said, consisted merely of guerillas who moved about on foot, so the major road bridges could not be military targets since we did not even use them. But I am fairly sure that the British had a very good idea of what was really going on – and I could not discuss that with them without giving our whole secret operation away.

On the swift conclusion of the Lancaster House talks, in success or in failure, depended the start of a military operation that would certainly have involved an intensification of the war, and could have escalated into an international conflict. Nobody outside my inner circle knew exactly how much was at stake in a speedy conclusion to the conference.

The last stage of the argument dragged on, and was the hardest. It concerned the cease-fire and what happened to the fighting men of both sides during it. We had wanted a UN force to keep the peace, on the lines tentatively discussed with General Chand in Malta and later. In the end we settled for a Commonwealth force under British command, which was enough (perhaps because it was never threatened by either side). Our great anxiety was lest the Rhodesian forces, perhaps with South African support, should use the cease-fire period to attack our people: a token international supervisory force could not prevent this, and our soldiers would be wide open to attack while moving in from their bases outside the country to concentrate in the designated assembly points.

The British and the Rhodesians were used to armies with radios and telephones and trucks for transport. They could hardly imagine troops who got their messages physically, by messengers, and who moved around the country on foot. When we explained this, they thought we were confessing that we did not really control our soldiers, that they were just uncoordinated bands of guerillas. In the end we proved to them, by the efficiency and discipline of our redeployment, that even without modern equipment our armies could be moved efficiently and in disciplined bodies of men. It struck me that they had no idea how strong our human organisation was: they really did not believe that we could create such a fighting force.

The last point was to persuade them that, if the Rhodesian army was to be described as 'security forces', our soldiers should be called by the same name. But in the end a form of words was found, and the conference document was ready for signature.

Of course the new constitution was not satisfactory. It was the result of muddle and compromise, reached in haste to stop the bloodshed. It was dangerous to reserve twenty of the one hundred seats in parliament for white members elected by a whites-only electorate. It was foolish to provide for a president with no power. But at least the so-called 'entrenched clauses' in the constitution were watered down. A constitution that cannot be changed if the people want change is not a democratic constitution, and democracy was what Zimbabwe needed. That was what I thought we had won when I signed the formal agreement on 21 December 1979.

At that moment I had expected to feel triumph in our victory. Instead what I felt was gratitude to all those who had struggled with us, in Zimbabwe and outside. In particular I thought of what we owed to the peoples of our neighbouring countries, who had stood firm alongside our own people under bombing and terror as our nation struggled to be born. I thought that now at last we could all stand together. The names we were putting at the bottom of that piece of paper were not for Zapu and Zanu, not even for the Patriotic Front, but for all the people of Zimbabwe – those who had made the sacrifice for independence and those who had fought against majority rule, black and white and coloured and Asian. In the new country we were about to create, I believed that the rights of all would be respected equally, and that our suffering would at last be rewarded by justice.

Next morning the task of building the nation was to begin. Robert Mugabe and I had agreed to meet and discuss the procedure for the elections that were due in three months' time. The Patriotic Front, formed in Dar es Salaam in 1976, had its own constitution as a political party, agreed between the central committees of Zapu and Zanu and signed in Addis Ababa early in 1979. Despite our long-standing difficulties, the two wings of the party had negotiated together at Lancaster House and established a working relationship and a degree of mutual confidence, at least at the top level.

It seemed to me, and to many others in the leaderships of both the Zapu and Zanu wings of the PF, that when the elections came we must fight them as a single party. But there was plenty to discuss about how that would be done, concerning the allocation of places on the party lists, the drawing up of a manifesto and the processes which would be most likely to lead both to the largest possible victory at the elections and to stable government after them. All this we were to tackle peacefully, before our return home to start the campaign and the difficult process of pulling back our armies within our own borders. This was our agenda.

As agreed, on the morning after the signing of the Lancaster House agreement, I went to Robert Mugabe's flat for our first talk. Nobody answered: the place was empty. I waited, with my good friend and colleague Ariston Chambati, who had kept a detailed account of all the proceedings at Lancaster House. After a while one of the junior Zanu people arrived.

'Where is Mr Mugabe?' I asked.

'Oh, he left this morning for Dar es Salaam,' came the reply.

That was the end of our agreement to talk, broken not by me but by Robert Mugabe and the leadership of Zanu. Next morning I heard on the radio that Robert, on arrival in Dar, had announced that he and Zanu would be fighting the elections on their own. The smiles of Lancaster House were left behind in London. The national campaign of reconciliation that I dreamed of remained a dream. I, and the fighters and followers of Zapu, had been deceived.

Chapter 19
The Doubtful Elections

We had fought and beaten the illegal regime in Zimbabwe. But
victory had not brought unity. I speeded up my return to
Lusaka and began the necessary work to ensure that our
triumph was completed in peace and good order. Our
arrangement with the Soviet Union for intensification of the
war had automatically lapsed as the cease-fire was agreed. I
asked my deputy, Josiah Chinamano, to go to Maputo and find
out from Robert Mugabe in person whether he was determined
to break our agreement and fight the election as a separate
party. I myself set out to prepare our troops for an orderly
return to the agreed assembly points within Zimbabwe.

I began by visiting one of our large camps just outside Lusaka
itself, accompanied by Lookout Masuku, the Zipra commander,
and Dumiso Dabengwa, the head of security. The soldiers were
full of enthusiasm, but also understandably anxious to know
exactly what their role would be over the next few weeks.
Dabengwa approached me with a shocking piece of news. The
man who had given me most hope of a peaceful settlement
between the two parties and their two armies was dead.

Josiah Tongogara was the member of the Zanu central
committee for military affairs. His personality, which had
already impressed me at the Geneva conference in 1976, had
been the great revelation of the Lancaster House conference.
Even the British officials who might have been most prejudiced
against a man of his militant background came to admire and
like him. He was a true patriot, dedicated to the unity of
Zimbabwe and impatient of unnecessary divisions, a key
member of the Zanu central committee who had won the
admiration of his Zapu counterparts.

I was confident that, within Zanu, Tongogara would be a
powerful voice for unity – all the more so because he would be
talking the same language within Zanla, their army. His key
role was, indeed, within that army, and on leaving Lancaster
House he had travelled straight back to Maputo to get in touch

with his soldiers. From there he had set off urgently, by night, for Zanla headquarters at Chimoio. On the road, in a crash, he had met his death. Chinamano was on the point of leaving for Mozambique. As well as my appeal for unity to Mugabe, he now carried another message of sorrow at their loss to Tongagara's party and family.

Zipra and Zanla were very different armies. Zipra, based in Zambia and operating into Rhodesia across the Zambezi, was organised purely as a fighting force under strict military discipline and political control. Zanla, on the other hand, had combined military action with political indoctrination. The terrain along the border between Mozambique and Zimbabwe allowed them much more freedom of movement. Their forces had cooperated closely with those of the Mozambican liberation movement, Frelimo, during the fighting against the Portuguese, and in the last days of the Smith regime President Samora Machel had authorised Mozambican forces to enter Rhodesia in cooperation with Zanla.

The task of the Zanla forces, with their Frelimo allies, was less to fight Smith's forces than to win support for Zanu at the expense of Zapu. Dangerous confusions arose. We received reports of unidentified bands of armed men speaking Portuguese, who raided communities that had hitherto been faithful to Zapu, beating or even killing Zapu party organisers, and compelling the people to shout slogans of which the clearest was 'Down with Nkomo'. Even before the cease-fire, when all energies should have been concentrated on defeating the Smith regime, Zanu was building up its political organisation in eastern Zimbabwe, along the Mozambique border.

After the war was over, President Samora Machel let me know that he had been well aware of his people's interference in Zimbabwe – he told me that Frelimo units had been sent right across Zimbabwe to the Botswana border, just, as the president put it, 'to find out how the fighting was going'. They did not do any fighting themselves. I protested that these men had harassed the population and organised anti-Nkomo propaganda, and President Samora did express his regret. President Nyerere in the same period knew well what was going on. He approached both the Soviet Union and the Cubans to persuade them to divert their arms supplies from Zipra to his friends in Zanla. Fortunately the Soviets would have none of it, and maintained their support for Zimbabwe through Zapu.

This was the regrettable political climate in which the difficult military task of bringing our troops back into the country had to be tackled. To me the most important fact appeared to be that we had fought the war on the same side, negotiated as one, and been victorious. It seemed a great disservice to the people of Zimbabwe to launch their independent history divided by party quarrels, not united by national feeling.

Robert Mugabe had shown by his quick get-away from Lancaster House that national unity was not his top priority. My messages inviting him to name the place for personal discussions on the approach to the election met no response. It was impossible to find out what he thought or what his party intended to do. The immediate problem was that of registering parties to contest the election. In the hope that, after all, it would be possible to fight the campaign as one party, under the Patriotic Front banner, I refrained until the very last moment from registering my own party.

If he would not join with us, we presumed that Mugabe would choose to campaign as Zanu, the name his political soldiers had drilled into the people in the areas under their control. But it turned out that the name was not available. Mugabe's former leader, Ndabaningi Sithole, had contested the 1978 elections, held under Ian Smith's tailor-made constitution, under the name of Zanu. He claimed the right to do the same this time, so Zanu was not available to Mugabe's party. At the very last moment our Zapu central committee learned that Mugabe's party had decided to campaign as Zanu (PF); we decided in a hurry to use the name Patriotic Front (Zapu). But so much time had passed that we were only able to qualify by a technicality.

Registrations should have been made at the British government offices in Salisbury. We sent ours to the British High Commission in Lusaka, and it arrived with only a few minutes to spare before the deadline expired. To avoid bad trouble this was accepted as a valid registration, so under our unfamiliar labels the campaign officially began. Now it was time to go home.

I had flown in often to Salisbury airport, sometimes in danger, sometimes in triumph. I had been greeted there by all sorts of receptions, from throngs of thousands to teams from the police Special Branch. This time was unlike all the others. After almost a century the signatures on that agreement at Lancaster House had brought in a constitution which, if operated in good faith, would protect the liberty of all the people – of the snakes and the lions of Zimbabwe, even the frogs, everything that moves in that country. The season of Christmas and the New Year, the height of the summer rains, had since my childhood been the time for celebrations and for friendship. There was never such a celebration in people's hearts as now, and I was thankful to have played my part in bringing it about.

The British were in charge of security for the transitional period of the elections, and they were playing it safe. At the airport itself the crowd was strictly limited. In the airport building I saw the tense faces of the immigration men, the customs officials and the police, who had turned out not to examine our bags and our passports, but to stare nervously at this unknown figure whom they had been taught to hate for so long, and who now might be preparing a terrible revenge. At my press conference they lined up at the back of the room, powerless and fearful of what I might say.

I spoke of reconciliation, of the war that was over, of the need to forget the past and start to build a nation in peace, where the people would not be divided by artificial barriers. I warned against the spirit of revenge: we were all citizens now, and must work together. I could see the relief on the faces of those white officials, and when the press conference was over the fear had dropped away from them. That was the start I had wanted.

The meeting with the people was planned for Highfields, near my home – not in the stadium, which was far too small, but on a vast patch of open ground beside it. The British military helicopter lifted off and swung round in a wide arc out of the city limits, and back into Highfields from the wrong direction. I realised that they were not leaving my safety to chance: anyone waiting along the predictable route would not have seen us pass over, or been able to take a shot if he had planned one.

Then I was down in front of the crowd, a mass of

Zimbabwean humanity united in the confidence that at last freedom was on its way. I spoke to them as I had so often spoken, but now with a message not of hope but of achievement, of thanks to the neighbouring countries who had made our struggle possible, of the need to forget hatred and start afresh. I felt that the people were speaking with my voice: there was no difference between us: we were one. The official estimate of the crowd that greeted me was over 150,000 people. When Robert Mugabe returned to the same airport two weeks later he was greeted by a similar gathering. I have no doubt that many of the same people turned out to see both of us come back: that was the mood of unity in the nation at the time.

Of course the work that followed was hard. The cease-fire arrangements contained obvious dangers and difficulties for our soldiers, and for our clandestine party workers, who had to come out of their secrecy and expose themselves to public view. Our people were fearful of treachery, of sudden air-strikes on the assembly points by the beaten defenders of the Smith-Muzorewa regime, even of an attack with South African backing on our people who were now out in the open. The discussions in our Zapu central committee were heated – whom could we trust, how should we proceed? Some of our units were too well hidden in the bush to be rapidly informed that the fighting was over, and radio messages might be taken by them as decoys set by the enemy. For their own sake and for the peace of the country we had to find them and convince them that they were no longer hunted men. As we located our people and gave them their new orders it was remarkable how they accepted discipline, took up their posts as soldiers in an organised army and rejoiced that peace was coming.

Lancaster House had provided for a brief and nominal period of British rule over the time of the elections. In truth I did not want them there – and I do not think they wished to be there. The arrangement was that there would be a British governor at the head of a British team to organise the elections. Military supervision of the three rival armies – the Rhodesian one, Zipra and Zanla – was by a Commonwealth monitoring force of soldiers from Britain, Australia, New Zealand, Kenya and Fiji, with the officer commanding, General Acland, being British. The Commonwealth also provided a small team of observers to report on the elections, and a group of British parliamentarians was also present.

The country was full of dangers. Some undercover units of the Smith regime continued their old dirty tricks, killing and provoking disorders. Bishop Muzorewa during his period in office had recruited a small force of so-called auxiliaries, dangerous and irresponsible gangs that refused to be confined to barracks along with the official forces of the Smith regime. Throughout the election campaign South African units remained inside Zimbabwe – perhaps ready for action, certainly gathering intelligence, anyway a danger.

The greatest threat to the fair conduct of the elections came not from any of these but from Zanla guerillas in the eastern areas of the country. At the cease-fire large numbers of fighting men loyal to Zanu were not withdrawn into the scheduled assembly points. They stayed on in the villages they had organised on a war footing, refusing to move or to allow anyone else to campaign there. No outsider was allowed in those places, on pain of death. The people were not allowed to know that there was an alternative to voting for Zanu (PF). Exercising our democratic rights, PF (Zapu) put up candidates and tried to campaign throughout the country. Two of our candidates and eighteen of our party campaigners were killed by these adversaries. Many more were terrorised.

The key figure, whose job it was to see that the elections were fairly carried out, was the governor, Lord Soames, a veteran Conservative politician (and a son-in-law of Winston Churchill). He was a friendly and genial man. Personally I always had excellent relations with him. I had the impression that his health was not good, and that his main concern was to get home. Certainly, when it came to ensuring free elections, he broke his faith with me.

As the evidence accumulated of terrorism and mass intimidation in the eastern provinces of the country, Lord Soames summoned all the party leaders to Government House. He told us frankly that in certain areas intimidation was on such a scale that free and fair elections could not be conducted. I asked him to clarify this statement, and he made it clear that the offences were being committed by members of Robert Mugabe's Zanu (PF) party. I confirmed that my own PF (Zapu) party was unable to campaign in those areas, adding that neither Ian Smith's (all-white) party, nor Sithole's Zanu nor Bishop Muzorewa's so-called United African National Council, could campaign there either.

I argued that the governor faced a grave decision. If he withheld the right to vote from the people of those areas, he would be denying them what was in the constitution that it was his duty to uphold. If elections could not be fairly held in some areas, I said, the voting there should be postponed for up to six months; I did not maintain that voting should be postponed throughout the country. Lord Soames at the time agreed, and said so.

Yet two days before the poll the governor changed his mind and decided that elections could be held on the due date even in the disturbed eastern districts. He never called me in to explain this decision, nor did he give me the chance to put my case against his change of mind. I am convinced that his conduct was wrong, and can only be explained by Lord Soames's wish to get clear of the situation as soon as he could. But such a grave decision cannot have been made by the governor alone. It must have been confirmed by orders from Whitehall. Somewhere locked away in Government House for this whole period was Sir Anthony Duff, the senior Foreign Office official whom I had regarded at Lancaster House as the chief of the hard-line British faction. I do not think Lord Soames acted on his own initiative, but I think he acted wrongly all the same.

I raised the question of intimidation personally with Robert Mugabe. He brushed it aside, and paid no attention. Some of my party officials tried to discuss the matter with their Zanu (PF) opposite numbers – people they knew well and had worked with for years. Their response was simply to deny that the intimidation had anything to do with the party leadership. If there was intimidation that was entirely the responsibility of local people, and outside the control of party headquarters.

In some districts I do not believe that my party's candidates could have won, intimidation or not. But the British election supervisors in an interim report had told the governor that more than half of the electorate was living in conditions where a free vote could not take place. Zapu was cheated out of some seats that it could have won, given a fair campaign. I suspect that Bishop Muzorewa's party was also cheated out of several seats. I was aware of this before the votes were counted. But there were two compelling reasons why I could not force my justified objections to a head and call for a full investigation. To do so would have delayed the whole electoral process until well after the date when our people had been promised their independence. Worse, Zanu (PF) would undoubtedly have resisted the claim, probably with violence. There was a real risk that the price of fair elections would have been a renewed civil war – this time between Africans.

Lord Soames's other breach of faith with me came four days before the elections were due. Perhaps sensing that the result would not be a fair one, he asked me to go to the assembly points at which my Zipra soldiers were concentrated and appeal to them to accept the result of the elections however they might turn out. I did so. I went to the people and told them that we had fought for our independence, and we were on the verge of getting it. These elections were in remembrance of those who suffered and those who died in the fight for freedom. Many had no graves, and could have no stone over them. Their memorial would be the elections which, in a rough and ready way, would tell us the views of the people, by which we were bound to abide.

Robert Mugabe had been asked by the governor to deliver the same message to the men in the camps which his party controlled. Mugabe had not done so, Lord Soames knew he had not done so, and Lord Soames did not inform me of that. I do not think that was honourable.

Voting took place on three days: 27, 28, and 29 February, Wednesday, Thursday and Friday. The count took place on the Sunday and Monday; the results were announced on the Tuesday. During that period the following things happened. On the Saturday, President Julius Nyerere publicly announced that the elections had not been free and fair. About the same time Robert Mugabe left Zimbabwe and later met General Walls, the commander of the former Rhodesian army. The two men went to Maputo in Mozambique, where they met General Malan, the top man in the South African army.

Mugabe went on to Dar es Salaam. On his arrival there he

stated – before the result was announced – that his party, Zanu (PF), was going to win fifty-six out of the one hundred seats in the new parliament of Zimbabwe. (He was out by one: they won fifty-seven seats.) Mugabe then visited President Nyerere, and at once Nyerere made a statement that the elections had been free and fair. Nyerere had reason to be glad. Robert had not been his first choice as leader of Zanu: Julius originally preferred Ndabaningi Sithole, and only switched his support to Mugabe when Ndabaningi was definitively rejected by the commanders of his Zanla army. Mugabe's great virtue in Nyerere's eyes was that he was not Nkomo.

The British role in the elections I do not pretend to understand. Up to the end, the governor's staff were still predicting that no party would get an outright majority; they certainly very much overestimated the support that Bishop Muzorewa's discredited party would receive. But one thing makes me very suspicious. After the count, the used ballot papers were flown specially to Britain, not to be stored as historic documents, but to be burned. It is hard to believe that that would have been done if there were nothing to hide.

On the Monday after the vote, at midnight, I received a phone call from the governor's spokesman, Nicholas Fenn: 'I am very sorry, but you have lost the elections.' Zanu (PF), he said, had won. With the count still not complete, Robert Mugabe's party had already got more than the fifty seats needed for an overall majority in parliament. The bishop's people had been knocked out. Mugabe would therefore be asked to form a government.

I could not believe it. But the official results confirmed the information. Leaving aside the twenty white seats, all won by Ian Smith's Rhodesian Front, Zanu (PF) had fifty-seven seats, PF (Zapu) twenty seats, the bishop's UANC three. It was beyond belief. I was deeply distressed. I desperately needed to talk to the one person who could comfort me, and who would surely need comfort.

I telephoned maFuyana in East Berlin. She had already heard the forecasts of the results on the BBC, gradually becoming firmer all evening in the view that my party had done very badly. MaFuyana was very emotional in her disappointment. So far away, we could not come to terms with this thing until we had spoken. I calmed her down, and she took part of the load from me. We had lived for so many long years, sometimes together, more often apart, but always waiting and working for this moment when the people of Zimbabwe would speak with their own clear voice. Now we heard this muddled sound. But it was easier to bear once we had spoken.

That my party should have won not a single seat in Salisbury, and only twenty seats in the whole western strip from Kariba right down to Beitbridge, I could not believe and still do not believe. Even the known and massive campaign of intimidation could not have achieved that. That the first elections in free Zimbabwe failed to reflect the people's will is something of which I am sure.

Chapter 20
Zimbabwe's False Start

I slept off the shock of the election's declared result and awoke still as firmly convinced that my party and my followers had been cheated. But I never seriously doubted what I had to do. Our nation had gained its independence by years of sacrifice. Any bickering now would inflame passions, divide the people and encourage the enemies waiting on our borders to destabilise the country. We had to accept what we were told. If we argued and won our argument it was possible that the results would be set aside. But then the only prospect was that Britain – whose colony we still in theory remained – would take control for a year, or two, or three, or five. Neither we nor the British could possibly want that.

First I had to consult my senior party colleagues. They were deeply disappointed and angry. Some had been candidates, declared defeated in constituencies where they knew a large majority of voters wanted them to win. The soldiers in particular were distraught: the Zipra commanders had used every ounce of their personal authority to persuade the men to stay quietly in their assembly points throughout the election campaign, despite many provocations. Now they would have to go back to those soldiers and tell them they had been cheated but must accept it.

To my relief and gratitude I found that my colleagues accepted my bitter analysis: there was nothing for it but to swallow the result and trust that the alleged victors would use their triumph generously and in good faith. So the message was passed along the party's well-tried chain of command, through the members of the central committee and the officers of Zipra. I myself gave them full support. It was not easy. The people knew as well as I did that the election was a cheat.

I told them that they had fought, and their comrades had died, so that the people of Zimbabwe could rule themselves. Everything else was secondary. What we had failed to win was government by our own party. But these elections had been run by the British: the next round, in five years or less, would be under the control of Zimbabweans themselves, and it was our duty to prepare for that, and to win fairly then. For the present the task was to create a national army and a national police force, and once those national institutions were created, free of foreign interference, they would – I really believed it – start to work on behalf of all the people of the nation.

This was what I told my people. I was careful never to put the question to a vote: there was a real danger that it might have gone the wrong way, unleashing forces that I could no longer control. I spoke, won their assent, and started planning for government.

Robert Mugabe did make an attempt to reconcile the nation to itself. In his cabinet of twenty-two members of parliament he included two white members of Ian Smith's Rhodesian Front party and four members of my own Patriotic Front. Between his naming as prime minister-designate on 4 March and the announcement of the cabinet list on 11 March he offered me the ceremonial post of president of the new republic, and I declined it.

I could not possibly have taken the presidency. Both Robert and I had often, publicly, criticised the constitution given to us by Britain specifically because it provided for this purely ceremonial office. In Britain the Queen – sanctified by tradition, standing as symbol of the nation far above day-to-day politics – fills an invaluable role. I can see why the British think other countries would benefit from imitating constitutional arrangements which work so well for them. But the historic British institution of the monarchy cannot just be exported to countries with quite different national traditions. Certainly I, as an active politician, could not possibly perform that role.

The ceremonial head of state would be obliged to sign documents and make public speeches composed by Zanu, embracing policies that I disagreed with and had in the past often denounced. By pretending to agree with those policies I would only bring myself, and the office of the presidency, into ridicule: if I expressed my disagreement I would be abusing my constitutional powers. Robert told me that the office of president was the most exalted in the country, and constitutionally he was right. But personally he was entirely wrong. For me, acceptance of the presidency would have meant retreating into an official prison, deprived of my right to speak my mind and take a lead on matters of great national importance. I had spent too much of my life in prisons for that to be attractive, or even possible. I was obliged to decline.

But the prime minister did see the importance of having me inside the government, to give a lead to that important section of the population that looked to me. His next offer was of the ministry of local government and housing. This was an important post, in which I believe I could have done much valuable work. In fact I longed to do it, and to get in contact once again with the ordinary people of the towns and the country areas that I knew so well. But there were still more important things to be done. I had visited the Zipra camps: I knew the mood of disillusion in which our young fighting people were living, after their long years of insecurity and combat, and the distrust born of the false election results that I had struggled to persuade them to accept. It was essential that one of the ministers responsible for security matters in the new government should have their absolute confidence.

With the full backing of my party colleagues it was therefore agreed that I should demand a senior ministry dealing with security matters. Robert Mugabe himself took the ministry of defence, responsible for the armed forces. I took the ministry of home affairs, in charge of the police. That seemed the formula best calculated to win the confidence of the fighting men of both armies and to contribute to the building of a real sense of impartial national security.

I moved into the same office from which for decades the ministers of the former regimes had watched and schemed. At this same desk that I now occupied they had signed the restriction orders and detention orders and exclusion orders, they had received the prison reports and operated the whole apparatus of a repressive state. At last, I thought, I had the chance to make sure that those bad days do not come back again, that the rule of law and the rights of the citizen are upheld at the same time as peace and order are preserved.

I was greeted on arrival at the ministry by the permanent secretary, Mr Claypole. We had met once before. That was when, in the early 1970s, the then minister for law and order,

Mr Lardner-Burke, visited the regime's prize prisoner in the Gonakudzingwa detention camp. What I best remembered of that visit was Lardner-Burke's polished shoe, crushing the intricate ants' nest that had given me so much pleasure. Mr Claypole was an efficient administrator in charge of an efficient office. Now, as minister, I had the chance to use this good machine for good ends.

Our nation had been divided, first by the foolish refusal of the ruling minority to share the fruits of development with those who had made it possible, and who outnumbered them at least twenty-five to one. Then the African leadership had been split by the period of forced exile or imprisonment and the conspiracies that festered in it. The people as a whole had taken no part in this division of their leadership. They had fought heroically for their freedom, and now it was won they wished to enjoy it in unity. This was the mood which the independence celebrations of Zimbabwe should have consecrated. But the event itself foreshadowed what was to come.

I had been a guest at the birth of many African nations, taking my place to represent the future of my country on the platform. I had sat with the Queen's representative, the outgoing governor, the new president and prime minister, the honoured guests, as the troops marched past, the old flag came down and the symbol of a new nationhood broke out at the top of the flagpole.

At midnight on 17 April 1980, Zimbabwe's turn had come at last. We were a nation as rich as any on the continent, well endowed with natural resources, with an infrastructure second to none in Africa. Our people, tried in the fire of combat, craved for peace, prosperity and, above all, unity. Many of those in the crowd at Rufaro stadium, of all parties and all colours, would not have grudged me the name of Father Zimbabwe. I had struggled for thirty years and more to see this moment come.

The stadium was crammed with people, packed on the rising terraces around the football pitch where the ceremony was to take place. On the saluting base, built out into the field, were the dignitaries: Prince Charles to represent the Queen; Lord Carrington and Lord Soames, the architects of Britain's hand-over; Mr Waldheim and Mr Ramphal, from the United

Nations and the Commonwealth; the front-line presidents; Mrs Gandhi of India and President Zia of Pakistan; the leaders and the ambassadors of so many countries that wished us well; the representatives of liberation movements that, like ours for so long, were struggling for freedom – the South Africans, the Namibians, the Palestinians.

Behind the saluting base were the benches for the junior ministers, the party officials and the supporting cast. At the back of those rows, in the dark by the radio commentators' box, where the television cameras could not see us and our supporters in the crowd could not single us out for their applause, places were reserved for maFuyana and myself. In the stadiums of Zimbabwe I had so often stood up to address the crowds, and found the words to express what they wished to say but had not yet articulated. Now I was hidden away like something to be scared of. My wife could scarcely restrain her tears at this symbolic humiliation.

Two hours before the midnight ceremony we had to be in our places. The time was passed with marches and demonstrations on the football pitch, transformed for the night into a parade ground. There was one great show-business attraction too. Michael Manley, the Jamaican prime minister who had helped our cause so much within the Commonwealth and the non-aligned nations, had brought with him the famous Bob Marley and his musicians. Outside the stadium swarms of people struggled to get in. The police, over-reacting, used tear-gas to repel them. Coughing and choking in our rear seats, maFuyana and I were helped and supplied with water for our streaming eyes not by the security services, but by a visiting journalist from London – an old friend, who would be embarrassed in this context to be named.

But even this squalid confusion could not spoil the ceremony. Back in the 1940s at Tjolotjo Government School I had been the prize student who hoisted the Union Jack in honour of our visiting prime minister, the disappointingly tiny Sir Godfrey Huggins with his glittering shoes. Now for the very last time that flag came down, and the colours of free Zimbabwe broke out into the air. I am not ashamed to say that I wept for joy.

We had accepted from Britain a constitution of whose

imperfections I was well aware, since I had methodically argued against them at Lancaster House. But we had signed it in the name of the people of Zimbabwe, and in their name we had to make it work. Whatever its faults, it enshrined the rule of law and the rights of the individual, and asserted the supremacy of the people through their representatives in parliament. Yet I was uncomfortably aware that previous regimes in our country had been subject to many of the same laws and conventions, but had nevertheless governed as if they did not exist.

The first months of the republic were bound to be dangerous times. At home, we had to transform three separate fighting forces – the former Rhodesian army, Zipra and Zanla – into a single national army and police. We had to try to meet the pent-up economic expectations of our people, and reassure the former privileged caste that they too were safe. Externally, we had to reestablish our commercial links with neighbouring countries, and face the probability that our most powerful neighbour, South Africa, would do her best to upset our progress.

It was my firm view that all these objectives could be most surely met if we stood strictly by the rule of law at home: no privileges, no exceptions, fairness and openness all round. But fairness and openness in government had to start at the top, in a cabinet fully answerable to parliament. If we wanted to change the system we had to keep the rules. We could not start from scratch, forgetting the history that had made our country what it was.

When we first walked into the cabinet offices, the white people could hardly believe it. Here were these terrorists from the jungle walking into a civilised building where civilised ceremonies take place – how could they understand this sophisticated machinery and make it work? In parliament the wigs and gowns of the speaker and the clerks, the pictures of past governors and prime ministers on the walls, the intricate rules of procedure – all these things were strange. We had been given a Westminster constitution, built up on hundreds of years of conventions, and we had to operate it through people many of whom found it an effort to express themselves in English, a foreign language. The block of twenty white MPs, veterans of the old parliament, were openly contemptuous of the inexperience of many of the new members. I did not mind: I knew that the new African members were speaking for the people.

In cabinet we had behind us many years of experience in running guerilla organisations. The cabinet system is much the same as any managerial committee system: each minister concentrates on his special functions, while the prime minister tries to keep the whole picture in sight and to ensure that general policy is followed by all. At the start I was so busy on the details of my own job that I had no time to think about rivalries and plots. Perhaps the things that others were up to slipped by me because of that.

The underlying problem was that the Zanu ministers – sixteen out of the twenty-two of the cabinet – regarded their party central committee as more important than the cabinet or parliament itself. This was unconstitutional, and in practice it was dangerous. Zanu had been set up on the back of tribal feelings, stirred up in the first place by Shona-speaking exiles who exploited it as a way of attacking my own leadership. Once that spirit is out of the bottle there is no telling where it will go. The Zanu central committee had developed into a balancing act between the various Shona-speaking groups. Nothing could be decided rationally: everything rested on the calculation of advantage between those groups.

Robert Mugabe, whose intelligence should have set him above this faction-fighting, had become its servant. He had included in his cabinet several ministers whose only qualification for the job was their membership of some Zanu faction. Gross acts of irresponsibility by ministers went unchecked, because the prime minister appeared unwilling to upset his internal party balance. The interests of those outside Zanu – including those of the two non-Zanu parties represented in the cabinet, Zapu and the whites-only Rhodesian Front – were forgotten. White people, as much citizens of Zimbabwe as anyone else, felt themselves under threat. My own job began to seem impossible.

As minister of home affairs my main task was to create a new national police force from three separate elements – the former white-run police, Zanla and Zipra. After the cease-fire the guerilla armies had been confined, by agreement, to assembly points under their own commanders. These areas contained their fair share of tough and turbulent young men – a guerilla army is not created out of quiet stay-at-homes. For the peace of the country it was essential to offer them a stable future. Some could be absorbed in the national army and police, some had to be offered jobs or land. Demobilisation began much more slowly than any of us would have wished. Unemployment, spreading in Zimbabwe as in practically every other country in the early 1980s, made the quest for jobs unexpectedly hard. The promised international aid for rebuilding our shattered economy was coming through less generously than we had been led to believe.

The Zipra boys were getting the worst of it. The private deals of Zanu ministers produced some results for their own Zanla people, but much less for ours. Men of the former Zanla army were moving around the country, acting as Zanu agents and stirring up antagonism against Zipra, who were cooped up in their camps with little to do and often without adequate food and supplies. The two ex-Zipra commanders now serving as generals on the Joint Military Command were Lookout Masuku, the former commander, and Dumiso Dabengwa, the former head of security. They both regularly visited the camps and tried to reassure the lads that their interests were being looked after in difficult circumstances. I was careful not to show partiality to Zipra, but I accompanied the generals from time to time and spoke to the men of the need for national unity.

Of course there were outbreaks and breaches of discipline. I detested the powers vested in me as minister of home affairs under the continuing emergency legislation: it had been introduced under the former Smith regime in 1965, and kept intact by the new government. But if I was satisfied of the need, I was prepared to sign orders for detention without trial, and I did so against more than two hundred soldiers guilty of breaches of the peace. All of them were members of my ex-Zipra army.

Shortly an unforgiveable breach of the peace occurred. Ndabaningi Sithole and some of his remaining followers were travelling on political business – talking, I thought, nonsense, but perfectly lawful nonsense. They were attacked by a group of ex-soldiers. One of Sithole's followers was killed, Sithole himself survived only by spending the night in hiding. It was clear where the attackers had come from. The police were unable to track them down. They were Zanla people, and the Zanu hierarchy frustrated the attempt to identify them.

On a separate occasion nine Zapu officials were arrested and detained without trial. The police did not inform me as minister. It turned out that it was not the official police force that had effected the arrests. After thirty days the detention orders fell due for confirmation by me as minister. I refused to sign the orders, since I did not know the reason for them. The ministerial seal was taken from my office during my absence and new orders were illegally prepared without my signature. It was official gangsterism, with a majority within the government preventing ministers from doing their duty.

I was determined to keep the young men of both armies under control. I did not want them hanging around the towns, and I knew that if trouble did break out among them it would be more easily controlled in the countryside. Some of my Zanu ministerial colleagues argued – understandably enough – that the soldiers deserved some relaxation, and could not be shut away for ever in remote districts. I argued publicly against this, but was overruled. Ex-Zanla and ex-Zipra camps were set up side by side on the outskirts of the big cities. Sure enough, trouble broke out there.

The first fighting occurred in Bulawayo early in November 1980. Zanu organised a party rally at the White City stadium in the western suburbs of Bulawayo. The speakers, including several Zanu ministers, insulted Zapu, insulted me as its leader, and said that all minority parties should be crushed. The most violent speaker was my fellow-minister Enos Nkala. Immediately afterwards rifle shots were fired into the Zipra camp at Entumbane nearby. Zipra fired back into the neighbouring Zanla camp.

The soldiers of both forces had been allowed by agreement to keep their personal weapons. But Zanla now brought out and used heavy weapons, mortars and rocket-launchers, which they were not entitled to possess. Civilian lives were lost and much property damaged in the firing. Sixty people on all sides were killed. When the news reached the camps in Salisbury similar disturbances broke out on a smaller scale. Senior officers of both sides had to go to the camps of their own men and arrange a cease-fire.

It was apparent – and the subsequent commission of inquiry confirmed it – that Zipra had kept its bargain to retain only personal weapons, while Zanla had hoarded away heavy weapons in contravention of the general cease-fire agreement. Following the fighting a curfew was imposed, but only on pedestrians from 6 p.m. to 6 a.m. Vehicles were free to move about, and I am convinced that it was in this period that stocks began to be built up of unauthorised heavy arms.

Early in January 1981 I was sacked from my job as minister of home affairs. The prime minister announced without warning that there was to be a cabinet reshuffle, and I was to take over the job of minister of the public service – a politically insignificant post, in charge of the bureaucracy. Robert Mugabe explained my demotion in the following terms: it was, he said, 'because of public expressions of criticism of the police, which were entirely unjustified'. In other words, the man who dismissed me stated that there was no good reason for my dismissal. I suppose he was trying to find a reason for obeying the orders he received from his central committee.

Perhaps I should have resigned from the cabinet there and then, as the Zapu central committee wanted me to do. But I argued that I should stay, and persuaded my colleagues. I went to Robert Mugabe and spelled out to him the unrest that might arise among our young men if Zapu were stripped of all responsibility for security. Robert at first told me that he could not persuade his party committees to agree: then, after further persuasion, he granted me the meaningless title of minister without portfolio. I was to assist the prime minister on defence matters and some public service functions, and to remain a member of the cabinet committee on security. The official announcement was meant to satisfy the army and police that these would be ministers of both parties in charge of their interests. But once again the Zanu central committee kept the real decisions in its hands. I saw no official papers on security. I was not even consulted about appointments to the public service.

In February 1981 fighting between Zipra and Zanla broke out again. There had been trouble at a National Army camp near

Bulawayo, at Ntabazinduna: the ex-Zipra soldiers were given leave, and in their absence the ex-Zanla elements took over the armoury. The hostility at once spread to Entumbane, the site of the previous fighting, where a Zipra and a Zanla assembly point had been imprudently sited side by side. Full-scale fighting broke out there, and also at Connemara Barracks, near Gweru, where the National Army camp split into its ex-Zipra and ex-Zanla elements. The Connemara fighting was quelled when some fighter aircraft – flown, ironically enough, by pilots of the former Smith regime – flew over and scared some sense into the warring factions.

At Bulawayo I was called in to take over the command room at Brady Barracks. A combination of negotiation and threats enabled senior officers of the former guerilla armies to approach their own men and secure a cease-fire. The senior ex-Zipra officers, Masuku and Dabengwa, faced up to their own men and ordered them to lay down their arms. As the former commander-in-chief of Zipra I added my authority to theirs. It was a dangerous assignment: the risk of outright mutiny was always there. But we brought it off. The government later staged an important criminal trial as a result of this and subsequent incidents. The judge confirmed: 'The attitude of the leaders was, "You shall obey the government".' It had proved worthwhile to keep me in the cabinet after all.

But one grave error was made, over my strong objections. Emmerson Munangagwa, the minister of state in charge of security, insisted that all the men be disarmed even before they had moved back into their own barracks. The result was that many soldiers and ex-soldiers must have hidden their weapons rather than return to their dangerous camps without them. The stocks of concealed weapons in the country were dangerously swelled by this order. Men of both guerilla armies had their secret arms dumps. This became apparent later in circumstances of extreme danger for me and for the country.

The final demobilisation of the guerilla armies began in May 1981, starting with the disarming of the ex-soldiers. I went to the biggest of the ex-Zipra camps, at Gwaai River Mine, where over 5,000 armed men were encamped with their personal weapons, mortars, rocket-launchers and armoured personnel carriers. It was an emotional moment. These people had been recruited and trained for the liberation of our country. I told them that the need to remain an organised force was gone. They must give up their weapons and hand them over for use by the new National Army, to defend our country against internal disruption and external invasion. The external threat, I knew, was real enough: South African destabilisation of our country was under way, with its agents often disguised as 'former Rhodesian soldiers'. I feared, but I certainly did not say, that the internal disruption was coming from the same government that I was telling my people to trust.

It was, I believe, a dangerous mistake to disarm the ex-soldiers before disbanding their camps. For many months they were left as complete units, with their uniforms and their military organisation, but without the weapons that give a soldier's life its purpose. If, as I suspect, many of them had hidden their guns at the time of the second Entumbane fighting, it is possible that they were continuing to train in secret: I do not know, but I fear it. They were in any case deeply disillusioned, and with good reason. For the many who could not be found a place in the National Army and police the future was empty. They had no jobs to go to, and the government's resettlement schemes were proving a failure.

The men were sometimes disgracefully treated, even by the officers of the National Army who were supposed to supervise them. At Christmas 1981 the final dispersal of the men took place. The National Army brigadier at Gwaai River telephoned me on my holiday, asking for my help in persuading the 3,000 men under his charge to leave quietly. I drove down from Bulawayo, over 150 kilometres to the camp. I told the soldiers that the nation was grateful for their services, but their time in the forces was now over. There was no alternative: they must return peacefully to their homes, settle down, get married and find jobs – I especially recommended the local village cooperatives that I had been trying to promote.

The men accepted their demobilisation. I went off to have a meal in a local hotel. When I drove back past the crossroads to the camp I saw these young soldiers lined up at the roadside, literally taking off their uniforms in the open air and putting on their civilian clothes before climbing into trucks to be driven home. It was humiliating: I felt humiliated just watching.

I called for the brigadier and asked him how he could do this thing. If he needed the men to change out of their uniforms, why did he not ask me to persuade them to change right there in the camp, not out here on the open road? The officer apologised. He said he had just not thought about it. It was an insult to the men, really disgraceful. That was how the army treated some of the men who had volunteered to serve their country.

I had been assured that the Zanu party leaders would also be visiting their ex-soldiers to tell them to disband. Three months after the final dispersal of Zipra I discovered that they had done exactly the opposite. Over in the east of the country by the Mozambique border a brigade strength of Zanla guerilla fighters had been kept in being. More than a hundred instructors had been brought in from North Korea – a country with which we had hitherto had no connection at all – to arm and train the brigade as a special force outside the command structure of the Zimbabwe army, responsible directly to the Zanu central committee. The Fifth Brigade was being formed. In Matabeleland we were to get to know it all too well.

Once Zipra was disbanded, my usefulness to Robert Mugabe's government was at an end. My office became more than ever a backwater. Cabinet documents arrived too late for me to consider them. I was not consulted on security matters. I was not even told about appointments to the civilian public service. The Zanu central committee had taken over the functions of the cabinet and of parliament.

I spoke out against all this, in parliament and on public platforms. But I stayed strictly within the limits of a free democracy – although in the admittedly strange role of a member of the government who was also its severest critic. I could not bring myself to believe that democracy was breaking down so soon after it had been introduced. The alternative to open criticism was a retreat into illegal opposition, with all the dangers – including that of renewed civil war – that it could bring to Zimbabwe. This I utterly rejected. Yet now I was to be accused of exactly the conduct that I had done so much to avoid.

Chapter 21
Outcast

Prime Minister Robert Mugabe had every opportunity to tell me face to face why he was sacking me from his government, and what the substance was of the grave charges he made against me. Perhaps he did not dare; perhaps his conscience would not let him. On 5 February 1982, Robert met me at my request to discuss the serious problems of the country, and in particular rising unemployment and the resulting discontent. During the meeting I was handed an urgent telephone message saying that the police had raided Ascot and Woodville farms, near Bulawayo, properties associated with my party and centres of employment schemes for former Zipra soldiers. I briefly mentioned the matter at the end of the meeting. The prime minister said he knew about it and we could discuss it later.

That afternoon I travelled on the plane to Bulawayo with two ministers close to Robert Mugabe, Emmerson Munangagwa, the minister of state responsible for security in the prime minister's office, and Sidney Sekeramayi, minister of lands and resettlement. There was nothing out of the ordinary about the journey: no problems were raised, no suspicions. Munangagwa, without mentioning it to me, went straight to Ascot Farm, to which he had summoned the press, radio and television. Next day first he and then the prime minister announced on radio and TV that massive stocks of weapons had been found at the two farms. There was, they said, a plot to overthrow the government with the help of South Africa. The man responsible was Joshua Nkomo.

The charges were ridiculous, and soon became even more exaggerated. I had amassed a huge secret arsenal, with heavy weapons and armoured personnel carriers, using my party's resettlement schemes as cover. I was plotting with South Africa to overthrow the state. But the fact that the accusations were false did not make them less serious. After this, my life within the normal political structures of the country was at an end.

I was not only a minister in the government, but a member of the cabinet committee on security. If there were indeed suspicions against me, I had the right to be asked by the prime minister to offer my own explanation. If stocks of weapons had indeed been found on properties under my control, I would expect to be shown the evidence and asked to account for its presence: even if I were a common criminal, that would be the correct procedure. Instead I was told nothing about the allegations – although I had been in personal conversation with the prime minister and his chief of security – until they had been given the widest possible publicity by the state press and broadcasting monopolies.

In all, the government announced a total of thirty-five alleged finds of arms on properties owned by Zapu, by myself, or by my political associates. Most of them were pure invention. One find was said to include enough electronic equipment to jam the communications of the entire Zimbabwe security forces. It turned out to consist of camera parts and the complete fittings (including X-ray equipment) for a dental surgery, which had been supplied to Zapu in Zambia by the German Democratic Republic as part of their humanitarian aid, and which was due to be installed in a clinic as part of a cooperative project. The armoured personnel carriers turned out to be ordinary trucks.

But two large dumps of arms were found, filmed and photographed. There was no doubt of their existence. They were at two sites: Ascot Farm near Bulawayo, and Hampton Ranch in the Midlands not far from Gweru. Both properties were owned by a private company called Nitram, which I had helped to set up as the nucleus of resettlement schemes for ex-Zipra soldiers who could not be found places in the new National Army or police. Two things therefore need explaining – the arms themselves, and the organisation on whose property they were found.

First, the weapons. I am convinced that, although there were weapons in those places, the numbers found were swollen by the ferrying in of arms from elsewhere by the investigators. I also know, and the prime minister knew as well, that the process of collecting weapons from the former combatants was not completed when the two guerilla armies were disbanded. Robert Mugabe himself said: 'If all arms cached by Zipra were found in or near assembly places only, my government and I would not have minded.' Ascot Farm is less than eleven kilometres from the Entumbane assembly points where two rounds of fighting between ex-Zipra and ex-Zanla soldiers had taken place. On his own words the prime minister should have accepted the possibility that there were arms in that area. Hampton Ranch is close to Connemara Barracks, where the National Army had split into warring sides just a year previously. The arms stolen in that mutiny must have been hidden somewhere nearby: Emmerson Munangagwa, the minister of state, confirmed that this was the source of 600 rifles found at Hampton.

It was not lawful, but by common knowledge both Zanla and Zipra ex-combatants had held onto arms after their entitlement to do so had ceased. This recognised problem should have been solved by recognised procedures. Instead, the discovery was exaggerated by the government, then exploited as a means of discrediting my party, Zapu, and expelling me from the government.

As for Nitram, it was established with my backing to buy properties at which Zipra ex-combatants could find useful work. This was entirely open: I had reported on the experiment to the cabinet, and invited fellow-ministers to see the places. The idea was to create cooperative enterprises. The ex-fighters – more than 4,000 of them were involved – contributed $50 a month from their service pensions in order to buy shares in the establishments where they were working, which would give them a stake in their success. I had discussed this plan in detail with Emmerson Munangagwa himself, who had expressed the view that it could be dangerous to set up farms where all the workers were ex-combatants. I had entirely agreed with him, and the policy was to integrate local farm-workers with the soldiers. The details of how it would all work were still being elaborated, but this was one resettlement scheme which – unlike most of those set up by the government itself – was starting to be productive, and at no cost to public funds.

Nitram was by no means the only enterprise being started under the auspices of Zapu and of people associated with it. There was no set pattern, we were experimenting with resettlement projects at a time when, as Robert Mugabe had agreed with me in a private meeting just before the arms finds, official resettlement policies were a 'national disaster'. Zapu itself owned two farms and five business enterprises. Nitram had four farms and four businesses. Individual party members had five farms and three business enterprises, which were being used for resettlement.

My personal involvement in all this was deep. I had myself raised funds for the establishment of collectively owned African enterprises. The enterprises – I have described the different patterns of ownership – included a thousand-hectare vegetable farm on the outskirts of Bulawayo, growing mostly tomatoes, onions and carrots, with maize as the break crop. There was a small ranch with two hundred cattle just outside Gweru, a motel and entertainment complex (including a snake-park, a big tourist attraction) outside Harare, a garage in the town, and a clothing factory with its own retail outlet.

There was a chicken farm, a pig-breeding establishment and a farm set up as an experimental women's cooperative. We had started a secretarial college and established the first of what was intended to be a chain of rural health clinics. We had bought some urban housing with the intention of selling it by instalments to its occupiers. The whole idea was to give people a stake of their own in the country, to free them from dependence on the state or the municipalities by encouraging home ownership and cooperative enterprises. A main source of funds was the allowances of $150 a month paid to ex-combatants, who set aside a fixed proportion of that for investment in the cooperatives.

These ideas, I emphasise, had been presented to and discussed with other cabinet ministers; there was no question of a secret network controlled by Zapu, rather the reverse. Dignitaries, including President Canaan Banana and senior Zanu ministers, had been invited to the opening ceremonies of our schemes.

All this was ended by the arms scandal. Under the infamous Unlawful Organisations Act of the previous Smith regime all the properties associated in various ways with Zapu were declared unlawful, confiscated and put in the hands of a liquidator. (He, poor man, did not know quite what to do: his usual job was to sort out the debts of bankrupt firms, not to help destroy viable enterprises.) No compensation was offered for the loss of personal property found on the farms. Among the party's property removed from one Nitram farm were the complete historical records of Zapu and of Zipra, in exile and at home, including all lists of our casualties. As a result, no names of the Zipra dead are included in the Roll of Honour kept at Heroes' Acre outside Harare. Even our national history is distorted.

My own losses were very large indeed; other party members much less able to afford any loss at all were ruined. Hundreds of young men and women who had been given a start on a peaceful and productive life were left to wander off with no means of support. Since many of them had never known life outside a refugee camp or a guerilla base, this was dangerous as well as cruel. They left angry with the authorities and disillusioned about our party's ability to protect them and give them work.

On 17 February 1982, eleven days after the arms finds were announced, the prime minister held a press conference at which he stated that I and three of my colleagues had been dismissed from the government: Josiah Chinamano, Joseph Msika and Jini Ntuta joined me in my disgrace. Two days later my old colleague Clement Muchachi resigned in sympathy. The leaders of Zapu had been eliminated from the ruling coalition. Robert Mugabe had ruled out a policy of reconciliation, and gone for confrontation.

Worse was to follow. The two senior officers of Zipra were Lookout Masuku and Dumiso Dabengwa. They had forged the army in its Zambian bases into an effective fighting force. After the cease-fire they had led their men into the planned assembly points, earning the generous praise of, among others, General Acland, the commander of the Commonwealth Monitoring Force. They then played their full part in the building of a national army, in close cooperation with their colleagues from Zanla and the former Rhodesian forces. When fighting broke out between Zipra and Zanla they had bravely faced it, and been chiefly responsible for pacifying their own men. They were loyal citizens and able professional soldiers.

By early 1982 Lookout Masuku held the rank of lieutenant-general and the position of deputy commander of the National

Army. Dumiso Dabengwa had resigned from the service when the interim joint military command was dissolved and the National Army took over as a unified force: he had set up in business and was doing well. On 11 March these two men were arrested, along with five other senior ex-Zipra officers, and charged with treason and other grave offences arising, for the most part, in connection with the at Ascot Farm and Hampton Ranch arms finds.

Thus the people best able to keep the remaining dissatisfied elements of Zipra under control were removed from the scene. The accused men were kept in prison for over a year awaiting trial, much of the time in solitary confinement. When they were brought before the court in April 1983, one relatively minor charge was found proven against one of the less senior accused men. All the others were acquitted of all the charges.

On their release from custody the men were all rearrested outside the court on detention orders. As I write, they remain in detention without trial. Similar treatment – wholly unjustified on any legal grounds – was extended to a group of white air force officers accused and acquitted of sabotage. There were vigorous international complaints about the unjust treatment of the whites. I noted, and was grateful for, a public protest by General Acland at the treatment of his black former colleagues.

Following my dismissal from the government, my life became dangerous. Hostile publicity was directed against me in the government-controlled press. My wife became seriously worried, especially when the prime minister likened Zapu to a cobra and said: 'The only way to deal effectively with a snake is to strike and destroy its head.' That seemed a direct incitement to violence against me. This was no fantasy. Over the next year ten people close to me, all of them connected with the cooperative movement I was fostering, were killed. In each case witnesses said the attacks were carried out by armed and uniformed men. Six district councillors elected as Zapu representatives were killed in similar circumstances.

In this climate of terror I do not blame anyone for keeping away from me. I am only grateful to those who stayed by me. In particular my friend and companion in the dark days after my dismissal from the government was Vote Moyo. He was always good company, and his seniority as a member of parliament as well as of the Zapu central committee seemed to give him some protection. But in August 1982, the government acted. Vote Moyo was arrested within the grounds of parliament, on his lawful business as a member of parliament. He was detained: the government said that criminal charges would be brought against him, but the charges never came to court. Vote appealed to the courts for release from detention: the courts ordered his release, and he was promptly redetained. As I write he is still in detention. His crime was to be my friend.

My replies to the verbal attacks were passed over in silence, ignored by the press, radio and television. The government spoke of a problem of 'dissidence' – a problem that it did not define, and that was hard to understand. That there were gangsters at work, especially in Matabeleland, was clear. There were many unexplained deaths, robberies and beatings. A significant number of white farmers in the open ranch-land of Matabeleland were killed without explanation. By lumping all these deplorable incidents together as 'dissidence', the government implied that they were the result of an organised and politically motivated movement: the clear indication was that ex-Zipra people were at work, and that I was behind their crimes. In parliament the prime minister pointed the finger at me and proclaimed before the television cameras that the father of Zimbabwe had become the father of the dissidents.

One thing is perfectly clear from the repeated accounts of eyewitnesses: that many of the attacks on lives and property were the work of men wearing uniforms that looked like government uniforms, and carrying weapons that looked like government guns. It is not unknown for armed soldiers to use their weapons for freelance crime in their off-duty hours. But the pattern and frequency of the events led many people to believe that this was a deliberate and coordinated campaign to create insecurity in the Matabeleland countryside. In the wake of the arms finds a climate was being developed which would be used to justify full-scale repression.

In parliament I called for a select committee of all parties to examine the problem of dissidence: the government said there was no need for an inquiry, they knew who the guilty ones were. I insisted that I did not know, nor did the people of Zimbabwe, nor did our increasingly worried friends abroad. Still the inquiry was refused. People very close to members of my family felt I should leave the country for my safety. I refused to go. I am a citizen of Zimbabwe. I do not wish to live in other people's countries, but in my own.

When I ceased to be a minister I lost my police protection. But I could not in that atmosphere feel safe without a guard. I asked leave to keep weapons for my personal escort, and was allowed two pistols and two assault rifles. In October 1982, when I was in Harare, my wife telephoned from Bulawayo to say that a group of uniformed men had come three times in the one day to search my house. I was extremely worried. I telephoned the minister of home affairs, Herbert Ushewokunze, at his home. He said he knew nothing of such a search; his voice became blurred, as though he was unwell, then he seemed to drop the telephone off the hook, and for the rest of the evening he was unobtainable. I therefore telephoned Emmerson Munangagwa of the prime minister's office. He too said he knew nothing: he even called back to say he had asked his men, who reported that they knew nothing of any raid on my Bulawayo home.

About 10 p.m. I was just going to bed when one of my young security guards came in. He told me a group of men claiming to be police had jumped over the outer wall, demanding to speak to me. As he was speaking, there was a noise in the passage outside my room: it is a small house, nothing spacious about it. My guard opened the door and told me: 'They are here, they are inside in the passage.'

I called out, 'What do you want?' – no reply. So I went into the corridor. They were there with their AK rifles at the ready: they would not answer my questions, only saying there was someone to speak to me. Finally a man claiming to be a superintendent of the Central Intelligence Organisation arrived and told me he had been ordered to search my premises.

The officer collected the weapons belonging to my guards, then conducted a thorough search of the house. Of course he found nothing significant – but after a time he produced some small, rough objects that he said looked like precious stones. Maybe they were: a man who had stayed in the house is a miner by profession, and it is possible they were samples. The superintendent took and listed the weapons and a few harmless papers, asking me to sign for them. (There was no mention of any emeralds, an allegation that was to arise later.) I protested that there was specific ministerial authorisation for the weapons carried by my security guards: nevertheless they took them away, claiming they were needed for ballistics tests after a wave of robberies in the area.

Three months later, in January 1983, they suddenly returned our guns. I told my men to be sure never to shoot first, however much they suspected that intruders might be thieves: I strongly feared that the police were only looking for an excuse to shoot back. All those months I was undefended: I regularly changed the house where I spent the night, and several times the houses I had just left were raided by police. My friends were woken in the night and turned out of their beds: once these so-called policemen turned out a little girl of fourteen in the middle of the night, with her hands on her head, just to see if I was in the house. They brought tracker dogs with them, and when they got into the room where I had slept they tore the bed apart, even ripping open the mattress: the dog had my scent, they were on my trail.

Despite all this I could not just be idle. It was government policy to promote economic development and employment by encouraging people to set up joint business ventures with local or foreign companies. But most black businessmen had no security, so could not raise the necessary capital. I found a formula which I believed would work.

I began to discuss a joint venture for the manufacture of bottles and containers, to replace the imported bottles used by our drink and pharmaceutical industries. I also started talking to some manufacturers about producing something like the Puma blankets which are so popular that Zimbabwean women often smuggle them in from Botswana or South Africa. I got in touch with a firm making electrical insulators, such as our government spends millions of dollars a year importing from South Africa. The managers of the blanket company – black and white – were detained for a week. The managers of the other companies were heavily reprimanded. Their offence was to have had dealings with Nkomo. That was forbidden, even if it brought jobs and useful products to the nation.

I could speak in parliament, but elsewhere I was not allowed to make public speeches. In fact I made only two appearances at meetings all that time after my expulsion from the government. One was in the Matopos hills, and there I made my way by a devious route, because I had good reason to believe that an ambush was planned along the usual road. The other occasion was at Manama, a drive of about 160 kilometres: I had obtained the necessary permit from the minister of home affairs. While on my way to the place I was told that the permit had been revoked and the meeting was banned.

Several thousand people had assembled to hear me. The organisers of the meeting were extremely worried: they said they would be blamed if I did not appear and that the crowd would believe they had used my name on false pretences, to attract a big turnout. At their request I did make a speech, which went like this: 'The meeting has been stopped by the minister, so you had better go home.' The boys from the police support unit surrounded me, fingers on the trigger: the organiser of the meeting was arrested before my eyes. I had to shout at them to let him go and to point their guns somewhere else, and they fell back. I think they were really ashamed. But it was intimidation, both of me and of my supporters.

The problem of so-called dissidence became more serious, especially in Matabeleland. One particularly dreadful incident was the abduction of six young tourists on the road from Victoria Falls to Bulawayo. According to reports their vehicle was stopped at a makeshift road-block which they assumed was manned by the army: there were three cars at the block. Some shots were fired, and the tourists' vehicle's radiator was damaged. The driver and three women passengers were released, the six men were taken into the bush, and shortly afterwards a ransom note was received.

The note contained three demands – that Masuku and Dabengwa be released, that Zapu's property be returned and that Nkomo be reinstated in the cabinet. That was already contradictory. Why should men trying to destroy the government seek to have me reinstated in it? And how did it come about that of all the hundreds of cars that pass along that road every day the one to be stopped should contain two young Britons, two young Australians and two young Americans –

from the leading country in the West and two of the leading countries in the Commonwealth? The car had passed through the immigration post at Victoria Falls, coming from Zambia: only government forces could have known the potential for diplomatic pressure of the passengers in that particular vehicle.

I absolutely guarantee that neither I nor Zapu had anything to do with that kidnapping. The diplomats of those very important countries came to my house to ask for my and my party's help in obtaining their release. I asked why they came to see me: Zimbabwe was run by Robert Mugabe. They said he had approved their visit. But I told them they were being used to divide my country, by treating me as though I ran my own little republic within it.

One of the cars seen by the released women passengers to have been involved in the ambush was later used by the police to transport the driver of the damaged vehicle back to town. Then the car disappeared. I really do not believe in dissidents who drive about in private cars that are later used by the police and disappear without trace in a country with road-blocks everywhere. I do not believe that six young white men could be hidden and eventually killed in the villages without anyone seeing them or reporting their presence.

I had nothing to do with that cruel kidnap. I had great sympathy with the young men's parents, who came to Zimbabwe to try to trace them, and on their behalf I made two extended visits to the area where they disappeared, calling upon anyone who had any information to come forward. I next planned to tour the Tjolotjo area to continue my inquiries there, but the government stopped that. The curfew was brought in, and that was the end of my travels. It was also the start of the real repression in Matabeleland.

Chapter 22

Repression

In January 1983 the killings began in Matabeleland. The first reports reached me from Mbembesi on the 25th, then from Bubi and from Tjolotjo in the country north-west of Bulawayo, areas already subject to curfew. The police had, I was told, been instructed not to intervene, the National Army was confined to barracks clear of the area. The perpetrators were young men in camouflage uniforms with distinctive red berets, calling themselves the Fifth Brigade. In the first week of these events I had reliable reports of ninety-five deaths. Eyewitnesses of the killings and beatings had reported to my party offices, asking for justice. I could not ignore their claims, which soon turned out to be tragically justified.

There had, just before the killings started, been a glimmer of hope. During December President Canaan Banana and Enos Nkala, minister of supply, had approached me as emissaries of the prime minister. At two meetings with them in Bulawayo I had the impression that progress had been made, and I requested a meeting with Robert Mugabe himself. The prime minister was less forthcoming than his messengers, and the meeting made little progress, but at least a joint committee of three Zanu and three Zapu representatives was set up to discuss our differences.

The killings made our joint committee seem irrelevant. The Fifth Brigade, I knew, was a force recruited almost entirely from ex-Zanla combatants and specially trained by over one hundred North Korean instructors in operations 'in aid of the civil power' – that is, against civilians. Officially they were hunting down the so-called dissidents, gangsters who were said to be politically motivated by loyalty to Joshua Nkomo. In reality they were out to terrorise the people. They burned villages, slaughtered cattle, assaulted women and killed simply to instil fear.

The prime minister was by now absent on business abroad. I asked to see his deputy, Simon Muzenda. Muzenda passed me on to the minister of home affairs, Herbert Ushewokunze. Ushewokunze first agreed to meet me and then failed to keep his appointment, so I called a press conference to which I presented twelve eyewitnesses to the horrors. I emphasised that I was not attacking the government, but the unlawful acts being done in its name. I appealed for the government to stop the carnage.

The police responded by warning me that my statement might have contravened the Law and Order Maintenance Act – the worst of the Smith regime's instruments of repression, under which almost any criticism of any act by an official was subject to severe penalties. The government itself responded by putting down in parliament a censure motion against Zapu for exposing the carnage, which had now spread to Nkayi and to Lupane. In the debate I called for an impartial inquiry. My speech was shouted down and my request refused. My statements were distorted or ignored by the press and the broadcasting organisation.

The one point the government emphasised was that Josiah Gumede had survived. Gumede, whose death I had reported, was the former president of Zimbabwe-Rhodesia. The fact that he had been cruelly beaten and left for dead in his house for two days, in an attack by men of the Fifth Brigade, was passed over in silence.

The scale of the Matabeleland brutality is understandably questioned by some reasonable observers. Why, they ask, should such excesses be permitted – whatever was the point of it all? I cannot say why Zanu should have allowed its men to do such things: to me also it seems senseless. But that it happened I am certain. As impartial witnesses I can quote the priests of the Roman Catholic church in Matabeleland. Their church is not a dissident organisation. It had bravely spoken out against the crimes committed by the forces of the Smith regime.

At their conference at Easter 1983, six Catholic bishops made a statement including the following words:

We entirely support the use of the army in a peace-keeping role. What we view with dismay are methods that have been adopted for doing so. . . . Methods which should be firm and just have degenerated into brutality and atrocity. We censure the frightful consequences of such methods.

Violent reaction against dissident activity has, to our certain knowledge, brought about the maiming and death of hundreds and hundreds of innocent people who are neither dissidents nor collaborators. We are convinced by incontrovertible evidence that many wanton atrocities and brutalities have been and are still being perpetrated. We have already forwarded such evidence to the government.

This is the witness of disinterested men, priests in close daily contact with the people of their parishes. They have everything to gain from preserving good relations with the government, much to lose from a failure to do so. I return to their statement:

The facts point to a reign of terror caused by wanton killings, woundings, beatings, burnings and rapings. Many homes have been burnt down. People in rural areas are starving, not only because of the drought, but because in some cases supplies of food have been deliberately cut off and in other cases access to food supplies has been restricted or stopped. The innocent have no recourse or redress, for fear of reprisals.

Dr Nathan Shamuyarira, the minister of information, described the Catholic bishops' statement as 'irresponsible, contrived propaganda'. The prime minister said the bishops were 'mere megaphone agents of their external manipulative masters'; he called them 'a band of Jeremiahs'. But abuse is not a reasoned answer. If anything, the bishops, writing while the campaign of repression was still in progress, underrated its frightfulness. The latest reports, from the same sources as gathered the evidence for the bishops, now puts the number of casualties at the hands of the Fifth Brigade in Matabeleland in 1983 at around 20,000 people.

The damage went well beyond that. Houses, villages, whole communities were burned to the ground. At the end of the dry season, after two years when the rains had failed, the rural people were anyway on the point of starvation. The government then prohibited the sending of food to the worst affected districts on the pretence that it would be used to sustain the bands of dissidents. Travel was restricted, access to watering points for cattle and for people was controlled by soldiers. To take a bus, to buy a bag of meal, to bring the livestock to the water-hole, they demanded what they called a proof of loyalty to the government. The only proof accepted was a membership card of the ruling Zanu party.

My own first cousin, Sihle Nkomo, lives still in the *umuzi* where he gave me shelter when I was restricted to his home by the Rhodesian government in 1962. By October 1983, cut off from food supplies, his children were showing the dreaded symptoms – swollen bellies, yellowing hair – of the disease kwashiorkor, which is caused by malnutrition. As the bishops had declared at Easter: 'These brutal methods will have the opposite effect to what the government is intending to achieve.'

One small story which illustrates it all is of a killing that took place on Monday 17 October 1983, in the Somnene purchase area, near Soluswe mission. There were four victims: a former teacher at Tjolotjo school, Roger Malusalila, a Zapu member and a farmer; Roger's farmer neighbour, Nyathi; Nyathi's nephew; and a visiting friend of the nephew.

The Fifth Brigade had set up a small camp near Roger's farm, in a dry place with no water. The soldiers had issued an order that all nearby households should send a young girl to fetch water for the camp. In some cases girls had carried water in the evening, and been told to stay to bring it again in the morning. That meant remaining all night in the camp with the soldiers. Some girls, perhaps, stayed willingly, others because they were frightened.

Roger and Nyathi refused to allow the young women of their households to go to the soldiers' camp. The soldiers came first to Roger's house and took him out, then to Nyathi's house and took him and his two guests. All four were taken into a field and shot. The bodies lay there for a day until the police came and took them to Plumtree. Those of Nyathi and his guests were soon returned to Somnene and buried.

But Roger's sons live in Bulawayo, and wished to bury their father there. It took two days of negotiations before the police would allow the body to be moved from Plumtree: the problem was with the death certificate. It was eventually issued, with the cause of death described as 'gunshot wounds'. By now it was the weekend, and the funeral could not be arranged before Monday. So, a clear week after his murder by the men of the Fifth Brigade, Roger Malusalila was buried. His body, with its open wounds, had been several days in the African sun. There is no way of tracing his killers, and anyone who tried to do so would be in immediate danger of his life.

I had a long-standing engagement to attend an international body of which I am a member – the executive committee of the World Peace Council, due to meet in Prague on 21 and 22 February 1983. I was isolated from influence in my own country. Perhaps, I thought, my friends abroad might hear what I had to say, and perhaps persuade my government to listen too. I had informed the government of my intention to travel, and had as a courtesy handed a copy of the invitation for the meeting to the prime minister's office.

On Saturday 19 February, I went to catch my plane at Bulawayo airport. The route was Johannesburg, Zurich, London, then Prague. I passed through customs and handed my passport to the immigration officer. He stamped it and handed it on to a uniformed policeman standing beside him. The policeman escorted me through to the departure lounge, and said formally: 'I have been told by the commissioner of police to inform you that you are not to leave the country.' I asked why, and he replied that his instructions were simply to pass me that message. The other passengers immediately saw that something was going on: tension could be felt in the lounge. I told the policeman to find us a private room and fetch the security people, so that we could get out of the public eye.

There was a wait of two hours: nobody seemed to know what was going on. Then some men of the paramilitary support unit arrived and took me to the office of the assistant commissioner of police, Mvere. He was not there and they had to contact him by radio.

'The man you want is here in the office,' they said.

The assistant commissioner, who obviously did not realise I was listening, became angry: 'Take him out of there – put him in some other little office,' he shouted over the radio. He obviously thought his office was too important to have me in it, so I was moved along to some smaller room and told I would be searched.

'Fine,' I said, 'you go ahead.' They searched my bags and they searched my body: the three comrades I was travelling with were taken round to some other office.

After the search the young police officer accompanying me tried to find a senior man to tell him what to do next. He said the police were helping out the Special Branch, who are meant to deal with political and subversive offences. I told him to contact the commissioner of police in person: he too could not be traced. It was a Saturday – I suppose they were all out boozing. After seven hours of this the young officer decided to take action on his own: 'Old man,' he said (the term is respectful among our people), 'I will allow you to go home.' He stated that he would keep certain things found in my luggage. They were a copy of the statement I had made in parliament about the killings in Matabeleland; the handwritten draft of points for discussion with the prime minister on that problem; and $300 in Zimbabwe currency.

I told the officer that the parliamentary speech was a privileged document, and that the notes had not yet been communicated to the prime minister or any other person, so could not be regarded as published documents which might make their possession an offence. I also explained that the $300 was spending money for my wife during my absence, which she had mistakenly packed up with my air ticket and passport. The policeman kept all the documents anyway, saying I could explain all that on Monday. My wife arrived, and I went home. I had been harassed but not harmed. My three travelling companions were not so lucky. They spent over six months in detention, their only offence being to have been with me.

My interrogation on the Monday was absurd. The Special Branch man, Inspector Ngwenya, told me that the documents in my parliamentary folder appeared to contravene the Law and Order Maintenance Act. I explained that they could not possibly be regarded as subversive, and told him to go ahead and investigate. As far as the $300 was concerned, I said that exporting the money might constitute a technical offence, but would hardly make me rich since nobody outside the country will accept Zimbabwe currency anyway. They let me go.

That afternoon my solicitor telephoned to say there was yet another charge against me, and I should go once more to the police. They informed me of a cable from the Harare police claiming that emeralds had been found in my house on 5 October 1982. This was obviously a reference to the small stones produced by the police when they raided my house in the middle of the night: I pointed out that under our law unauthorised possession of precious stones is an offence leading to immediate arrest, and if I was accused of that they should have put me in the cells at once. Of course, no charges were made against me, and I left for home, but the news media reported that I had been officially accused of all sorts of crimes.

On the Sunday I saw a small car leaving my house as I arrived, with men in it looking like detectives. Sure enough, they had left a note with my security guards requesting me to notify the police in future if I left the house. I notified my lawyer, who wrote a letter pointing out that I was a member of parliament and charged with no offence. A week passed uneventfully. The following Friday began the chain of events which left two of my people dead in my house, and carried me across the border fence into Botswana.

I awoke in Botswana with the uneasy feeling that I had been in this position before, when I was much younger – homeless, penniless and uncertain where I was going next. I was deeply grateful to President Quett Masire for authorising my brief stay in his country, in government hospitality. But I knew my presence could be embarrassing to his government, which was already having to cope with many thousands of refugees driven across the border from Matabeleland by Robert Mugabe's operations against the civilian population there.

I knew I could not stay long. Soon after I woke from my exhausted sleep, I authorised a public statement that I was neither a refugee nor seeking political asylum, and said nothing more. I was both surprised and pleased when, shortly afterwards, I received a telephone call from my old friend Tiny Rowland in London. Not for the first time Tiny offered to help. He had already been busy. In the absence of Prime Minister Mugabe at a conference in New Delhi, he had spoken to two senior ministers in the Zimbabwe government, Deputy Prime Minister Simon Muzenda and Minister of State Emmerson Munangagwa. He asked me to telephone them, and I did.

The two ministers requested me to return home at once. I replied that I had only left because it was impossible to feel safe in my own country, and that whatever happened I needed time to rest and think. They then asked me to receive a high-level deputation, consisting of Munangagwa himself, General Rex Nhongo, the army commander, and one senior official. To this I gladly agreed, hoping that the Mugabe government was at last prepared to talk seriously about the real issues of repression and reconciliation. The Botswana government made arrangements to greet its distinguished guests, and we sat down to wait.

The first telex said the visitors were due at 3 p.m. The time came, but not the people. Three-thirty came, then four o'clock and another telex saying the visit was off. I tried to telephone Munangagwa: every time I said who I was the line was cut off. With Muzenda it was the same.

After a while I got back to Tiny Rowland. He advised me to stay put: I explained that my presence would embarrass the Botswana government, and I must therefore make some move. So he too advised me to return home, and again I explained to him that I could hardly return to a place where my life was under constant threat. On that inconclusive note our talk ended. I resolved that the only place I could go was to Britain.

Through the Botswana authorities I got in touch with the British High Commissioner, who courteously came to see me at my borrowed house. I told him I intended to visit London. He went away and on his return formally read me a statement from the Home Office pointing out that, under the Fugitive Offenders' Act, I might be subject to extradition from Britain to Zimbabwe on a warrant for crimes allegedly committed in that country. I asked for a copy of the document, but the high commissioner said it needed interpretation by a lawyer; so I said I was going to Britain anyway.

I flew by light aircraft to Jan Smuts airport outside Johannesburg to transfer to the London plane, and there the press were waiting. I had to be extremely discreet: I allowed photographs but no interviews, and boarded the British Airways flight. In London the immigration people explained that they would give me a week to apply formally for entry to Britain, handed me a bundle of documents explaining the rules and admitted me as a visitor. So there I was, a free man, at London airport without a penny to my name.

Once again, despite his wish that I should not come to Britain, Tiny Rowland came to my rescue. A young man representing him approached me to say that he had been authorised to arrange transport and accommodation. So I arrived by car at the Penta Hotel. For that I was truly grateful. No conditions were laid down for my stay, although I was well aware that Tiny would prefer me to be in Zimbabwe. Rest and quiet, after the hunted life I had led, restored my health and confidence. By Easter I had almost made up my mind to go home.

At this moment the Catholic bishops published their overwhelmingly detailed and convincing report on the Matabeleland atrocities, committed by the soldiers of the Fifth Brigade, Robert Mugabe's North Korean-trained private army. The prime minister poured scorn on the report, which was if anything understated. I could not keep silent: to do so would have been to betray my own suffering people. I called a press conference, declared that I knew the reports of atrocities were true, and announced that I would not be going home until I had put my views to Robert.

Tiny Rowland, according to my information, was at this time in Latin America on business. But on my return to the Penta Hotel after speaking to the press I received a telephone call from a member of his staff, Mr Dunlop. Tiny had decided his assistance was to end that night: from the following day I was to be responsible for my own expenses. I was very, very angry. If Rowland could talk to Dunlop from Latin America, surely he could have spoken to me? I was furious that my friend should go through an intermediary to tell me what to do.

I thought it best both for Tiny and for myself to handle the problem as discreetly as possible. I told Dunlop that I would not move out of the hotel at once. I would stay on for a few days at my own expense, and meanwhile I would try to raise a little money to help me carry on. In the event some Zimbabweans in London – not well-off people at all – managed to get some money together for me, and thus enabled me to move discreetly out of the expensive hotel and into a flat.

After a few days, inevitably, the news leaked out that I was no longer getting financial support for my stay in London. Newspaper reports stated that Lonrho and Dunlop, the companies that had been supporting me, had withdrawn their backing. I can only think this was the result of someone listening in to my telephone. Lonrho as such had never given me any support: the only Dunlop involved was Tiny Rowland's personal assistant, not the tyre company.

So, at the darkest moment of my life, the man I regarded as my friend withdrew his help and left me without either money or a place to live, at twelve hours' notice. I understand why he did it. People were pressing him. If he went on helping, his investments in Zimbabwe might be threatened. My friends in the Zimbabwe government wanted me to starve, although I do not see what good it would do them to see me in the gutter. As for Tiny Rowland, I am sincerely grateful for all he did for me over the decade since we were introduced by President Kaunda at the end of my years in prison. The last message I sent to him expressed my thanks.

The rest of the story is soon told. From London I wrote two carefully considered letters to Prime Minister Mugabe. One detailed his political mistreatment of Zimbabwe since taking office. The other proposed a non-political national conference chaired by himself of all the major interest groups in our country – churches, trade unions, farmers' organisations, professional bodies, local councils, political parties, together with representatives of student societies, the armed forces, ex-combatants and youth groups – in order to thrash out an agreed understanding of our problems and to work towards a reconciliation of the nation with itself.

The ruling party responded by attempting to expel me from parliament on the ground of my absence without leave. I went home, to take my seat and face them, and to join my wife and children after their five months in house arrest. For many long years maFuyana had believed that once the struggle was over we could settle down to a respected place in the nation for which she too had suffered. I was more sad than I can say to have only this anxious existence to offer her.

I have never abandoned hope that I might contribute to a reasonable solution to our national problems, by discussion rather than by confrontation. Sometimes it looks as though progress is possible, sometimes I have to fight back despair. I have come to see that our national difficulties are shared with most of the new nations of Africa. I shall devote my final chapter to describing the problems of our heritage, and looking forward to a cure.

Chapter 23

Freedom Lies Ahead

The hardest lesson of my life has come to me late. It is that a nation can win freedom without its people becoming free. I have told in this book how all my experience from my earliest childhood taught me to oppose, first by argument and then by armed struggle, the domination of the black people of Zimbabwe by the tiny white minority within the country. I have told of the triumph of that struggle, and then of how the new African government adopted as its own the repressive techniques of its illegitimate predecessor.

I am a Zimbabwean patriot and an African patriot too. I refuse to accept that we cannot do better than we have so far done, or to reach for the easy excuse that all our mistakes are simply a colonial inheritance that can conveniently be blamed on the invaders. Of course our history has made us what we are, and the recent period of that history was distorted first by the influence of remote empires, then for ninety years by direct colonial rule. It is up to us to do better now.

Under colonial rule the development of our social and political life was controlled, and could not change naturally with the changing times. In the best of the traditional African communities the group was governed by consent: the leader summoned his council, the council debated, a decision emerged, and that decision became binding law. Those outside the ruling council who criticised its decisions were regarded as treasonable: the idea that authority can be controlled and its decisions improved by independent discussion and criticism did not exist. Nor could it develop during the colonial century, when all authority was vested in a governor subject to the orders of a remote metropolitan power. Even the few Africans invited to take part in legislative councils or local authorities had to accept the law as it was given to them, not participate in making or correcting it.

The new African rulers who came to power at independence have all too often claimed the same unquestioned authority as their traditional and colonial predecessors. Instead of welcoming debate as the necessary means for improving government, they have confused opposition to particular policies with general disloyalty. Constructive criticism is brushed aside, and suggested improvements are described as attempts to undermine the state.

Far too often in Africa authority has become intolerant. The easy answer is to claim that opposition must be absorbed within a one-party state, a modern version of the traditional chief's council within which full discussion took place before an acceptable and unchallengeable policy emerged. This misses the point. A one-party state, sincerely operated, may indeed be a way of encouraging open and constructive debate. A multi-party state, badly operated, may be just another way of keeping an elite in power. It is not the formal system that matters, but the spirit in which a single- or multi-party state is encouraged to operate.

What matters is that the leadership should encourage diverse opinions to be heard – the opinions of different social groups, different economic interests, different regions. Since regions within African nations tend to be inhabited by people of different languages and cultural backgrounds, the regional aspect is vitally important: recognising and accommodating regional differences is the best way to prevent them turning into tribal rivalries.

Of course many African nations are decently and humanely ruled, by leaders who listen to and take account of the opinions of the people. But far too many leaders have come to believe that their own interests and those of the people are the same. They confuse self-preservation with national security, and to preserve their own regimes throw the safeguards of the law and of individual rights out of the window. When the rights of the individual – even of a few individuals – are suppressed, there can be no respect for the rights of the people as a whole. The state begins to govern against its citizens, rather than with them.

When in prison, I was visited by the representatives of the International Red Cross. I heard with dismay of the conditions in which political prisoners were existing in other African states. They did not claim I was well treated – they knew about prisons, they understood that a man or woman deprived of liberty is deprived of the most precious thing in life. But they had observed how in some black-ruled nations the loss of liberty was made far more evil by the inhumanity with which prisoners were treated. In South Africa, they told me, the wicked system of political imprisonment imposed by the racist government was made worse because the jailers hardly treated their charges as human beings; nevertheless, there, the physical conditions of the prisons were at least clean. But too often in black Africa, they told me, the injustice of imprisonment was compounded by squalor and personal brutality.

African leaders must improve their record on human rights, and African peoples too must have greater regard to their responsibilities. I appeal in particular to our young people, especially the students and the soldiers, to accept the challenge of political development. They too often see in their governments the signs of corruption, of nepotism, of tribalism, sapping the legitimate authority of the state. To this the young react by setting up redemption councils, salvation councils, revolutionary councils, thus themselves going outside the law in an attempt to rectify the lawlessness of government. But once they have ignored the constitutional procedures for setting things right, they are themselves undermining the rule of law. Inevitably the new structures that they put in place fall victim to the same sins that beset the old ones. Then it is the masses who suffer once more.

Patience in the face of injustice is hard, but it is necessary. It would be easier to achieve if our rulers would accept a shared standard by which to judge their own conduct and seek to improve it; and such a standard already exists, in the Universal Declaration of Human Rights which all our governments have signed. We share a problem, largely for the historical reasons that I have outlined. We should begin to look for a shared solution.

But Africa has not done well in the quest for shared remedies. Twenty years ago, when I attended the inaugural session of the Organisation of African Unity, I was proud of our continent. Despite our differences we had come together to express our common will. No such group of nations in history had ever done that before, and it still remains a great achievement. Cooperation in the OAU has averted many dangers and contributed to the security of all its members.

But so many of the things we should be doing together remain undone. Our communications are still dominated by extinct colonial needs – our airline routes, our telephone links, pass through remote ex-imperial capitals instead of binding together the nations within the same landmass. Our students must travel for their higher qualifications to distant countries, where they lose touch with the communities they came from. Our raw materials are exported almost unprocessed to rich nations outside our continent instead of providing work and income for our own people.

There are so many practical endeavours which the nations of Africa should be tackling in partnership, through the OAU, that are still governed by bilateral arrangements with the countries that once called us their 'possessions'. Because we are fragmented, we are weak, and when we face the outside world it is all too often as suppliants rather than as equal partners. It is through practical working together that we could learn to develop the will for political cooperation, and the establishment of African standards that are as high as any in the world.

Less than thirty years ago I was a guest in Kwame Nkrumah's Ghana at the ceremonies heralding the end of colonialism in Africa. Since then, at different speeds and in different styles, Britain, France and Portugal have removed their occupying forces and their alien institutions from our continent. Only in South Africa and in Namibia do regimes directly descended from the imperial process linger on to face the resistance of the subject people, who will eventually prevail there too.

Southern Rhodesia, although constitutionally a colony, shared the main characteristic of those neighbouring regimes, which is why its freedom as Zimbabwe had to be won with such pain. In southern Africa, unlike the rest of the continent, the white people came to settle and to stay, not just to exploit and go home. Our problem was not alien rule, but minority rule backed by alien commercial interests. Most Zimbabweans are black, and their rights were for far too long denied. That is all the more reason why, now that the problem of minority rule has been solved, the rights of all the people of Zimbabwe should be equally respected. The white people fought so hard because they feared that, if they handed over power, we, the black people, would treat them as badly as they had treated us. It is up to us now to prove them wrong, to show we really believed in the equality we said we were fighting for. We owe special care, too, to the coloured Zimbabweans, cousins to the white people as well as to the black people, and to the Zimbabweans of Indian origin, who are in our country not because their ancestors were oppressors but because they were themselves oppressed.

The strange racial policies of our past governments have grossly distorted the way we use our most precious resource. We have rich mines and prosperous factories, but our main wealth comes from the land. We feed our own growing population, and we normally export large quantities of tobacco, grain and meat. But about half of our usable land produces our entire surplus of food. It is owned by only about 6,000 commercial farmers, all of whom were until very recently white. The other half of our productive land is communally farmed, exclusively by Africans, and is home to about 6 million of our total population of 7.5 million.

The success of the white farmers had several causes. The colonial governments made sure that the best land was allocated to the whites. Public investment, especially in irrigation, roads and power supplies, was for whites, not blacks. The whites received free technical advice on how to work their land most profitably. Since they owned their land, they were able to borrow on security from the banks for investment in their farms. They worked hard, and had almost absolute authority over their black employees, who therefore worked even harder. All this made Zimbabwe's white-owned commercial farms highly productive.

Our communal – that is to say, African – farms are by contrast among the most wretched on the continent. While the best land was being grabbed for the whites, the black farmers were herded into the poorest and driest areas, denied public investment and the education that would have enabled them to do better. Since their land was in communal rather than private ownership, they could not borrow from the banks for investment. Any successful African farmer found his stocks limited by the order of government officials, as the growth of population forced more and more people into the communal lands.

As a result, the pattern of land use that has developed in the communal areas is terribly wasteful. Homes are scattered widely across the country, the intervening ground beaten by footpaths rather than used for grazing. Cultivated fields are small, and each one must be wastefully fenced against wandering livestock. Fuel is obtained by random cutting of trees, which damages the fertility of the soil and the climate itself. The women, whose traditional task it is to fetch wood and water, must travel greater and greater distances to find them. Since the homes are scattered, it is expensive or even impossible to supply them with electricity or clean running water. Because there can be no communal sanitation, water is often polluted, leading to the spread of disease.

This great national problem arises from past policies of racial discrimination which made a tiny minority rich and the vast majority poor. Now all of us in Zimbabwe must face the consequences together.

There is no reason why our country, properly cultivated and organised, should not provide food and clothing for several times the present population. Ironically enough, the areas formerly set aside for white farmers represent our most precious asset. There were never enough white people to farm the vast tracts of land set aside for their exclusive use. Over much of our best soil the trees and the grass and the wildlife have been left untouched. The commercial farms are so huge that they have hitherto been profitable with low yields per hectare: more intensive production, with more labour on the same area, would make possible far greater production.

But the wasteful farm practices that have been encouraged to grow up in the communal areas would soon destroy that precious asset: and it would be disastrous to encourage new settlements on hitherto underused land without at the same time ensuring that the communal lands do not continue to be laid waste. The full use of unexploited commercial land, the development of planned communities there, and the reallocation of badly farmed land in the communal areas must go hand in hand. In particular the unused water resources of the communal areas, in the form of underground aquifers and of potential dam sites, must be tapped.

New settlements in the commercial areas must be real, productive farm communities – not scattered huts, uncontrolled grazing and loose dogs on the run, but planned villages, fields and paddocks carefully laid out to get the most from the land. These new communities must include three important groups: land-hungry people from the existing communal areas, workers on existing commercial farms and ex-combatants disbanded from the former guerilla armies. Above all, they must be offered the technical advice they will need if they are to use the land well. Such rational settlements, whether on unused land or on farms bought from their white owners, would be positively welcomed by commercial farmers. Their confidence will be won not by speeches, but by seeing that new settlers make good neighbours.

Equally, in the towns, an answer must be found to the problems of those hundreds of thousands of people who have jobs if they are lucky, but who have no stake in the community because they have no property. Housing there has been managed and developed not by the people but by impersonal town councils. Individual ownership is a mirage for most, who can neither earn nor borrow the money to buy property. But collective ownership by the people of a neighbourhood should be encouraged, to give them real responsibility for the places where they live, and a share in the decisions that most closely concern their lives and those of their families.

But all this, in the towns and the countryside alike, depends on the active and willing cooperation of those involved. (The failure of the *ujamaa* resettlement policy in Tanzania shows how wrong things can go when plans are imposed on the people and not developed with their participation.) Human beings will work together, and be the happier for it, if they feel that their ideas and their initiatives are taken into account in the final decision of what is to be done.

Zimbabweans have lately fought a long and terrible war. It has disrupted their lives. But it has also left them with an extraordinary sense of national solidarity which binds together people of all races and colours, whichever side they fought on. That energy is being dissipated by a government which seems to feel the need to exercise a partisan authority rather than to mobilise the national will.

It is not too late to change all that, to muster the collective energy of our people and build the new Zimbabwe we promised through all those long years of suffering and struggle. During my brief exile in 1983 I appealed in this sense to Prime Minister Robert Mugabe, calling as a start for a national conference of all the country's interest groups, under his chairmanship, to begin the process of reconciliation. He did not answer then. Perhaps in the interval between the writing of this book and its publication he will change his mind and reply constructively. For my part, I shall continue working to that end.

Long live Zimbabwe!

Appendix A

Zimbabwe Declaration of Unity made at Lusaka, Republic of Zambia, on 7 December 1974

1. Zanu, Zapu, Frolizi and ANC hereby agree to unite in the ANC.
2. The parties recognise the ANC as the unifying force of the people of Zimbabwe.
3. (a) They agreed to consolidate the leadership of the ANC by the inclusion into it of the presidents of Zanu, Zapu and Frolizi under the chairmanship of the president of the ANC
   (b) Zapu, Zanu and Frolizi shall each appoint three other persons to join the enlarged ANC Executive.
4. The enlarged ANC Executive shall have the following functions:
   (a) To prepare for any conference for the transfer of power to the majority that might be called
   (b) To prepare for the holding of a Congress within four months at which:
      i. A revised ANC constitution shall be adopted
      ii. The leadership of the united people of Zimbabwe shall be elected
      iii. A statement of policy for the ANC will be considered
   (c) To organise the people for such conference and congress.
5. The leaders of Zapu, Zanu and Frolizi call upon their supporters and all Zimbabweans to rally behind the ANC under its enlarged executive.
6. Zapu, Zanu and Frolizi will take steps to merge their respective organs and structures into the ANC before the congress to be held within four months.
7. The leaders recognise the inevitability of continued armed struggle and all other forms of struggle until the total liberation of Zimbabwe.

Signed:

Abel Tendekayi Muzorewa
PRESIDENT OF ANC

Ndabaningi Sithole
PRESIDENT OF ZANU

Joshua Mqabuko Nkomo
PRESIDENT OF ZAPU

James Robert Dambaza Chikerema
PRESIDENT OF FROLIZI

State House, Lusaka, Zambia

Appendix B

Declaration of Intention to Negotiate a Settlement

1. The prime minister and other cabinet ministers of the Rhodesian government and the president and other representatives of the African National Council met at Victoria Falls on 25 August 1975, and subsequently in Salisbury on 31 October 1975, and thereafter.
2. Both parties took this opportunity of expressing their genuine desire to negotiate a constitutional settlement.
3. Both parties publicly expressed their commitment to work out immediately a constitutional settlement which will be acceptable to all the people of our country.
4. In pursuance of this objective, the negotiating teams from both sides shall arrange a plenary meeting in Rhodesia of nominated representatives chosen respectively by the government of Rhodesia and the ANC. At this meeting detailed discussions of all aspects of the constitutional issue will commence and, where appropriate, sub-committees will be established to consider and report to the plenary meeting on particular aspects.
5. (1) Representatives of the ANC at any meeting or meetings in Rhodesia whether formal or informal and including both plenary and committee or sub-committee meetings, held in terms of Clause 4 hereof shall have full freedom and/or diplomatic immunity in respect of the following.

   (a) from preventive detention or restriction for any act or omission in or outside Rhodesia; and
   (b) to enter and depart freely from Rhodesia; and
   (c) subject to the confidentiality of the discussions agreed Clause 8 hereof, to exercise freedom of expression and speech at any meeting or meetings in Rhodesia as described hereinbefore in this clause and to communicate freely with any person inside or outside Rhodesia; and
   (d) not be subjected to any observation, harassment or recording by film, tape, other mechanical device, or other means not expressly authorised by themselves.

   (2) For the purposes of subclause (1) of this Clause –
       (i) any reference to 'Representatives of the ANC' shall be construed as a reference to all persons nominated by the ANC to attend any meeting or meetings in Rhodesia as

described hereinbefore in subclause (1) in any capacity whatsoever, whether as delegates, advisers, aides or in any other capacity;

(ii) the freedom and immunities referred to in subclause (1) shall apply and be enjoyed as aforesaid not only at and/or during any of the meetings mentioned hereinbefore, but at all times from and including 31 October 1975, until the conclusion of the Constitutional Conference referred to in Clause 7 hereof;

(iii) any reference to 'preventive detention' shall be construed as a reference to detention in terms of any regulations made under the Emergency Powers Act [Chapter 33].

6. Because of the urgent need to end the present uncertainty it was agreed that every effort should be made to expedite the proceedings.

7. When agreement has been reached on the form and content of the Constitutional Settlement, a final Constitutional Conference will be arranged at a mutually agreed venue, which shall be outside Rhodesia. The purpose of this Conference will be to ratify formally the terms of the Constitutional document giving effect to the agreement reached.

8. All those present agreed on the importance of preserving the confidentiality of the Constitutional discussions and undertook not to reveal any details to the press and other media.

Signed: *Signed*:

Joshua Mqabuko Nkomo   Ian Douglas Smith
THE ANC PRESIDENT   THE RHODESIAN
                           PRIME MINISTER

Witnessed: *Witnessed*:

Salisbury, 1 December 1975

Index

Index

Ibbotson, Rev. Percy, 48, 49, 67, 68
Idris, King, 77
India, 47, 72; JN visits, 73, 74; National Congress, 73, 85, 139, 192, 215
Indian Zimbabweans, 23, 27, 65, 95, 105, 126, 134, 166, 199, 249
Iraq, 170
Israel, 77, 78, 86, 166

Jairos Jiri charity, 111
Jamaica, 192, 193, 215
Jan Hofmeyr school, 34, 40, 64
Jirira, Amon, 156
Johannesburg, 29, 30, 34–7, 47, 50, 239, 242
Jones, Sir Elwyn, 128
Juba, 63
Jukuda, Miss, 32

Kabwe prison, 160
Kalanga language and people, 13, 26, 68
Kale, John, 77–80
Kambona, Oscar, 75
Kangai, Kumbirai, 160
Kano, 50, 51
Kapwepwe, Simon, 60
Karanga language and people, 69, 159
Kariba, 161, 167, 168, 210
Kaunda, President Kenneth, 48, 60, 76, 99, 103; supports liberation, 147–64, 170, 182, 183, 189, 192, 193
Kennedy, Mr (trader), 18
Kenya, 75, 86, 88, 93, 196, 205
Kezi, 17, 104
Khama, President Sir Seretse, 35, 159, 163

Khama, Sikhume, 14
Khartoum, 63
Khona, William, 156
Kissinger, Dr Henry, 170, 171
Kiwanuka, Joseph, 77
de Koch, Mr, 33
Krim, Arthur and Matilde, 89, 182
Kumbai, Patrick, 103
Ku Klux Klan, 182
Kwekwe prison, 149, 151

Labour party (British), 47, 53, 54, 55, 126, 172, 191
Lagos, 77, 91
Lalapansi, 120
Lancaster House conference (1979), 54, 194–200, 201, 204, 207, 216
Land Husbandry Act (1951), 69
Land-Rover, 94
Lardner-Burke, Mr, 136, 154, 214
Latin America, 86, 243
Latin language, 31
Law and Order Maintenance Act, 115, 236, 240
Lear jet, 149
Legion gold mine, 19
Lennox-Boyd, Alan (Lord Boyd), 92, 191
Lesabe, Thenjiwe, 164
Lestor, Joan, 81
Liberal Party (British), 138
Liberia, 75, 87, 88
Libya, 77, 78, 102, 185
Lincoln's Inn, 83
Livingstone, 50
Lobengula, King, 13, 14, 15, 74
London, 47, 63, 75, 98, 110, 134; JN visits, 51–9, 81–3, 89, 92, 94, 176, 194–200, 239, 241–3